Environmental change. We experience these words so frequently with regards to a danger to the lifestyle we have become used to in the twentieth and mid 21st hundreds of years. Shockingly, the expression "environmental change" is connected to an undeniably hostile discussion, that gives no indication of being settled.

here are the individuals who accept the world is getting hotter and the further expansion in temperature – joined with related changes in precipitation, ocean levels, mountain glaciation, polar ice cap inclusion and thickness and so forth – they hope to happen all through the remainder of this century will have the most significant and unfortunate results in the historical backdrop of mankind.

thers will let you know the flow warming pattern finished in 1998 or somewhere around there and there isn't anything to stress about.

Undoubtedly, there are different suppositions that don't exactly squeeze into both of these classes, however generally, public, administrative and logical assessment is separated into these two camps. The two sides are persuaded science backs up their arguments.

One other issue separates the two arrangements of sentiments: the greater part of the researchers and government officials who accept environmental change/an Earth-wide temperature boost represents a genuine danger to our reality additionally accept a lot of this warming is anthropogenic for example brought about by human action. Modern action, exhaust from transport utilizing non-renewable energy sources, ignition of warming and cooking materials and the purposeful consuming of fields and woodlands are exercises that numerous researchers specifically are persuaded causes an Earth-wide temperature boost through what is regularly alluded to as the "nursery impact" by which gases in the air, like carbon dioxide, ingest infrared radiation discharged by the earth when daylight arrives at the surface. These researchers accept human movement has significantly expanded the measure of carbon dioxide and other "nursery" gases and, subsequently, has prompted the expanded warming of our planet.

hose who question this hypothesis will quite often either debate the warming is really occurring or fight that human action isn't responsible.

Contrary to what exactly individuals from either camp might say, the science isn't settled. The people who propose humankind is causing environmental change can highlight a great

arrangement of proof to back up what they say, yet there are an adequate number of inconsistencies in the information to cause sensible uncertainty and request further unprejudiced and straightforward review. The people who deny human movement is causing environmental change disregard a critical verifiable truth: human action has caused huge environmental change previously, basically through deforestation and the consuming of farmland.

There is little point recorded as a hard copy this book to attempt to resolve a contention that has caused limits of poison, abuse, prejudice and intransigence.

his book plans to clarify the number of cutting edge civilisations all through the whole history of humankind as we aggregately comprehend that term were obliterated by environmental change – some rapidly and others considerably more leisurely – and how that exact same shared factor represents a danger to our reality in the 21st century and then some. It ought to be noticed that in spite of the fact that adjustments of environment have made numerous domains rise and fall all over the planet, human action isn't generally a contributing factor.

The name "Atlantis" is in the book's title since I need to show why Atlantis might have existed and, all the more significantly, how it is completely conceivable it might have been annihilated in a solitary day by an environmental change-initiated catastrophic event. A definitive reason for this book is to demonstrate environmental change can prompt the passing of a civilisation over a time of a few ages or only a couple hours.

Before we take a gander at the dangerous effect of environmental change on countries and societies, maybe we ought to analyze the harmless impacts of environmental change on the development of civilisation. Release us back on schedule to a moment that civilisation as we comprehend it didn't exist.

Twenty 5,000 years prior, the world was altogether different to the conditions we are utilized to now. The environment was a lot colder and drier than it is currently. A lot of Europe, North America and Northern Asia was covered under ice sheets. The Neanderthals had in all likelihood become extinct.

Their latest gatherings are accepted to have died of starvation in southern Spain. This period is usually alluded to as the last Ice Age. This

term is somewhat deceptive as periods known as ice ages were not generally one long, constant time of extraordinary virus. There were hundreds of years of moderately warm, sodden climate scattered with longer times of extraordinary cool, dry weather.

These conditions were excessively unforgiving and undermining for any gathering of people to shape what we would think about a civilisation. Life was probably frightful, brutish and short. A consistent battle to observe sufficient food and safe house for little family gatherings or clans while keeping away from the consideration of bigger predators

.

hen, after two or three bogus beginnings, the Ice Age finished inside the range of a human existence cycle around 12,800 years prior. All in all, we know the temperature of our planet can increment (or diminishing) by a few degrees in under a century since we realize it occurred toward the finish of the Ice Age, and at different occasions previously. Woods became over a significant part of the world. Ocean levels rose and the ice sheets withdrew to the polar locales and the most elevated mountains. Also inside a century or thereabouts, the primary unmistakable civilisations prospered. The speed at which mankind advanced to building complex mass settlements and creating farming proposes man had the scholarly potential for progress before conditions became ideal enough for these achievements.

As the following sections of this book will clarify, what environmental change gave, environmental change additionally removed. Environment is anything but a steady or predictable power of nature – which is unequivocally why we have "environmental change" – and from the time of 12,800 years prior, one more component became an integral factor what begun to influence the environment, and subsequently the climate, for the absolute first time in our planet's set of experiences: enormous scope human activity.

Göbekli Tepe

The accompanying Google Earth map shows Göbekli Tepe and Tell Qaramel, with Babylon and the Sumerian city of Ur as reference points.

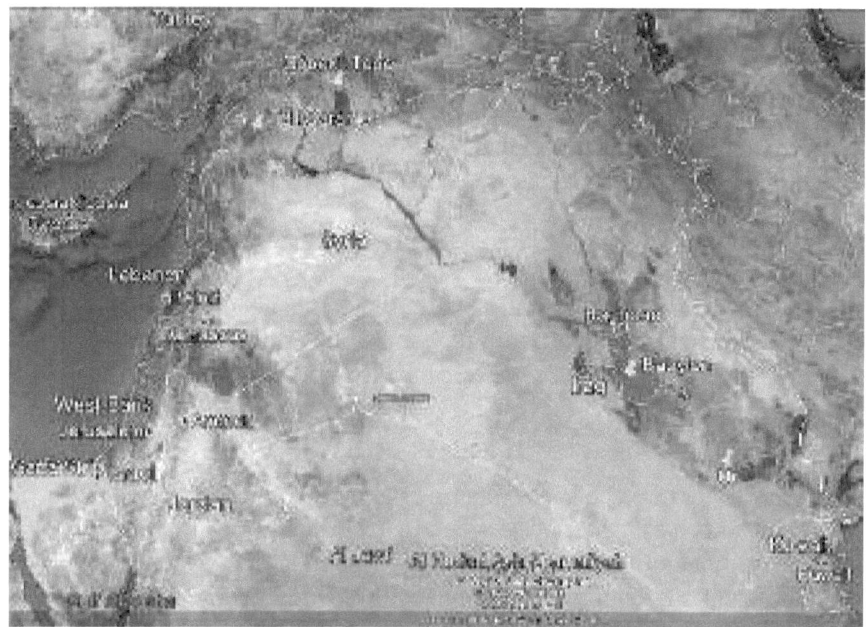

The words "Göbekli Tepe" are Turkish for "potbelly slope" – not the most moving of names for what may be the most seasoned civilisation on the planet. It is in south-eastern Turkey, close to the Syrian boundary and 15 km upper east of the town Sanlıurfa (recently known as Urfa/Edessa). Just piece of the peak settlement has been unearthed, so archeologists can just give halfway rundowns of this site. What they have found is maybe the main ancient archeological site on the planet since it may clarify an incredible arrangement regarding how man developed from tracker finders in little family or ancestral groupings to ranchers with super durable metropolitan settlements and coordinated societies.

Since 1994 unearthings have been completed by the German Archeological Institute (Istanbul branch) and Sanlıurfa Museum, under the course of the German excavator Klaus Schmidt. As indicated by Schmidt, somewhere around five percent of the site has been uncovered and the archeological burrow could undoubtedly proceed for more than 50 years before completion.

Göbekli Tepe was established in the Mesolithic or "Center Stone Age" period, somewhere in the range of 10,000 and 9,500 years BC, or as long as 12,000 years prior. There is

proof the site was involved and fundamental development began considerably before, around 11,000 BC. All in all, the site may be 13,000 years of age. The site gives one of the most punctual known connections between the tracker finders of the stone age – absolute first progenitors of humanity – and old civilisations that had known dialects, writing, coordinated religion and a culture we know about. To be more exact, "we" is characterized as the way of life that have created in what is frequently alluded to as the Middle East, in addition to Europe. Associations with the way of life overwhelmed by the Indian sub-mainland and China, Korea and Japan without a doubt exist, yet it very well may be contended the advancement of these societies was regularly autonomous of any impacts from the relatives of Göbekli Tepe. This is much more relevant while considering the incredible societies of the Americas.

The most seasoned occupation layer in the settlement (layer III) highlights solid columns connected by coarsely assembled dividers to shape roundabout or oval constructions. Up until now, four such structures, with measurements of 10-30m have been excavated.
Geophysical reviews show the presence of 16 extra structures.

Stratum II, has been dated to Pre-Pottery Neolithic B (7500–6000 BC), and has uncovered a few neighboring rectangular rooms with floors of cleaned lime, like the terrazzo floors made by the Romans. The latest layer comprises of dregs stored as the aftereffect of horticultural activity.

s the photographs beneath show, these stone monuments are brightened with cut reliefs of creatures and unique pictograms. The pictograms may address generally comprehended hallowed images, as known from Neolithic cavern artistic creations somewhere else. The painstakingly cut allegorical reliefs portray lions, bulls, hogs, foxes, gazelles, asses, snakes and different reptiles, creepy crawlies, 8-legged creature, and birds, especially vultures and water fowl. Obviously, the hallowed place was developed when the encompassing nation was a lot lusher and equipped for supporting a lot more extensive assortment of natural life, before centuries of settlement, development and environmental change brought about the more bone-dry conditions winning in current occasions. Additionally, the authenticity and specialized detail of these carvings infer a degree of mindfulness and generally speaking knowledge of the craftsmen that are just as modern as any age that has succeeded them.

Vultures likewise include in the iconography of the moderately close by Neolithic destinations of Çatalhöyük and Jericho; it is accepted that in the early Neolithic culture of Anatolia and the Near East the expired were intentionally presented to be devoured by vultures and different flying predators. (The head of the

deceased was sometimes removed and preserved – possibly a ritual of ancestor worship.) This represents an early form of "sky burial", as practiced today by Tibetan Buddhists and Zoroastrians in India and Persia (Iran).

The image above is from Wikimedia Commons and is provided by Teomanimit

The image above is public area from Wikimedia Commons

The image above is public space from Wikimedia Commons

The image above is from Wikimedia Commons and is provided by Teomanimit

Only a couple of humanoid structures have been found so far at Göbekli Tepe. One of the chief finds is an alleviation of an exposed lady, presented visually in a hunkered position, that paleologist Schmidt compares to the Venus accueillante figures found in Neolithic North Africa; and of something like one beheaded carcass encompassed by vultures. A portion of the columns, in particular the T-formed ones, have cut arms, which might demonstrate that they address adapted people (or human divine beings). One more model is adorned with human hands in what could be deciphered as a supplication motion, with a straightforward took or surplice engraved over; this might be planned to address a sanctuary cleric. There is additionally a day to day existence size sculpture of a man with bruised eyes and wearing what has all the earmarks of being a yellow necklace.

Some of the reliefs cut on the columns have been intentionally deleted, maybe in anticipation of new plans. There are unsupported models also that might address wild pigs or foxes. As they are intensely encrusted with lime, archeologists have had extraordinary trouble choosing their careful structure. Practically identical sculptures have been found at neighboring Nevalı Çori and Nahal Hemar.

The quarries for these sculptures are on a similar level as the settlement; some incomplete columns have been uncovered there in situ. The greatest incomplete column is as yet 6.9 m long; and is accepted to have been 9m long initially. This is a lot bigger than any of the completed columns saw as up until now. The stone was quarried with stone picks. Bowl-like melancholies in the limestone rocks may as of now have filled in as mortars or fire-beginning dishes in the epipalaeolithic. There are a few phalli and mathematical examples cut into the stone too; their dating is uncertain.

The houses or sanctuaries are gather massive structures together to 30m in width. The dividers comprise of unworked dry stone and incorporate various T-formed solid mainstays of limestone that are up to 3m high. Another, greater pair of columns is put in the focal point of the constructions. There is proof that the designs were roofed; the focal pair of columns might have upheld the rooftop. The floors are a type of terrazzo (consumed lime), and there is a low seat running along the entire of the outside divider. The sheer size of these structures is solid proof of a general public that was efficient and could rely upon the works of hundreds, and maybe thousands, of people.

While the primary constructions are fundamentally sanctuaries, resulting unearthings have uncovered more modest homegrown structures. Notwithstanding this, it appears to be clear the essential utilization of the site was cultic and not homegrown. In interviews, Schmidt has portrayed Göbekli Tepe as a "house of prayer on a slope" and maybe the world's first journey objective , drawing in admirers up to 100 miles/160 km away. Butchered bones of deer, gazelle, pigs, and geese have been found in huge amounts and are viewed as deny got from hunting and food ready for the visitors.

The occupants, and the individuals who visited, were trackers and finders who lived in towns for at minimum piece of the year. Schmidt hypothesizes that the site played a critical capacity in the progress to agribusiness; he accepts that the essential social association required for the formation of these designs went inseparably with the coordinated abuse of wild yields. For food, wild cereals might have been utilized more seriously than previously; maybe they were even purposely developed. Ongoing DNA examination of present day tamed wheat contrasted and wild wheat has shown that its DNA is nearest in construction to wild wheat found on Mount Karaca Dağ 20 miles/32 km from the site, persuading one to think that this is the place where current wheat was first domesticated.

Schmidt considers Göbekli Tepe a focal area for a religion of the dead. He recommends that the cut creatures are there to ensure the dead. This hypothesis is dubious as no burial chambers or graves have been seen as up until now. Schmidt has communicated certainty they still need to be found underneath the hallowed circles' floors. Schmidt additionally deciphers it regarding the underlying phases of an early Neolithic. It is one of a few Neolithic destinations nearby Mount Karaca Dağ Recent examination proposes that the Neolithic upheaval, i.e., the beginnings of grain development, occurred around here. Schmidt and others accept that versatile gatherings in the space had to help out one another to shield early centralizations of wild grains from wild creatures (groups of gazelles and wild jackasses). This would have prompted an early friendly association of different gatherings in the space of Göbekli Tepe. Hence, as indicated by Schmidt, the Neolithic didn't start on a limited scale as individual cases of nursery development, however began very quickly as an enormous scope social association .

Put another way, assuming that the disclosure of how to make fire and fundamental stone apparatuses prompted the advancement of people as an animal varieties unmistakable from different sorts of primate, the revelations and improvements nearby Göbekli Tepe and close by Tell Qaramel gave the quantum jump to mankind to advance from family gatherings of tracker finders living from hand to mouth, to coordinated, common society with plainly characterized settlements, wellsprings of food, order structures and a bunch of normal purposes.

All assertions about the site ought to be viewed as starter, as just a little level of its complete region has been exhumed at this point; floor levels have been reached in just the subsequent (complex B), which likewise contained a terrazzo-like floor. Through the radiocarbon technique, the finish of layer III can be fixed at c. 9000 BC; its beginnings are assessed to 11,000 BC or prior. Layer II dates to around 8000 BC.

Thus, the constructions not just originate before ceramics, metallurgy, and the innovation of composing or the wheel; they were worked before the supposed Neolithic Revolution, i.e., the start of horticulture and creature farming around 9000 BC. Yet, the development of Göbekli Tepe infers association of a request for intricacy not until recently connected with pre-Neolithic social orders. The archeologists gauge that up to 500 people were needed to extricate the
10-20 ton columns (indeed, some weigh as much as 50 tons) from neighborhood quarries and move them 100 to 500m to the site. Remember this was accomplished with practically no trend setting innovation available to them. All they needed to design into instruments were sticks and stones. It is by and large accepted that an exclusive class of strict pioneers directed

the work and later controlled whatever functions took

place here. Assuming this is the case, this would be the most seasoned known proof for a clerical caste
— significantly sooner than such friendly differentiations grew somewhere else in the Near East.

Göbekli Tepe is viewed as an archeological disclosure of the best significance since it significantly changes our comprehension of a urgent stage in the advancement of human social orders. It is obvious the erection of amazing edifices was inside the limits of tracker finders and not just of stationary cultivating networks as had been recently accepted. At the end of the day, as earthmover Klaus Schmidt puts it: "First came the sanctuary, then, at that point, the city." This progressive theory should be upheld or adjusted by future research.

ot just its huge aspects, yet the next to each other presence of numerous column sanctums makes the area interesting. There are no tantamount stupendous buildings from its time anyplace on the planet. Nevalı Çori, a notable Neolithic settlement additionally exhumed by the German Archeological Institute, and lowered by the Atatürk Dam starting around 1992, is 500 years more youthful, its T-molded columns are significantly more modest, and its hallowed place was situated inside a town; the generally contemporary engineering at Jericho is without imaginative legitimacy or enormous scope figure; and Çatalhöyük, maybe the most popular of all Anatolian Neolithic towns, was assembled 2,000 years after the fact. Tell Qaramel is roughly as old as (might even be more established) and is amazingly noteworthy by its own doing, however its structures have a more useful and basic design.

Schmidt has attempted to decipher the conviction frameworks of the gatherings that made Göbekli Tepe, in light of correlations with different altars and settlements. He expects shamanic rehearses and recommends that the T-molded columns might address legendary animals, maybe predecessors, while he sees a completely expressed faith in divine beings just growing later in Mesopotamia, related with broad sanctuaries and royal residences. This compares well with an old Sumerian conviction that farming, animal cultivation and weaving had been brought to humankind from the hallowed mountain Du-Ku, which was occupied by Annuna— divinities, exceptionally antiquated divine beings without individual names. It is additionally clear that the creature and different pictures give no sign of coordinated brutality, i.e., there are no portrayals of hunting attacks or injured creatures, and the column carvings disregard game on which the general public for the most part remained alive, similar to deer, for imposing animals like lions, snakes, bugs and

scorpions. Likewise, it is probably the case this was a general public that didn't have fighting or decided not to portray it in their art.

Klaus Schmidt recognizes this story as an oriental antiquated legend that protects a halfway memory of the Neolithic.

All in all, whatever religion was explained at Göbekli Tepe address an amassing of the convictions and information on stone age agrarian clans we are unequipped for naming, extending back potentially north of 100,000 years. The pictograms cut on the sanctuary columns may be the world's first endeavor at writing, and recommend a typical language for the occupants and guests from up to 100 miles/160 km away.

tand on top of the "potbelly slope" and you are in a land where civilisation as far as we might be concerned most likely began. Filter the skyline toward the south-west and you are confronting Tell Qaramel and Jericho. Look north and you are pointing towards Nevalı Çori. Go toward the east and you are pointing towards Karahan Tepe. Toward the west falsehood the remnants of Çatalhöyük, and keeping in mind that this settlement might have been worked after Göbekli Tepe was deserted (it is conceivable the two spots coincided for years and years), it was impacted by the more seasoned complex and is essential for the equivalent culture.

hen one thinks about the area of Göbekli Tepe, it appears to be probable this strict complex gave at minimum a portion of the social material for the Sumerians. Besides, the complex is uphill and upstream from the streams Tigris and Euphrates. It appears to be plausible that when assets were depleted on the slopes that were home to Göbekli Tepe, Tell Qaramel, Nevalı Çori and Çatalhöyük that their occupants would advance downhill to the ripe bow and proceed their development.

Some archeologists like to talk of a "missing connection" that could show when and how people advanced from chimps. Göbekli Tepe gives off an impression of being a connection among clans and families that are forgotten always and societies that have added to social orders of the 21st century. There is something like one sculpture that demonstrates unequivocally individuals of Göbekli Tepe impacted more renowned civilisations that succeeded them: it is a cut stone figure, half man and half lion – a sphinx.

Based on the pace of exhuming starting at 2011, Göbekli Tepe brings up a bigger number of issues for antiquarianism and ancient times than it replies. We don't have the foggiest idea how a power sufficiently enormous to build, expand, and keep up with such a

generous complex was activated and paid or took care of in the states of pre-Neolithic culture. We can't "read" the pictograms, and don't know for specific what which means the creature reliefs had for guests to the site; the assortment of fauna portrayed, from lions and pigs to birds and bugs, makes any single clarification tricky. As there is by all accounts practically no proof of home, and the creatures portrayed on the stones are mostly hunters, the stones might have been expected to fight off indecencies through some type of wizardry portrayal; it is additionally conceivable that they filled in as symbols. It isn't known why an ever increasing number of dividers were added to the insides while the safe-haven was being used, with the outcome that a portion of the engraved columns were darkened from view. Entombment might have happened at the site. The explanation the complex was at last covered remaining parts unexplained. Until more proof is assembled, it is hard to conclude anything with sureness about the starting culture.

Around the start of the eighth thousand years BC "Potbelly Hill" seems to have lost its motivation. The appearance of agribusiness and creature farming acquired new real factors to human existence the region, and the "stone-age zoo" (as Schmidt calls it) portrayed on the columns clearly lost whatever importance it had for the area's more established, rummaging, networks. However, the complex was not just deserted and neglected, to be step by step obliterated by the components. All things considered, it was purposely covered under 300 to 500 cubic meters of soil. The structures are covered with settlement reject that more likely than not been brought from somewhere else. These stores incorporate rock devices like scrubbers and pointed stones and creature bones. The lithic stock (stone apparatuses, prevalently rock) is described by Byblos focuses and various Nemrik-focuses. There are Helwan-focuses and Aswad-focuses as well.

Why the complex was covered is a secret, yet it protected the landmarks for posterity.

efore we consider the reason why this civilisation arrived at a clearly unexpected end, let us think about a portion of the other related settlements.

Tell Qaramel

A little more than 100 miles/160 km south-west of Göbekli Tepe, and 25 km north of the Syrian city of Aleppo, is a settlement that is basically as old, and comparably beguiling. Tell Qaramel had somewhere around five round stone pinnacles around six meters in tallness and width, with dividers up to 1.5 meters thick – rather

comparative in appearance to a middle age palace keep. Aftereffects of scientifically measuring tests recommend the pinnacles were worked around 10650 BC, making them just about 13,000 years of age and formally perceived as the most seasoned known stone constructions in the world.

The Polish archeological group that found the site and has done a large portion of the resulting research has tracked down stays of a much more established structure under one of the pinnacles, so it is conceivable the spot is more established than Göbekli Tepe.

The settlement at Tell Qaramel seems to have had a double purposes: it was a strict focus and potentially the primary spot on the planet where domesticated animals cultivating was rehearsed. We realize these individuals approached auroch (a terminated progenitor of homegrown cows) groups on the grounds that a whole body has been found consumed in a pit. Sheep and goats would have been the main animals tamed, trailed by cows and afterward pigs.

Nearby, the remaining parts of three onagers (a sort of wild ass, somewhat bigger than a jackass) have been found. Millennia after the fact, onagers were utilized by Sumerians to pull carts, and in Ur, they were even used to pull war chariots. There is proof onagers were saved for meat/conciliatory purposes, yet could individuals at Tell Qaramel have been quick to tame creatures for transportation?

The photos underneath from the Tell Qaramel site were mercifully provided by Prof. Ryszard Mazurowski of the University of Warsaw:

Photo by R.F.Mazurowski

Photo by R.F.Mazurowski

Excavations at the site have revealed various more modest, round houses encompassing the pinnacles, in addition to different structures that seem to have had strict capacities. A burial ground containing 27 human skeletons, some of whom had been beheaded posthumously.

The structure nearest to the graves estimated 10.5 meters by 5 meters and was partitioned into three sections. A stele improved with four breaks was found in its apse. There is a stage in the center which looks like a sort of raised area produced using a white lime mass. Close to it there are bow shape seats and a very much made hearth, where enormous creatures, for example, bison, gazelles and onagers were sacrificed.

In the eastern mass of the safe-haven, archeologists have gone over a total figure of a lady produced using chalk, and a somewhat gigantic rock Jericho-type hatchet, which was imported from that piece of Palestine.

The top of the Polish archeological group, Prof. Ryszard Mazurowski made a surprising disclosure in a magazine interview:

However Tell Qaramel is around 180 km away from the Mediterranean, we even tracked down portrayals of an octopus (which is partially a lady), shells and turtles," he asserted. The educator is persuaded this is obvious evidence, individuals at the settlement had some awareness of the ocean and had voyaged broadly, coming into contact with individuals residing in other places.

This disclosure makes it incredibly logical individuals at Tell Qaramel and Göbekli Tepe knew about one another as a flat out least, if not piece of a similar culture, having similar traditions and convictions. That arable cultivating seems to have been spearheaded in one of these settlements and animals cultivating in the other is of tremendous importance to the advancement of mankind as a whole.

Artifacts found at the site are of stone and earth, including ornamented stone bolt straighteners, showing mathematical plans, normally addressed and adapted pictures of snakes and human figures, stone querns, pounders, processors, enhanced dishes, tomahawks, picks, cleaning stones, borers and needles. As per Prof. Mazurowski, more objects of this nature have been recovered from this site than some other spot in the "Close to East".

The bolts and hatchet heads recommend the occupants actually chased after a portion of their meat. One of the pinnacles was annihilated by fire, which raises the chance this was the consequence of an antagonistic demonstration by outcasts. Could this be the site of the world's first war?

At the hour of composing, the archeologists had not distributed a hypothesis to clarify the downfall of Tell Qaramel, however it doesn't appear to be absurd to assume the environmental change that constrained individuals at Göbekli Tepe and close by destinations to relocate to more appropriate terrains additionally prompted the relinquishment of Tell Qaramel.

Nevalı Çori

Nevalı Çori was an early Neolithic settlement around 15 miles/25 km north of Göbekli Tepe on the center Euphrates, in the area of Sanlıurfa (Urfa),

eastern Turkey. The site is popular for having uncovered a portion of the world's most old known sanctuaries and amazing figure. Along with the site of Göbekli Tepe, it has upset logical comprehension of the Eurasian Neolithic.

he settlement was situated around 490 m above ocean level, in the lower regions of the Taurus mountains, on the two banks of the Kantara stream, a feeder of the Euphrates.

The site was analyzed in 1993 with regards to save unearthings during the erection of the Atatürk Dam underneath Samsat. Unearthings were led by a group from the University of Heidelberg under the course of Professor Harald Hauptmann. Along with various other archeological destinations nearby, Nevalı Çori has since been immersed by the dammed waters of the Euphrates. This makes further examination into what befell the site incomprehensible, yet we do realize it was a settlement from around 10,000 – 8,500 BC or maybe even later.

Nevalı Çori could be set inside the neighborhood relative sequence based on rock apparatuses uncovered there. A specialized summery is as per the following:-

The event of thin unretouched Byblos-type focuses places it on O. Aurenche's Phase 3, which, for example right on time to center PPNB. A few instruments demonstrate progression into Phase 4, which is comparative in date to Late PPNB. A significantly better ordered qualification inside Phase 3 is allowed by the settlement's design; the house type with under floor channels, normal of Nevalı Çori layers I-IV, additionally portrays the "Halfway Layer" at Çayönü, while the varying arrangement of the single structure in layer V, House 1, is all the more obviously associated with the structures of the "Cell Plan Layer" at Çayönü.

as far as outright dates, four radiocarbon dates not really set in stone for Nevalı Çori. Three are from Stratum II and date it with some conviction to the second 50% of the ninth thousand years BC, which matches with early dates from Çayönü and with Mureybet IVA and along these lines upholds the relative sequence above. The fourth dates to the tenth thousand years, which, if right, would show the presence of a very beginning stage of PPNB at Nevalı Çori.

The settlement had five engineering levels. The exhumed engineering remains were of long rectangular houses containing a few equal trips of rooms, deciphered as magazines. These are neighboring a similarly

rectangular bet structure, partitioned by divider projections, which ought to be viewed as a private space. This kind of house is described by thick,

complex establishments made of enormous rakish cobbles and rocks, the holes loaded up with more modest stones in order to give a somewhat even surface to
support the superstructure. These establishments are interfered with each 1-1.5m by under floor channels, at right points to the primary hub of the houses, which were canvassed in stone pieces however open to the sides. They might have served the seepage, air circulation or the cooling of the houses. 23 such designs were uncovered. They are strikingly like designs from the alleged diverted sub stage at Çayönü.

A region in the North-West piece of the town gives off an impression of being of extraordinary importance. Here, a religion complex had been cut into the slope slant. It had three resulting engineering stages, the latest having a place with Stratum III, the center one to Stratum II and the most seasoned to Stratum I. The two later stages likewise had a terrazzo-style lime concrete floor, which didn't make due from the most established stage. Matches are known from Cayönü and Göbekli Tepe. Solid columns like those at Göbekli Tepe were incorporated into its dry stone dividers, its inside contained two unsupported mainstays of 3 m tallness. The earthmover accepts light level rooftops. Comparative designs are just known from Göbekli Tepe so far.

Soundings slice to look at the western side of the valley likewise uncovered rectilinear engineering in 2-3 layers.

The nearby limestone was cut into various sculptures and more modest models, including a more than life-sized exposed human head with a snake or sikha-like tuft. There is likewise a sculpture of a bird. A portion of the columns likewise bore reliefs, including ones of human hands. The detached human figures of limestone unearthed at Nevalı Çori have a place with the most punctual known life-size models. Similar material has been found at Göbekli Tepe.

Several hundred little dirt puppets (around 5 cm high), the greater part of them portraying people, have been deciphered as votive contributions. They were terminated at temperatures between 500-600°C, which proposes the advancement of clay terminating innovation before the appearance of ceramics proper.

ome of the houses contained affidavits of human skulls and inadequate skeletons.

To place this data in setting, the complex had refined stone structures and lodging and was occupied for a period equivalent to London, Berlin or Paris, yet was deserted almost 10,000 years prior. This was no transient habitation of transitory tracker finders. Whatever general public the occupants shaped kept going longer than the Roman Empire, regardless of whether you date that foundation from Julius Caesar to the fall of Constantinople.

Karahan Tepe

Karahan Tepe is around 39 miles/63km east of Urfa and are arranged on the Tektek Mountains. The Tekteks are on the northern boundary of the Urfa-Harran plain, between the headwaters of the Tigris and Euphrates waterways. The site that was found in 1997 and was dated to c. 9500–9000 BC by Turkish classicist Bahattin Çelik. Covering a space of 325,000 square meters, it comprises of various stone T-columns and high reliefs portraying, among different pictures, a winding snake and the battered middle of a stripped man. There are additionally cleaned rock sculptures of goats, gazelles and rabbits.

öbekli Tepe and Nevalı Çori were in what is presently the Turkish territory of Sanlıurfa (Urfa) and existed together for around 1,500 years. As the previous was overwhelmingly a strict mind boggling and the last option was to a greater extent a homegrown settlement, it suggests an expanded region administered by a solitary culture. All in all, it's possible this was the main nation or state.

When these destinations were deserted, individuals who had lived there more likely than not remained genuinely nearby as the Neolithic town of Çatalhöyük gives plentiful proof of a continuation and social advancement from around 7,500 – 5,700 BC. Moreover, the strict, pictographical and rural improvement firmly recommend that whatever convictions were communicated at Göbekli Tepe and Nevalı Çori were progressively adjusted at Çatalhöyük and changed further still by the arising Sumerian civilisation.

Assuming individuals didn't vanish – for example they weren't completely cleared out in a disaster – when they deserted Göbekli Tepe and Nevalı Çori why was a flourishing social community that had kept going longer than a significant number of the world's most celebrated civilisations unexpectedly vacated?

Warfare can be limited as there is no proof of brutality at one or the other site. Illness might have been a variable. It may clarify the entombment of Göbekli Tepe by its last occupants. Provided that this is true, illness would have been a side effect of the issues confronting these individuals. Over a time of 3,000 years the clan who established Göbekli Tepe and Nevalı Çori and Tell Qaramel changed their little corner of the earth past recognition.

efore these spots were fabricated, mankind was made out of numerous little family bunches spread all over the planet. These individuals ate anything they might get or search and enhanced their eating regimen with wild products of the soil and grains they picked in season. Göbekli Tepe marks whenever we first know about that individuals got together in bunches bigger than family or faction size for a typical purpose.

at the end of the day, what initially united individuals in sensibly huge numbers was religion. Stones were quarried and cut and trees were chopped down to construct the fundamentally strict complex at Göbekli Tepe and later at Nevalı Çori later still at different destinations. Tell Qaramel is somewhat disparate as far as the plan of the settlement, and potentially its purpose.

hen came one more justification for individuals from various families to participate: agribusiness. As referenced before, research by the paleontologist Schmidt and others firmly proposes the main development of wheat occurred around here. Cultivating advanced after a time of collecting wheat and different grains from regions wherein they thought normally. Individuals would have needed to alternate to monitor these regions from touching creatures. This necessary association and surprisingly an order structure.

For the situation of Tell Qaramel, the site may have been the place where individuals originally created animals cultivating, so a few parts of the association would have been marginally unique. In many cultivating social orders, ranchers live with their animals and offer the equivalent defensive walls.

Archeologist Klaus Schmidt accepts there was a quantum jump from essential agrarian culture to enormous scope cultivating with extremely durable settlements. When one gathering dominated fundamental agrarian and social association, it would have spread to different families who might see the advantages of a reliable and copious food source. To accomplish this, the backwoods would have been chopped down for farmland and fuel. Normal assets would rapidly have become exhausted, particularly as populace development would have been exceptionally high because of the underlying achievement of agribusiness in supply food and the requirement for additional individuals to monitor and develop used farmlands and herds. Also, to be reasonable for these individuals, the thought of rationing assets and

securing the climate would have been an outsider idea on the grounds that there had not been a need to consider such things previously. The downside to being pioneers was an absence of direction from individuals who had effectively made mistakes.

Deforestation added to environmental change. Indeed, even after 10,000 years, we can perceive how this "development" in human conduct made long-lasting harm the climate around here. Individuals who assembled Göbekli Tepe and Nevalı Çori didn't vanish and bite the dust suddenly, yet they needed to leave these spots and start once more. Humanity's absolute first endeavor at a civilisation must be deserted.

This isn't to say the endeavor was a disappointment. Individuals met up and assembled settlements that went on for millennia. There is no proof of battle at Göbekli Tepe and Nevalı Çori despite the fact that graves of individuals who kicked the bucket fiercely around a similar period have been found somewhere else. Indeed, even the pinnacles at Tell Qaramel might have had purposes other than guard of the occupants. Quite a bit of what these individuals accomplished has been passed down to the remainder of humankind. In any case, in building Göbekli Tepe and Nevalı Çori humankind committed its first error: they didn't take appropriate consideration of their current circumstance. They addressed the cost, however unfortunately, in excess of 10,000 years after the fact the example actually has not been learned.

The uplifting news is at minimum a portion of these individuals advanced downhill and downstream to the fruitful, all around inundated terrains between the Tigris and Euphrates, and may well have turned into the originators of Sumeria and with it, such a great deal what is perceived as a feature of the aggregate Eurasian history.

Mohenjo-daro

The accompanying Google Earth map shows the urban communities of Harappa and Mohenjo-daro.

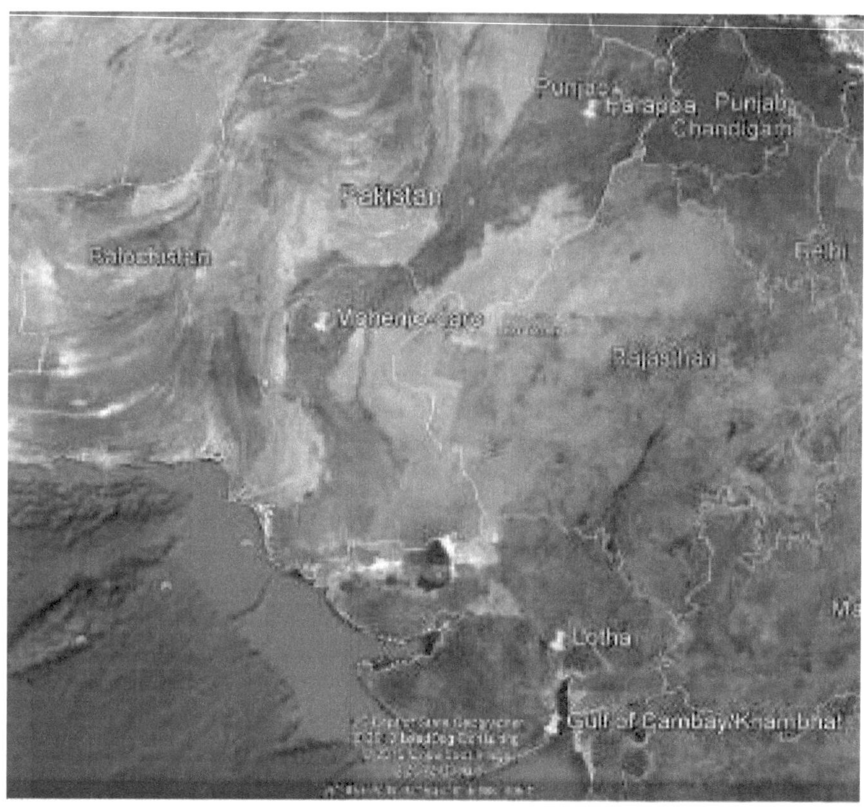

Mohenjo-daro is in the territory of Sindh, Pakistan, and was one of the biggest city-settlements of the Indus Valley Civilisation. Worked around 2600 BCE, it was one of the early metropolitan settlements on the planet, existing simultaneously as the civilisations of antiquated Egypt, Mesopotamia, and Crete. The archeological remains of the city are assigned an UNESCO World Heritage Site. It is in some cases alluded to as "an antiquated Indus valley metropolis".

here has been theory that the precursors of the Indus Valley civilisation moved from the space around Göbekli Tepe and Nevalı Çori before the establishing of Sumerian civilisation. It has been recommended certain individuals moved further South in the Tigris-Euphrates district while others moved East and afterward South towards the Indus.

Mohenjo-daro was worked around 2600 BC and deserted around 1500 BC. The city was rediscovered in 1922 by Rakhaldas Bandyopadhyay, an official of the Archeological Survey of India. He was directed to the hill by a Buddhist priest who trusted one of the principle structures to be a stupa. During the 1930s, huge unearthings were directed under the initiative of John Marshall, K. N. Dikshit, Ernest Mackay, and others. Further unearthings were completed in 1945 by Ahmad Hasan Dani and Mortimer Wheeler.

The last significant unearthings were directed in 1964-65 by Dr. George F. Dales. After this date, unearthings were prohibited because of harm caused for the uncovered designs by enduring. Starting around 1965, the main undertakings permitted at the site have been rescue uncovering, surface reviews and preservation projects. Regardless of the restriction on major archeological tasks, during the 1980s, groups of German and Italian review gatherings, driven by Dr. Michael Jansen and Dr. Maurizio Tosi, consolidated strategies like building documentation, surface studies, surface scratching and testing, to decide further pieces of information about this antiquated civilisation.

Mohenjo-daro is situated in Sindh Province, in southern Pakistan on a Pleistocene edge in the flood plain of the Indus River Valley. The edge is currently covered by the flooding of the fields, yet was conspicuous during the hour of the Indus Valley Civilisation. The edge permitted the city to remain over the encompassing plain. The site involves a focal situation between the Indus River valley on the west and the Ghaggar-Hakra stream on the east. The Indus actually streams toward the east of the site, however the Ghaggar-Hakra riverbed has dried up.

he edge that housed the city turned out to be overpopulated to the point that it was extended by the development of monster mud block stages. Eventually, the settlement developed to such extents that a few structures arrived at 12 m over the level of the advanced plain, and thusly a lot higher than this over the antiquated plain.

Mohenjo-daro in old occasions was most presumably perhaps the biggest city of the old Indus Valley Civilisation. It was the most evolved and progressed city in South Asia, during its prime. The preparation and designing are obvious proof of the significance of the city to individuals of the Indus valley.

The Indus Valley Civilisation (c. 3300–1700 BC, bloomed 2600–1900 BC), contracted IVC, was an antiquated riverine civilisation that prospered in the Indus stream valley (presently Pakistan and northwest India). One more name for this civilisation is the "Harappan Civilisation" (Harappa is another significant IVC site toward the north of Mohenjo-daro in Punjab).

The Indus culture bloomed throughout the long term and brought about the Indus Valley Civilisation around 3000 BC. The civilisation crossed a lot of what is presently Pakistan and North India, however abruptly went into decay around 1900 BC. Indus Civilisation settlements spread as far west as the Iranian line, with a station in Bactria, as far south as the Arabian Sea shoreline of western India in Gujarat. Among the settlements were the major metropolitan habitats of Harappa and Mohenjo-daro, just as Lothal.

There are striking similitudes among IVC and Ancient Egypt. The two civilisations relied on one extremely long waterway to flood a land that would some way or another have been totally barren.

Mohenjo-daro would be in a flash conspicuous to any individual who has lived in an unassuming community in America. It has an arranged design dependent on a road lattice of rectilinear structures. Most are of terminated and mortared block; some join sun dried mud-block with wooden superstructures. The sheer size of the city, and its arrangement of public structures and offices, proposes undeniable degrees of social association. At its pinnacle of advancement, Mohenjo-Daro might have housed around 35,000 residents.

The city had a focal commercial center, with an enormous focal well. Individual families or gatherings of families got their water from more modest wells. Squander water was directed to covered channels that lined the major streets.

Some houses, apparently those of more affluent occupants, incorporate rooms that seem to have been saved for washing, and one structure had an underground heater (hypocaust), conceivably for warmed washing. Most houses have inward yards, with entryways that opened onto side-paths. A few structures were two-storied.

In 1950, Sir Mortimer Wheeler assigned one huge, most likely open office as a "Incredible Granary". Certain divider divisions in its enormous wooden superstructure seemed, by all accounts, to be grain stockpiling sounds, complete with air-pipes to dry the grain. As per Wheeler, trucks would have brought grain from the open country and dumped them straightforwardly into the narrows. In any case, Jonathan

Mark Kenoyer noticed the total shortfall of grain at the "storage facility", which may accordingly be better depicted as a "Incredible Hall" of dubious function.

Adjacent to the "Incomparable Granary" is an enormous and elaborate public shower, some of the time alluded to as the "Incomparable Bath". From a colonnaded patio, steps lead down to the block assembled pool, which was waterproofed by a covering of bitumen. The pool is huge – 12m long, 7m wide and 2.4m profound. It might have been utilized for strict cleaning. Other huge structures incorporate a "Pillared Hall", thought to be a gathering corridor or the like. Close to the Great Bath is the alleged "School Hall", a complex of structures including 78 rooms and thought to have been a holy residence.

ohenjo-daro had no circuit of city dividers except for was generally very much strengthened, with pinnacles toward the west of the principle settlement, and guarded fortresses toward the south. Considering these fortresses and the design of other significant Indus valley urban communities like Harappa, it appears to be conceivable that Mohenjo-daro was a managerial focus. Both Harappa and Mohenjo-daro share moderately a similar engineering design, and were by and large not vigorously braced like other Indus Valley destinations. It is clear from the indistinguishable city designs of all Indus locales, that there was some sort of political or managerial centrality, but the degree and working of an authoritative focus remains unclear.

Mohenjo-daro was annihilated and afterward revamped something like multiple times. Each time, the new urban areas were fabricated straightforwardly on top of the old ones. Flooding by the Indus is accepted to have been the reason for destruction.

The city is separated into two sections, the alleged Citadel and the Lower City. The greater part of the Lower City is yet to be uncovered, however the Citadel is known to have the public shower, an enormous private construction intended to house 5,000 residents and two huge gathering halls.

The accompanying public space photographs provided by http://fr.wikipedia.orgcapture the substance of Mohenjo-daro for posterity.

Picture of Mohenjo daro ruins, with extraordinary public shower at front provided by world66.com and was additionally distributed by Wikipedia under the Creative Commons ShareAlike permit (CC-SA).

A bronze "Moving young lady" statuette (see picture above), 10.8 cm high and around 4,500 years of age, was found in Mohenjo-daro in 1926. In 1973, British prehistorian Mortimer Wheeler depicted her as his most loved statuette:

> "There is her little Balochi-style face with frowning lips and rude look at without flinching. She's around fifteen years of age I should think, not more, but rather she remains there with bangles as far as possible up her arm and nothing else on. A young lady impeccably, for the occasion, completely sure of herself and the world. There's nothing similar to her, I think, in the world."

John Marshall, one of the earthmovers at Mohenjo-daro, depicted her as a youthful ... young lady, her hand on her hip in a half-brash stance, and legs somewhat forward as she beats time to the music with her legs and feet.

The prehistorian Gregory Possehl says, "We may not be sure that she was an artist, yet she was great at what she did and she knew it". The sculpture could well be of some sovereign or other significant lady of the Indus Valley

Civilisation deciding from the power the figure commands.

In 1927 a situated male figure, 17.5 cm tall, was found in a structure with abnormally elaborate brickwork and a divider specialty. However there is no proof that clerics or rulers administered the city, archeologists named this honorable figure a "Minister King"; like the Dancing Girl, it has become emblematic of the Indus valley civilisation. The image was given by Mamoon Mengal at world66.com.

This hairy figure wears a filet around the head, an armband, and a shroud brightened with trefoil designs that were initially loaded up with red pigment.

The two closures of the filet fall along the back and however the hair is painstakingly brushed towards the rear of the head, no bun is available. The level back of the head might have held an independently cut bun as is conventional on the other situated figures, or it might have held a more intricate horn and plumed headdress.

wo openings underneath the profoundly adapted ears propose that a jewelry or other head adornment was appended to the model. The left shoulder is covered with a shroud beautified with trefoil, twofold circle and single circle plans that were initially loaded up with red color. Drill openings in the focal point of each circle demonstrate they were made with a particular drill and afterward cleaned up with an etch. Eyes are profoundly chiseled and may have held decorate. The upper lip is shaved and a short brushed facial hair growth outlines the face. The enormous break in the face is the aftereffect of enduring or it could be because of unique terminating of this object.

individuals of the Indus Valley Civilisation can guarantee various major logical accomplishments. With the conceivable exemption of the Mayans, they had the option to record extraordinary precision in estimating length, mass, and time. They were among quick to foster an arrangement of uniform loads and measures.

Their estimations are supposed to be incredibly exact; nonetheless, an examination of accessible articles shows huge scope variety across the Indus regions. Their littlest division, which is set apart on an ivory scale found in Lothal, was roughly 1.704 mm, the littlest division at any point recorded on a size of the Bronze Age. Harappan engineers followed the decimal division of estimation in every way that really matters, including the estimation of mass as uncovered by their hexahedron weights.

These chert loads were in an ideal proportion of 5:2:1 with loads of 0.05, 0.1, 0.2, 0.5, 1, 2, 5, 10, 20, 50, 100, 200, and 500 units, with every unit weighing roughly 28 grams, basically the same as the English Imperial ounce or Greek uncia, and more modest items were made an appearance comparable proportions with the units of 0.871. In any case, as in different societies, genuine loads were not uniform all through the space. The loads and measures later utilized in Kautilya's Arthashastra (fourth century BC) are as old as utilized in Lothal.[37]

Unique Harappan developments incorporate an instrument which was utilized to quantify entire segments of the skyline and the flowing lock. Furthermore, Harappans developed some new methods in metallurgy and created copper, bronze, lead, and tin. The designing ability of the Harappans was surprising, particularly in building docks after a cautious investigation of tides, waves, and flows. The capacity of the alleged "dock" at Lothal, notwithstanding, is disputed.

n 2001, archeologists concentrating on the remaining parts of two men from Mehrgarh, Pakistan, made the disclosure that individuals of the Indus Valley Civilisation, from the early Harappan periods, known about proto-dentistry. Afterward, in April 2006, it was declared in the logical diary Nature that the most established (and first early Neolithic) proof for the boring of human teeth in vivo (for example in a living individual) was found in Mehrgarh. Eleven bored molar crowns from nine grown-ups were found in a Neolithic memorial park in Mehrgarh that dates, from 7,500-9,000 years prior. As per the creators, their disclosures highlight a practice of proto-dentistry in the early cultivating societies of that region.

A standard bearing gold streaks was found in Banawali, which was presumably utilized for testing the virtue of gold (this procedure is as yet utilized in certain pieces of India).

The Indus civilisation's economy seems to have relied fundamentally upon exchange, which was worked with by significant advances in transport innovation. These advances included bullock trucks that are indistinguishable from those seen all through South Asia today, just as boats. The vast majority of these boats were most likely little, level lined art, maybe determined by sail, like those one can see on the Indus River today; be that as it may, there is auxiliary proof of maritime craft. Archeologists have found a monstrous, dug channel and what they see as a mooring office at the waterfront city of Lothal in western India (Gujarat state). A broad channel organization, utilized for water system, has anyway additionally been found by H.- P. Francfort.

During 4300–3200 BC of the chalcolithic period (copper age), the Indus Valley Civilisation region shows likenesses in its earthenware production with southern Turkmenistan and northern Iran which recommend impressive versatility and exchange. During the Early Harappan period (around 3200–2600 BC), similitudes in stoneware, seals, dolls, decorations, and so on, archive escalated band exchange with Central Asia and the Iranian plateau.

Judging from the dispersal of Indus civilisation ancient rarities, the exchange organizations, financially, coordinated a gigantic region, including segments of Afghanistan, the beach front areas of Persia, northern and western India, and Mesopotamia. This would mean contact with the relatives of the people who had left the upland settlements based on Göbekli Tepe and later Nevalı Çori and relocated down the Euphrates (potentially) to frame the Sumerian civilisation.

There was a broad oceanic exchange network working between the Harappan and Mesopotamian civilisations as ahead of schedule as the center Harappan Phase, with much business being taken care of by "agents traders from Dilmun" (present day Bahrain and Failaka situated in the Persian Gulf). Indeed, even in the soonest vestige, what we presently call the Gulf States depended on an immense exchange organization, that incorporated the Indian sub-mainland, for its abundance. Such significant distance ocean exchange became possible with the imaginative improvement of board constructed watercraft, outfitted with a solitary focal pole supporting a sail of woven surges or cloth.

Several beach front settlements like Sotkagen-dor (straddling Dasht River, north of Jiwani), Sokhta Koh (on the back of Shadi River, north of Pasni), and Balakot (close to Sonmiani) in Pakistan alongside Lothal in India vouch for their job as Harappan exchanging stations. Shallow harbors situated at the estuary of waterways opening into the ocean permitted lively sea exchange with Mesopotamian cities.

s with Göbekli Tepe and Nevalı Çori, Mohenjo-daro ,and the Indus Valley by and large, became unequipped for supporting its occupants. An early hypothesis for the death of this civilisation focused on attack by the Aryans who proceeded to secure themselves as the predominant ethnic gathering in the majority of the Indian subcontinent.

ubsequent exploration makes it practically certain environmental change was the reason. The Indus valley environment became fundamentally cooler and drier from around 1800 BC, connected to an overall debilitating of the rainstorm around then. Alternatively,

an essential element might have been the vanishing of significant segments of the Ghaggar Hakra waterway framework. A structural occasion might have redirected the framework's sources toward the Ganges Plain, however there is finished vulnerability about the date of this occasion, as most settlements inside Ghaggar-Hakra stream beds have not yet been dated. The genuine justification behind decay may be any blend of these elements. New geographical examination has as of late been led by a gathering drove by Peter Clift, from the University of Aberdeen, to research how the courses of streams have changed around here in the course of recent years, to test whether environment or waterway redesigns are more liable for the decay of the Harappan. A 2004 paper showed that the isotopes of the Ghaggar-Hakra framework don't come from the Himalayan ice sheets, and were downpour taken care of all things considered, going against a Harappan time powerful "Sarasvati' river.

These discoveries back up other proof that environmental change was the chief reason for the decay of the Indus Valley Civilisation. The amount of the progressions could be ascribed to human action is hazy. A general public that waters its territory cautiously, and constructs productive waste frameworks for effluents is probably going to be mindful with regards to its current circumstance. As the district was not intensely forested whenever during the IVC's presence, even enormous scope deforestation appears unlikely.

individuals of the IVC vanished without passing on many signs to the singular reasons for their destruction or where the survivors may have moved: the absence of mass graves make it improbable fighting or a pestilence was dependable. In any case, large numbers of the urban communities, including Mohenjo-daro were never possessed again. When Alexander the Great went through the Indus Valley in 325 BC, the extraordinary civilisation that had prospered there for more than 1,500 years had been forgotten for north of 1,000 years.

Gulf of Cambay/Khambhat

In May 2001, India's Union Minister for Human Resource Development, Science and Technology division, Murli Manohar Joshi, reported that the remnants of an antiquated civilisation had been found off the shoreline of Gujarat, in the Gulf of Khambhat. This is the most North-westerly piece of India's

coast and near the Indus estuary. The site was found by India's National Institute of Ocean Technology (NIOT) while they performed routine contamination concentrates on utilizing sonar, and was depicted as a space of consistently separated mathematical designs. The site is 20 km off the Gujarat coast, ranges
 km, and can be found at a profundity of 30–40 meters. In his declaration, Joshi claims the site is a metropolitan settlement that originates before the Indus Valley Civilisation. Later introductions of the site by Joshi depict it as containing routinely divided homes, a storage facility, a shower, a bastion, and a waste system.

A subsequent examination was done by NIOT in November 2001, which included digging to recuperate curios and sonar outputs to recognize structures. Among the ancient rarities recuperated were a piece of wood, ceramics shards, endured stones at first depicted as hand apparatuses, fossilized bones,

and a tooth. Ancient rarities were shipped off the National Geophysical Research Institute (NGRI) in Hyderabad, India, the Birbal Sahni Institute of Paleobotany (BSIP) in Lucknow, India, and the Physical Research Laboratory in Ahmedabad, India. Scientifically measuring of the piece of wood uncovered it was 9,500 years old.

NIOT returned for additional examination in the Gulf from October 2002 to January 2003. During these unearthings, NIOT found two paleochannels flanked by rectangular and square cellar like elements. Relics were recuperated by digging, including earthenware shards, microliths, wattle and wipe remains, and hearth materials. These items were sent for dating at the research centers of Manipur University and Oxford University. The wattle and smear remains are made out of locally accessible mud, reed, husk, ceramics pieces, and bits of new water shell. The wattle and smear likewise showed proof of halfway burning.

The latest work in the Gulf of Khambhat occurred from October 2003 to January 2004 and was basically a land overview. Strategies utilized during this examination included bathymetry overview, sub-base study, side-check study and attractive review. One significant finding from this examination concerns the direction of sand swells at the site. NIOT specialists revealed there are two arrangements of waves apparent at the site – one set is a characteristic element shaped by flowing flows while the other set has framed according to basic underlying features.

significant debate concerning this lowered settlement is the scientifically measured piece of wood. Dr. D.P. Agrawal, administrator of the Paleoclimate Group and originator of Carbon-14 testing offices in India uncovered in an article in Frontline Magazine that the piece was dated twice, at discrete research centers. The NGRI in Hyderabad reported a date of 7190 BC and the BSIP in Hannover, Germany, put it down on the calendar of 7545-7490 BC. A few archeologists, Agrawal specifically, have contended that the disclosure of an antiquated piece of wood doesn't infer the revelation of an old civilisation. Agrawal calls attention to that the wood piece is a typical find, considering that 20,000 years prior the Arabian Sea was 100 meters underneath its ebb and flow level, and that the slow ascent in ocean level lowered whole forests.

Another genuine disputed matter worries the stoneware shards recovered from the site during the different unearthings. Analysts portray them as demonstrative of hand-made and wheel-turned ceramics customs. The remaining parts found have straightforward edges with little chiseled lines. All of the remaining parts found so far have a place with little or small bits of earthenware. A few specialists have questioned these discoveries and guarantee the pieces may be normal geofacts; the little sizes of the recuperated pottery makes it hard to settle the issue. Be that as it may, in case the stoneware is veritable, archeologists say it should show a few likenesses to Harappan earthenware, which is ordinarily red and dark and stepped with seals. In light of the proof accessible, a complex coherence of Harappan civilisation isn't apparent.

While not every person is persuaded the studies have brought about a significant archeological revelation, one of the key work force included has no doubts.

Badrinaryan, boss geologist with the logical group from the National Institute of Ocean Technology (NIOT) liable for the submerged overviews in the Gulf of Cambay/Khambat has distributed his own report regarding the matter. Chosen separates are as per the following:-

"For a really long time archeologists have quarreled over the beginnings of the strange 'Harappan' (Indus Valley) civilisation that prospered across what is presently Pakistan and northwest India from around 3000 BC. Presently, new discoveries by Indian researchers working in the Gulf of Cambay propose that the Harappans were plunged from a high level mother culture that prospered toward the finish of the last Ice Age that was then lowered by rising ocean levels before 'history' began."

"It was for the most part accepted that an efficient civilisation couldn't have existed preceding 5500 BP. Many were hesitant to acknowledge that the flood legends referenced in numerous antiquated strict works held a few traces of validity. The new disclosure made in the Gulf of Cambay, India stunned many, and made some sit up and watch with interest. It unmistakably settled the presence of an old civilisation that was lowered in the ocean. The systems embraced to concentrate on this find, were novel and unique, wherein progressed marine advancements and the most current logical utilizations of different disciplines were put to use."

Mr. Badrinaryan's hypothesis is at finished chances with the theory that the

Indus Valley Civilisation was established by individuals who relocated from Asia Minor for example Göbekli Tepe and Nevalı Çori and related settlements. They would have relocated South-east from regions that were as of now not ripe enough or rich enough in assets to help a huge and developing complex society.
Instead, the authors of the IVC moved North-west because of rising ocean levels.

The undeniable inquiry is: the reason would they do this? To arrive at the locales of Mohenjo-daro and Harappa from the Gulf of Cambay, one would need to cross the Gujarat promontory and progressively bone-dry landscape prior to arriving at the River Indus. As expressed previously, without this strong stream and its feeders, the whole district would be a forlorn no man's land. Similarly as with Egypt and the Nile, the land is ripe just in places reached by the waters of the stream. Past that is only desert.

It would have been incredibly hard for individuals at Cambay to have moved East because of the tremendous desert of what is currently Rajasthan. Toward the South, based on what is presently Bombay the land is more fruitful, yet would a huge scope relocation along the coast have been attainable at that point? It isn't just land assets we should consider. Were there individuals previously possessing the coast who might have impeded this transitory path?

If we acknowledge the likelihood that the organizers of the settlements in the Gulf of Cambay might have chosen to move to the Indus Valley, the following inquiry is: the place where did they come from? On account of Göbekli Tepe and Nevalı, it is sensible to assume the precursors of the organizers of these spots were important for the mass relocation out of Africa (regardless of whether they went through the Levant or left Africa and moved along the southern shores of the Arabian promontory, or even addressed gatherings who had taken the two courses, still can't seem not set in stone) and the tracker assemble family bunches had shown up in the overall region millennia before their gatherings advanced into the relatively refined society that fabricated the settlements and began cultivating. This hypothesis may be off-base, however there is a line of progression that extends a huge number of years and gives basically incomplete responses to many inquiries concerning individuals' origins.

The equivalent can't be said for the authors of the Gulf of Cambay abodes. Until this point in time, we have no clue about where they came from, and can just supposition where

they went.

The most established civilisation of city-states is believed to be in Mesopotamia datable to 5500 years BP. A broad up until recently most seasoned mature civilisation happens in the North-western piece of India connecting Pakistan and Afghanistan. This is the notable 'Harappan' civilisation that kept going somewhere in the range of 5300 and 2800 years BP. This incorporates major destroyed urban communities like Mohenjo Daro, Harappa, Dholavira and towns, create focuses, camping areas, stream stations, invigorated spots, ports, and so on The urban communities had very much lined roads, organized in straight lines, with legitimate seepage and sterile game plans and magnificent water passing on frameworks including really look at dams for putting away water. Use of an assortment of relics, metallic articles, many sorts of ceramics, development of gigantic constructions, and so forth couldn't have happened all of a sudden. So clearly there was a significant missing connection between the antiquated agrarian gathering of individuals and the 'Harappan' civilisation. In India there were numerous Paleolithic, Mesolithic and Neolithic stone-age societies. However, not a solitary one of them have any distant likeness to the sort of civilisation found in the Harappan destinations. It is conceivable that the missing connection between the two is either under cover or has been lowered because of significant ocean level ascent brought about by softening of ice-sheets. It's obviously true that during the Last Glacial Maxima (ice-age), the oceans all around the world had contracted and the ocean level around 18000 years BP was around 130m beneath the current day ocean level. Thus, it is intelligent to search for such lowered civilisation close to regions encompassing the current day Indian seaside regions, particularly along the palaeo channel of different rivers."

Mr. Badrinaryan has not really said environmental change was the death of this newfound civilisation, yet that is the reason for the rising ocean levels. he Ice Age finished and ultimately, the majority of the water from the dissolved ice wound up in the ocean. This was an occasion that humankind had no impact over, and there was nothing left but to leave low lying settlements and move to higher ground.

"A progression of microlithic apparatuses were gathered at different areas. By and large microlithic instruments are normal for the Mesolithic time frame and are found among Paleolithic and Neolithic Stone Age periods. The trademark elements of Mesolithic apparatuses are that not normal for the previous Paleolithic stone tools

these are a lot more modest, regularly between 5cm to 1cm long and are made of finely created semi-valuable stones. These incorporate quartz, chert, jasper, stone, chalcedony, agate, corundum, and so forth Inspecting gathered around 248 such instruments. The devices incorporated a heated sharp edge with a serrated edge, point, and point on pieces, lunate, scrubber, centers with negative chipping and a drill. The instruments have both mathematical and non-mathematical forms."

"Since certain people have communicated questions about the ceramics pieces, an exhaustive logical review was made including the earthenware pieces to set up their realness. To decide the properties of different materials including ceramics, many examples were exposed to X-Ray diffraction (XRD) investigation. Since the materials that comprise ceramics and so on are dirts and heterogeneous combinations of an assortment of materials, these were likewise dissected. Each region has an exceptional unique finger impression design in the mud, which can be perceived in X-Ray diffraction (XRD)."

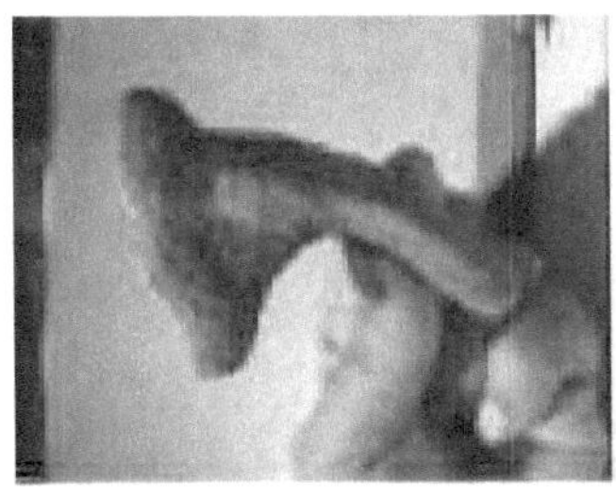

The image above comes from Mr. Badrinaryan's report on his discoveries in the Gulf of Cambay.

"In the Gulf of Cambay an assortment of microlithic devices have been gotten in continuation of late Paleolithic instruments. The presence of exceptionally developed test earthenware from 13000 BP, coordinated living, stationary very much arranged home, progressed sterile and town arranging exercises in the southern city demonstrates that it had created to be a set up civilisation from around 13000 BP. As of now there were confirmations for control of fire, making earthenware and so on from around 16840 BP. The southern city so far has given datable articles up to 8500 BP. The all around created northern

city has dates of civilisation from around 7506 BP."

It would be untimely to say there is consistent understanding as to definitively what has been found by NIOT, yet most would agree there was some type of settlement in a space that is at this point not livable because of rising ocean levels, which thus was brought about by environment change.

The accompanying Google Earth map shows one interesting side note that might give proof to help Mr. Badrinaryan's hypothesis that the occupants of the lowered city in the Gulf of Cambay happened to establish the Indus Valley Civilisation:

A little toward the North of the current limits of the Gulf of Cambay lies Lothal. This city traces all the way back to around 2400 BC and was a piece of the Indus Valley Civilisation. Lothal had the world's most seasoned known harbor which associated the city to an old course of the Sabarmati stream on the shipping lane between Harappan urban areas in Sindh and the promontory of Saurashtra when the encompassing Kutch desert of current occasions was a piece of the Arabian Sea.

It was a flourishing port in antiquated occasions, with its exchange of dabs, diamonds and important decorations arriving at the furthest corners of West Asia and even Africa. Methods and instruments spearheaded in the city for dab making and in metallurgy possess stood the trial of energy for more than four millennia.

Even before the appearance of the Harappan public, Lothal was a prosperous spot, with plentiful rice and cotton, in addition to bungalow businesses turning out dabs and ceramics. Archeologists have uncovered proof that the red fired product renowned all through the IVC was considerably refined in Lothal.

he dock was based on the eastern side of the city, and is believed by archeologists to be a designing accomplishment of the greatest request. It was constructed away from the primary ebb and flow of the stream to abstain from silting, however gave admittance to ships even at elevated tide. The metropolitan distribution center was assembled near the acropolis on a 3.5-meter-high (10.5 ft) platform of mud blocks. The city's rulers could accordingly direct movement on the dock and distribution center at the same time. Working with the development of freight was a mud-block wharf, 220 meters (720 ft) since a long time ago, based on the western arm of the dock, with a slope prompting the warehouse.

As with most IVC urban communities, Lothal was based on an all around requested framework, and life seems to have been very much arranged and managed. Each house had a sump, or assortment chamber to store strong waste to forestall the obstructing of city channels. Channels, sewer vents and cesspools kept the city clean and saved waste in the waterway, which was cleaned out during elevated tide. Individuals of Lothal spearheaded their own variations of Harappan workmanship and painting. Their developments remembered reasonable depictions of creatures for their normal environmental elements. The general plenitude of metal product, gold and adornments and elegantly embellished decorations authenticate the way of life and success of individuals of Lothal.

Most of the metal devices, loads, measures, seals, pottery and trimmings uncovered in Lothal are of the uniform norm and quality found across the IVC. The port was a significant exchange community, bringing in unrefined substances like copper, chert and semi-valuable stones from Mohenjo-daro and Harappa, and mass circulating to towns and towns inland. It was additionally a significant assembling base, creating enormous amounts of bronze celts, fish-snares, etches, lances and trimmings. Lothal sent out its globules, gemstones, ivory

and shells. The stone sharp edge industry took into account homegrown necessities—fine chert was imported from the Sukkur valley (Mohenjo-daro) or from Bijapur in present day Karnataka. Bhagatrav provided semi-valuable stones while chank shell came from Dholavira and Bet Dwarka. The exchange network extended to Egypt, Bahrain and Sumer. A vital piece of proof of exchange Lothal is the revelation of common Persian bay seals.

he overall closeness in reality proposes a type of connection between individuals of the lowered city and Lothal is unmistakably conceivable. This doesn't clarify a movement from the Gulf of Cambay to the Indus Valley and back once more. An absence of supporting proof doesn't preclude this, yet makes it very hard to show how, why and when such relocations occurred and regardless of whether they were the sole organizers to the IVC or impacted others as of now there. A more conceivable situation is whoever deserted the city that lowered would have moved to Lothal and coordinated with individuals who showed up from the Indus Valley around 2400 BC. This would clarify the obvious similitudes between what has been recovered from the seabed in the Gulf of Cambay and what has been found in Lothal and the Indus Valley.

There are various accounts of lowered old urban communities close to Asian shores, yet one of the primary concerns of this book is that civilisations all over the planet have been impacted by environmental change, so let us direct our concentration toward Africa.

The Garamantes

sooner or later somewhere in the range of 1000 and 500 BC, a civilisation arose in what is currently southern Libya. In the core of the Sahara Desert, individuals developed wheat, grain, grapes and figs and had groups of dairy cattle. They fostered their own letter set, assembled little pyramids rather like the Phoenicians, revered a divinity with the top of a canine – basically the same as their neighbors in Egypt – and their military rode into fight on four-horse chariots.

In 500 BC, these individuals were portrayed by Herodotus as the Garamantes – a "exceptionally incredible country". Pliny and Tacitus additionally went on about these people.

The Garamantes had the option to flourish in the Sahara for north of 1,000 years since they fostered an arrangement of water system that exploited

underground water stores. They constructed a complicated organization of passages (called "foggaras" in Berber)and wells that appropriated water to ranches and pastures.
While the Garamantes provided the architects, the difficult work came from slaves.

A realm was made in which clans from encompassing regions were oppressed and their labor used to assemble and keep huge number of miles of foggaras. As the Roman Empire ventured into North Africa, the Garamantes at first fought with their northern adversaries and afterward saw the advantages of exchange. The Romans acquired salt, jewels and (most likely) slaves and gave wine, glass and extravagance merchandise in return.

As the graph beneath by Samuel Bailey shows, the designing guideline behind a qanat/foggara was straightforward yet required a great deal of labor to implement.

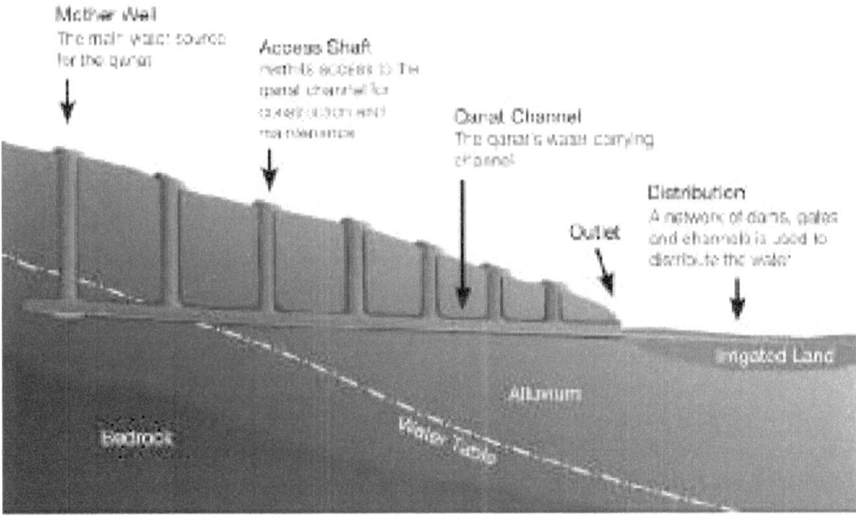

A Roman shower has been found at Garama, the capital. We realize Romans made it this far into the desert, initially in war and afterward as exchange missions and messengers. In 69 AD, Trajan sent Julius Maternus set for Garama,

and he is accepted to have been taken past the River Niger into what is presently northern Nigeria by his Garamantes hosts.

The beginnings of the Garamantes are difficult to decide. Their content proposes close connections with Berbers, yet does that mean the Berbers are their relatives or were the Garamantes one of the Berber clans? The five-meter high pyramids found at Garamantes urban areas look very similar to the pyramids of Meroe in Sudan rather than Egyptian plan. Their technique for internment consolidates protests all the more frequently connected with the Phoenicians. The foggaras are comparative in plan and capacity to the qanats of Persia.

Perhaps the appropriate response lies in the incredible tradition of the Garamantes: the advancement of shipping lanes and parade trails. From their base in southern Libya, the Garamantes associated the Ethiopians, the Egyptians, the Phoenicians and Carthaginians, the Greeks and Romans and the African clans past the Sahara. It would be completely normal for the Garamantes to "get" from the way of life they experienced. Thus, maybe they were an ingenious clan of Libyans (in the old feeling of the word) who saw nothing bad about duplicating the tactical strategies and hardware of the Egyptians and the washing propensities for the Romans.

The Garamantes were something beyond sly borrowers of others' traditions and innovation. Preserved remaining parts have been found that are more seasoned than any found in Egypt. In 1958, the mummy of a little youngster was found at Uan Muhuggiag in focal Libya. Tests uncovered it was around 5,500 years of age. It is conceivable another clan was capable, yet the mummy was found ashore that was subsequently administered by the Garamantes.

It is broadly accepted the camel was acquainted with the Sahara by the Garamantes. What is sure is these creatures were utilized along parade courses these individuals set up before they were utilized by other North African tribes.

The death of the Garamatean domain was brought about by an absence of water. They had relied upon fossil water on the grounds that there was essentially no precipitation on their territory. After north of 1,000 years of double-dealing, the underground lakes under the desert ran out of water. This implied individuals couldn't develop sufficient food to help such an unusually enormous populace in the center of

a tremendous desert. The endless loop was finished when the lessening populace couldn't stifle different clans and acquire adequate captives to extend the organization of foggaras.

By the time the Muslims vanquished Libya, the realm had turned into a dusty station on the train trails. At the point when the train trails were rerouted to consider new business sectors, Garama turned into a town in the desert and different settlements of the Garamantes were abandoned.

t is difficult to say of environmental change had an influence in the downfall of this one of a kind desert realm because of lacking proof, however there is no denying the way that for over a thousand years the Garamantes challenged the progressions in environment that burdened the remainder of the Sahara Desert.

The Vandals

The accompanying guide is gotten from the assortment of the Perry-Castañeda Library of the University of Texas:

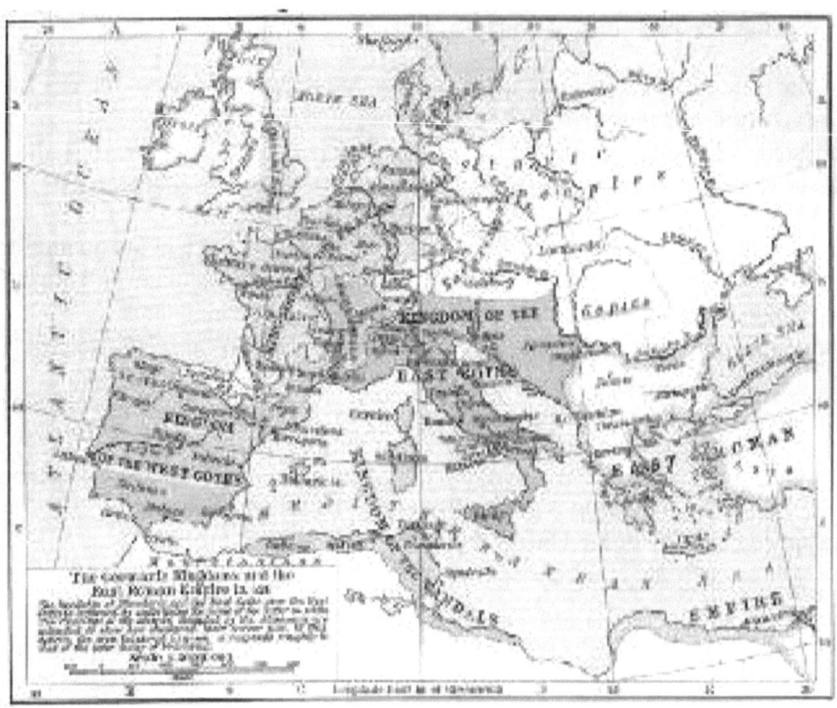

Considering their effect on North Africa and then some, it may appear to be abnormal to depict the Vandals as a civilisation. All things considered, the Vandals were an unmistakable clan from more prominent Germany who established a realm in northern Africa in the fifth and 6th hundreds of years AD. Their realm, and its capital Carthage, were caught by Belisarius in 534 AD and Berber clans attacked the majority of the region after the general had continued on to catch Rome. One can not ascribe the end of the Vandals to environmental change, however they are a superb illustration of what a culture can mean for the climate and climate.

Despite having their own realm for a little more than a century, the Vandals left a "heritage" that has kept going till the present. The harm they caused for North Africa, particularly the ecological demolition, have not been repaired. Millennia of improvement by Phoenicians, Carthaginians and Romans were scattered in a hundred years of silly, wanton obliteration. This is the reason we have the expressions "miscreant" and "vandalism".

Not all of the obliteration caused by the Vandals was purposeful. They had
the best naval force on the planet in the fourth and fifth hundreds of years,
and as boats were made of wood, that implied trees must be chopped down to
supply the natural substance for the Vandal naval force. A significant part of
the backwoods that bordered North Africa was cleaved down in about a
couple of ages to construct the Vandal warships. As this was managed with
no perceptible worry for the climate or preservation of regular assets, the
outcome was the finished annihilation of North Africa's woodlands, quite a
bit of which stays fruitless right up 'til the present time. Accordingly, the
environment has become more bone-dry and desert has infringed straight up
to the Mediterranean shore. This is the suffering tradition of the Vandals.

There have been endeavors by some cutting edge students of history to
depict the Vandals as distorted and no more awful for the Mediterranean
shores they visited than the 21st century German travelers one may find at
any ocean side resort.
ontemporary reports by the individuals who got very close with the
Vandals go against those revisions.

The Vikings of Greenland

Climate change doesn't really mean truly rising temperatures, and human
action can fuel a pattern towards cooler climate. The Viking colonization
of Greenland is an exemplary example.

When the Norse settlements were established, the inward areas of the long
fjords of western Greenland where the settlements were found were totally
different from conditions in the twentieth and 21st hundreds of years.
Unearthings show that there were impressive birch woods with trees up to 4
- 6 meters high nearby around the internal pieces of the Tunuliarfik-and
Aniaaq-fjords, the focal space of the Eastern settlement, and the slopes were
developed with grass and willow brushes.

According to the Icelandic adventures, Erik the Red was banished from
Iceland for a very long time, as discipline for a murder he submitted. He
cruised to Greenland, where he investigated the shoreline and asserted
specific grounds as his

own. He then, at that point, gotten back to Iceland to enlist individuals to choose Greenland. This is the reason he gave his revelation the name "Greenland" – it more likely than not sounded exceptionally alluring to individuals residing in a spot called Iceland. The date of foundation of the settlement is recorded in the Icelandic adventures as 985 AD, when 25 ships left with Erik the Red. Just 14 showed up securely in Greenland. This record has been somewhat affirmed by radiocarbon dating of some remaining parts at the primary settlement at Brattahlid (presently Qassiarsuk), which yielded a date of around 1000 AD. As indicated by the adventures, it was additionally in the year 1000 that Erik's child, Leif Erikson, passed on the settlement to find Vinland, for the most part thought to be situated in what is presently Newfoundland.

The accompanying guide from Archeology in Europe shows the settlement regions in Greenland:

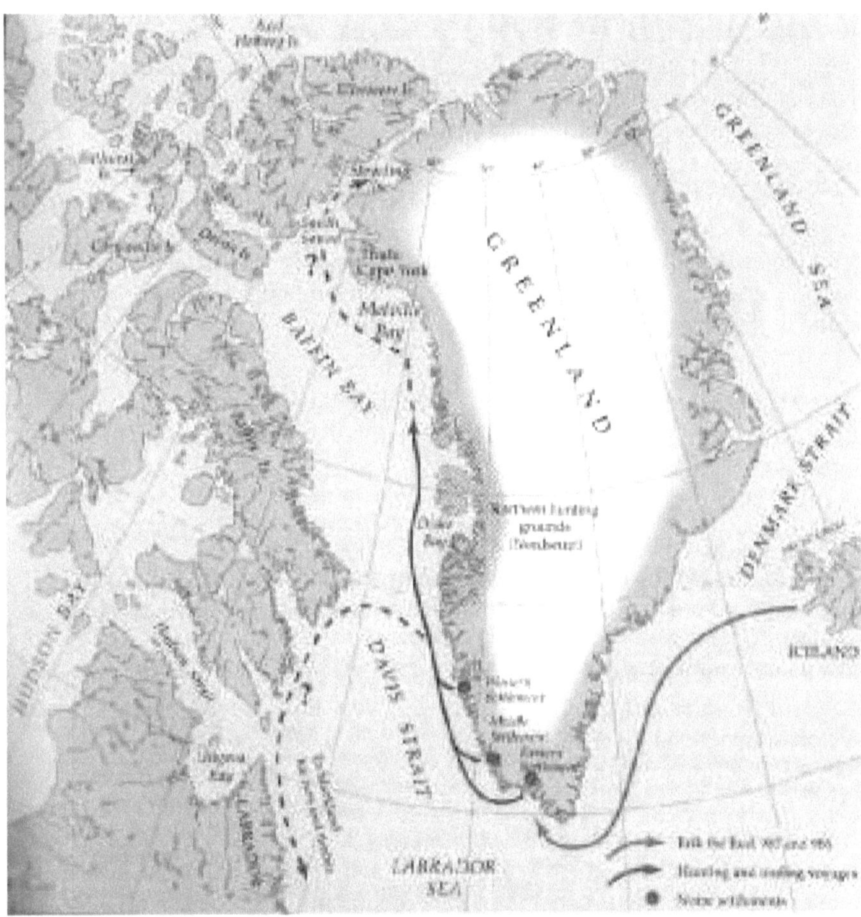

The Greenland province comprised of three settlement regions — the bigger Eastern settlement, the more modest Western settlement, the still more modest Middle Settlement (a few history specialists think of it as a feature of the Eastern).

Population gauges for the whole state range from maximums of simply 2,000 to upwards of 10,000 individuals. Later gauges, like that of Professor Niels Lynnerup in Vikings: The North Atlantic Saga, ed. by William W. Fitzhugh and Elisabeth I. Ward, have inclined toward the lower figure. Remnants of around 600 homesteads have been found in the settlements, 500 in the Eastern settlement, 95 in the Western settlement, and 20 in the Middle.

By Viking norms, this was a huge province (the number of inhabitants in present day Greenland is something like 56,000). The Greenlanders traded walrus tusk ivory to Europe, alongside rope, sheep, seals and dairy cattle stows away as per one thirteenth century account. The state imported iron devices, wood (particularly for boat building, which they additionally may have acquired from beach front Labrador), supplemental food varieties, and strict and social contacts. Exchange ships from Iceland and Norway (from the late thirteenth century all boats were legitimately constrained to cruise straightforwardly to Norway) ventured out to Greenland consistently and some of the time spent the colder time of year there.

In 1126, a ward was established at Garðar (presently Igaliku). It was dependent upon the Norwegian archdiocese of Nidaros (presently Trondheim); the remaining parts of something like five chapels in Norse Greenland have been found. In 1261, the populace acknowledged the power of the Norwegian King, albeit the province kept on having its own law. In 1380, Norway went into an association with the Kingdom of Denmark.

After flourishing for the initial three centuries, the Greenland settlements declined in the fourteenth century. The Western Settlement was deserted around 1350.
From 1378, there could have been at this point not a minister at Garðar. After 1408, when a marriage was recorded, very few set up accounts notice different insights regarding the pioneers. There was correspondence between the Pope and the Bishop Bertold af Garde from same year. The Danish Cartographer Claudius Clavus seems to have visited Greenland in 1420 dependent on archives by Nicolas Germanus and Henricus Martellus who approached unique cartographic notes and guides by Clavus. Two numerical compositions containing the second outline of the Claudius Clavus map from his movement to Greenland where he most definitely planned the region were found during the late twentieth century by the Danish researcher Bjönbo and Petersen.

Pope Nicholas V sent a letter in 1448 teaching the diocesans of Skálholt and Hólar (the two Icelandic episcopal sees) to guarantee the pilgrims of Greenland had ministers and a cleric. There had been no minister on the state for a considerable length of time since the appearance of Inuit trespassers who had obliterated the houses of worship and removed numerous Norse individuals as prisoners.

ithout a doubt the Eastern Settlement was ancient by the center fifteenth century albeit no definite date has been set up because of an absence of enduring records.

Greenland was consistently colder in winter than Iceland and Norway, and its landscape less agreeable to horticulture. Soil disintegration was a significant peril for cultivating right from the start, yet one that the pilgrims might not have perceived until it was past the point of no return. For the initial three centuries, the moderately warm West Greenland current streaming northwards along the south-western shore of Greenland would have made it feasible for the pilgrims to cultivate much as their progenitors had done in Iceland and northern Norway. Palynologists' tests on dust counts and fossilized plants give solid proof the Greenlanders more likely than not battled with soil disintegration and deforestation. As the inadmissibility of the land for farming turned out to be progressively obvious, the Greenlanders turn first to pastoralism and afterward hunting as their fundamental wellspring of food. Shockingly, they never scholarly the hunting procedures of the Inuit whose abilities may have permitted the pilgrims to adjust adequately to survive.

Extensive examination has been directed in Greenland to decide changes in environment during the medieval times. One key test includes boring into the Greenland ice covers to get center examples. The oxygen isotopes from the ice covers tests recommended that the "Middle age Warm Period" had caused a generally gentle environment in Greenland, enduring from around 800 to 1200 AD. From around 1300 AD, the environment started to cool. By 1420, we realize what was alluded to in Europe as the "Little Ice Age" had arrived at extraordinary levels in Greenland.

Excavations of midden or trash piles from Viking ranches in Greenland and Iceland show a shift from the bones of cows and pigs to those of sheep and goats. As the winters developed longer and crueler, and the springs and summers abbreviated, there probably been less and less an ideal opportunity for Greenlanders to develop feed to take care of cows. Unearthings of stores from a clan leader's ranch during the fourteenth century showed countless dairy cattle and caribou remains, though, a more unfortunate homestead just a few kilometers away had no hint of homegrown animal remaining parts, just seal. Bone examples from Greenland burial grounds affirm that the common Greenlander diet had expanded at this point from 20% ocean creatures to 80%.

There is no question the colder environment would have happened paying little mind to what the Greenlanders had done, however by similar token, their activities exacerbated things. Deforestation sped up the deficiency of soil and more likely than not exacerbated neighborhood climatic conditions. The appearance of Inuit, who were

threatening to the Norse and better prepared to living in the brutal cold climate was one more variable in the downfall of the Viking province of Greenland.

The Anasazi aka Ancient Pueblo People

The following map is taken from Wikipedia's commons files:

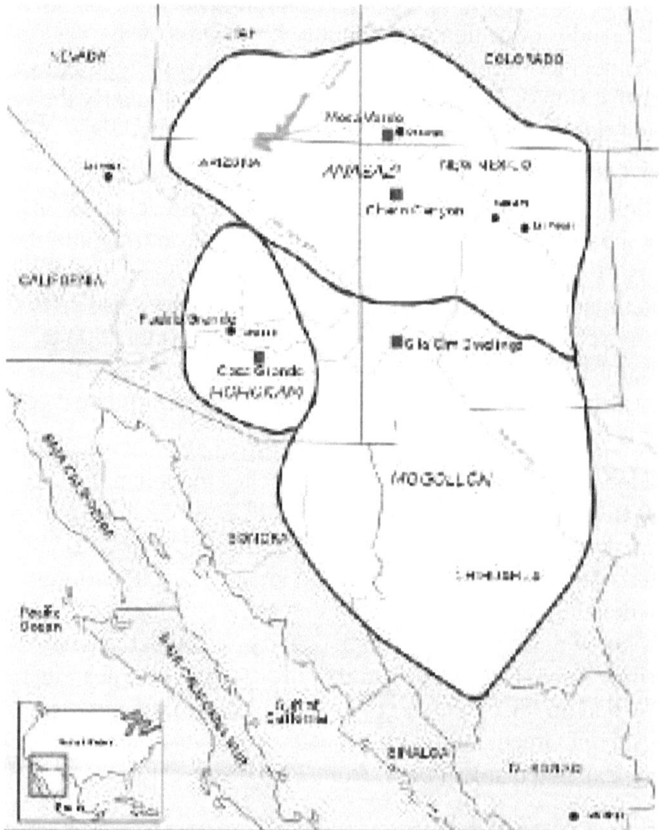

The Ancient Pueblo individuals or Ancestral Pueblo individuals were a pre-Columbian Native American culture jogged on the present-day "Four Corners" space of the United States, involving southern Utah, northern

Arizona, northwest New Mexico, and southern Colorado. These individuals have

regularly been alluded to as the Anasazi, albeit the term isn't liked by contemporary Pueblo people groups since "Anasazi" is Navajo for "Antiquated Ones" or "Old Enemy".

Archeologists are dubious with regards to when this unmistakable culture arose. The most famous hypothesis, in light of phrasing characterized by the Pecos Classification, is that this culture arose around the twelfth century BC, during the archeologically assigned Basketmaker II Era. It is accepted the Ancient Puebloans are progenitors of the cutting edge Pueblo people groups. As a general rule, present day Pueblo individuals guarantee these old individuals are their ancestors.

The Ancient Pueblo were one of four old societies perceived in the American South-west. The others are the Mogollon, Hohokam and Patayan. The Colorado Plateau is at the core of their memorable region. Spaces of southern Nevada, Utah and Colorado mark a free northern limit, while the southern edge is characterized by the Colorado and Little Colorado streams in Arizona and the Rio Puerco and Rio Grande in New Mexico. It ought to be noted constructions and other proof of Ancient Pueblo culture has been found as far East as the American Great Plains, in regions close to the Cimarron and Pecos waterways and in the Galisteo Basin (New Mexico).

The name "Pueblo" was given by the Spanish, and signifies "town" in that language. The Ancient Pueblo culture is likely most popular for the stone and adobe homes incorporated into bluff dividers, especially during the Pueblo II and Pueblo III times. Adobe structures were worked from blocks made of sand, mud, and water, alongside some sinewy or natural material, formed utilizing outlines and dried in the sun. The best-protected instances of these stone and adobe homes are in Chaco Canyon or Chaco Culture National Historical Park, Mesa Verde National Park, Aztec Ruins National Monument, Bandelier National Monument, Hovenweep National Monument, and Canyon de Chelly National Monument. These towns were regularly just available by rope or through rock climbing. These astounding structure accomplishments denoted a critical advancement from prior structures by these individuals. The principal Ancestral Puebloan homes and towns depended on the pit-house, a typical element in the Basketmaker periods.

The best-protected towns, like Chaco Canyon (outside Crownpoint, New

Mexico), Mesa Verde (outside Cortez, Colorado), and Bandelier (outside
Los Alamos, New Mexico), comprised of loft like complexes

and structures made from stone, adobe mud, and other local material, or were
carved into the sides of canyon walls. These ancient settlements usually
featured multi-storied and multi-purposed buildings surrounding open plazas
and viewsheds that were occupied by hundreds or sometimes thousands of
Ancestral Puebloan people. They hosted cultural and civic events and their
infrastructure supported a vast outlying region with settlements hundreds of
miles apart linked by custom-built roads.

The image above of the Mesaverde precipice royal residence is from
Wikimedia Commons and provided by Lorax.

Before anybody excuses the Anasazi/Puebloans as simply one more clan from
"crude" North America with some intriguing archeological remaining parts, it
merits remembering that in Europe preceding the Industrial Revolution in
Britain (Which occurred a few centuries after the death of the
Anasazi/Puebloan civilisation), the main individuals who coordinated with
their accomplishments in street fabricating and related foundation were the
Romans at the pinnacle of their turn of events. No other European power,
including those that vanquished North America, even came close.

To accomplish such a great amount with a populace of close to 20,000 individuals at any

point in their set of experiences is momentous. That the Anasazi/Puebloans dealt with this without the wheel, a type of composing or even load animals is nearly without equal in history.

One of the most entrancing and fascinating parts of Ancestral Puebloan framework is the Chaco Road that beginnings at Chaco Canyon. This is really an organization of streets transmitting out from numerous incredible house locales like Pueblo Bonito, Chetro Ketl and Una Vida, and driving towards little anomaly destinations and normal highlights inside and past the gorge limits.

sing satellite pictures and leading ground examinations have empowered archeologists to find something like eight principle streets that together are in excess of 180 miles/300 km long. These are streets in a literal sense: more than 30 feet/10 m wide and worked to a smooth evened out surface in bedrock or made through the evacuation of vegetation and soil. The Ancestral Puebloan/Anasazi pioneers of Chaco Canyon exhumed enormous inclines and flights of stairs into the bluffs to interface the streets on the edge highest points of the gulch to the destinations on the valley bottoms.

he biggest streets, which were worked simultaneously as large numbers of the extraordinary house locales (1000 - 1125 AD), are: known as the Great North Road, the South Road, the Coyote Canyon Road, the Chacra Face Road, Ahshislepah Road, Mexican Springs Road, the West Road and the more limited Pintado-Chaco Road. Essential designs like embankments and dividers are seen as now and then adjusted along the courses of these streets. Additionally, a few lots of the streets lead to normal highlights like springs, lakes, mountain ridges and pinnacles.

The longest and generally renowned of these streets is the Great North Road. The Great North Road begins from various courses close to Pueblo Bonito and Chetro Ketl. These minor streets join at Pueblo Alto and from that point go north past as far as possible. There are no networks along the street's course, aside from little, separated structures.

ome archeologists accept Chaco street framework filled essentially a financial need while others think the streets played a representative, philosophical job connected to genealogical Puebloan beliefs.

The framework was first found toward the finish of the nineteenth century, and first unearthed and contemplated during the 1970s. Archeologists at the time recommended the streets' fundamental intention was to move products inside the gully and then some. Somebody additionally proposed that these huge streets were utilized to rapidly move an

armed force from the ravine to the anomaly networks, a reason like the street frameworks developed by the Roman domain. This keep going situation has for quite some time been disposed of due to the shortfall of any proof of an extremely durable army.

The financial reason for the Chaco street framework is exhibited by the presence of extravagance things at Pueblo Bonito and somewhere else in the gulch. Things like macaws, turquoise, marine shells, and imported vessels demonstrate the significant distance business relations Chaco had with different areas. Additional proof is given by the inescapable utilization of lumber in Chacoan developments – a material not accessible locally – required an enormous and simple extremely durable transportation framework. Through investigation of different strontium isotopes, archeologists have found that a large part of the wood that used to construct Chacoan settlements came from various far off mountain ranges, characteristic likewise of the Chaco Road's financial significance.

One of the principle needs for the organizers of every settlement was that the site ought to be generally simple to guard. The absolute generally famous and notable authentic destinations are mostly up steep bluffs, yet the Ancient Pueblo individuals additionally exploited high, steep plateaus, for example, at Mesa Verde or present-day Acoma "Sky City" Pueblo, in New Mexico. This was worked before 900 AD and prospered until after 1300 AD.

n Chaco Canyon, the settlement organizers quarried sandstone impedes and pulled wood huge spans, developing 15 significant edifices which were the biggest structures in North America until the nineteenth century. Proof of archaeoastronomy at Chaco has been proposed, with the Sun Dagger petro glyph at Fajada Butte a well known model. Numerous Chacoan structures seem to have been adjusted to catch the sun oriented and lunar cycles. This would have required ages of cosmic perceptions and hundreds of years of skilfully organized development. As a harbinger to the downfall of the Ancient Pueblo individuals all in all, environmental change is thought to have prompted the displacement of Chacoans and the possible deserting of the gorge, following a 50-year dry spell that started in 1130.

Enormous buildings known as "Extraordinary Houses" were utilized for strict purposes at Chaco. As compositional styles developed over hundreds of years, these structures held a few center characteristics. Most importantly is their sheer size: Great Houses found the middle value of in excess of 200 rooms each, and some encased up to 700 rooms. Individual rooms were generous in region, with higher roofs than plans of going before periods. They were very much arranged and should have

utilized many development workers all at once in light of the fact that huge areas or wings were done in a solitary development stage, rather than in increases. Houses normally confronted the south, and square regions were quite often encircled by structures of fixed off rooms or high dividers. Houses were frequently four or five stories high, with single-story rooms confronting the square; room blocks were terraced to permit the tallest areas to turn into the pueblo's back building. Rooms were regularly separated into suites, with receiving areas bigger than back, inside, and extra spaces or areas.

Ceremonial constructions known as kivas were underlying extent to the quantity of rooms in a pueblo. There was an inexact proportion of one little kiva per 29 rooms. Nine edifices each facilitated a curiously large Great Kiva, each up to 63 feet (19 m) in measurement. T-formed entryways and stone lintels denoted all Chacoan kivas.

Great Houses normally had center and-facade dividers: two equal burden bearing dividers of dressed, level sandstone blocks bound in dirt mortar were raised. Holes between dividers were loaded with rubble, shaping the divider's center. Dividers were then shrouded in a facade of little sandstone pieces, which were squeezed into a layer of restricting mud. These surfacing stones were regularly positioned in particular examples. Between them, the Chacoan structures required the lumber from 200,000 coniferous trees, for the most part pulled by walking from mountain goes up to 70 miles (110 km) away.

The territory and normal assets constrained by the Puebloans changed significantly. The level locales are by and large high, with rises going from 4500 to 8,500 feet (2,600 m). Broad level plateaus are covered by sedimentary developments and backing forests of junipers, pinon, ponderosa pines, and yellow pines, each inclining toward various heights. Wind and water disintegration have made steep walled gorge, and etched windows and extensions out of the sandstone scene. In regions where disintegration safe layers (sedimentary stone layers, for example, sandstone or limestone overlie all the more effectively dissolved layers like shale, rock overhangs framed. These shades were favored destinations for havens and development sites.

ll spaces of the Ancient Pueblo country experienced intermittently dry spell. Wind and water disintegration additionally represented a danger in numerous settlements. Summer downpours could be unreliable and regularly showed up in ruinous thunderstorms.
While the measure of winter snowfall fluctuated enormously, the Ancient Pueblo relied upon the snow for a large portion of their water. Snow dissolve prompted the

germination of seeds, both wild and developed, in the spring. Where sandstone layers overlay shale, snow liquefy could amass and make leaks and springs and pools, which the Ancient Pueblo utilized as water sources. Snow additionally took care of the more modest, more unsurprising feeders, like the Chinle, Animas, Jemez and Taos streams. The bigger waterways were of less significance to them in light of the fact that the more modest streams were all the more effectively redirected or controlled for irrigation.

Ancestral Puebloans are likewise known for their stoneware. As a rule, ceramics product utilized for cooking or capacity was unpainted dark, either smooth or finished. In the northern or "Anasazi" part of the Ancestral Pueblo world, from around 500 to 1300 AD, the most widely recognized finished stoneware had dark painted plans on white or light dim foundations. The differentiating colors were delivered utilizing mineral-put together paint with respect to a pale foundation. Some tall chambers are viewed as stylized vessels, while limited necked containers might have been utilized to store fluids. Ceramics in the southern piece of the locale, especially after 1150 AD, is portrayed by heavier dark lines and the utilization of carbon-based colorants. In northern New Mexico, the neighborhood "dark on white" custom – the "Rio Grande" white products – proceeded until long after 1300 AD.

Changes in stoneware creation, design and beautification are signs of social change in the archeological record. This is especially obvious as the people groups of the American Southwest started to leave their customary homes and move south. As per archeologists Patricia Crown and Steadman Upham, the presence of the splendid shadings on Salada Polychromes in the fourteenth century might reflect strict or political unions on a territorial level. Late fourteenth and fifteenth century earthenware from focal Arizona, broadly exchanged the district, has tones and plans which might get from prior product by both Anasazi and Mogollon people groups. (Cordell, p. 142-143)

The Ancestral Puebloans additionally made numerous petro glyphs and pictographs.

The time frame from 700-1130 AD saw a generally quick expansion in populace because of steady and ordinary precipitation designs. Investigations of skeletal remaining parts show that this development was because of expanded ripeness rather than diminished mortality. Notwithstanding, this ten times expansion in populace throughout a couple of ages couldn't be accomplished by expanded rate of birth alone: in all likelihood little clans from encompassing regions moved and were ingested. Advancements like earthenware, food stockpiling, and horticulture empowered this rapid development. More than quite a few years, the Ancient Pueblo culture spread across the scene. Old Pueblo culture has been partitioned into three primary regions or branches, in light of geological area: Chaco Canyon (northwest New Mexico), Kayenta (upper east Arizona), and Northern San Juan (or Mesa Verde) (southwest Colorado).

Modern Pueblo oral customs express the Pueblo started toward the north of their present settlements, from Shibapu, where they arose out of the hidden world. For obscure ages they were driven by war bosses directed by "the Spirits" across North America. They settled first in the Ancient Pueblo regions for two or three hundred years, then, at that point, moved to their current location.

It isn't completely clear why the Ancestral Puebloans moved from their set up homes in the twelfth and thirteenth hundreds of years. The most probable reasons incorporate worldwide or territorial environmental change (what is presently alluded to as "the Little Ice Age" harmonized with the surrender of the settlements), delayed times of dry season, repeating times of dirt disintegration, natural corruption, de-forestation, antagonism from fresh debuts, strict or social change, and even impact from Mesoamerican societies. A large number of these potential outcomes are upheld by archeological evidence.

Current assessment holds that the Ancestral Puebloans reacted to a blend of tension from Numic-talking people groups moving onto the Colorado Plateau, just as environmental change that brought about farming disappointments. Archeological examinations show it was actually typical for old Pueblo people groups to adjust to climatic change by changing homes and locations.

arly Pueblo I destinations might have housed up to 600 people in a couple of discrete yet firmly divided settlement bunches. Notwithstanding, they were for the most part involved for a simple 30 years or less. Classicist Timothy A. Kohler unearthed enormous Pueblo I locales close to Dolores, Colorado, and found that they were set up during times of better than expected precipitation. This would permit harvests to be developed without advantage of water system. Simultaneously, close by regions encountering essentially drier examples were abandoned.

The Ancestral Puebloans achieved a social "Brilliant Age" between around 900 and 1130. During this period, by and large classed as Pueblo II, the environment was generally warm and precipitation was for the most part adequate. Networks became bigger and were occupied for longer timeframes. Exceptionally explicit neighborhood customs in engineering and ceramics arose, and exchange over significant distances seems to have been normal. Turkeys were domesticated.

After roughly 1150, North America experienced critical climatic change as a 300-year dry spell called the Great Drought. This adjustment of environment likewise prompted the breakdown of the Tiwanaku civilisation around Lake Titicaca in present-day Bolivia. The contemporary Mississippian culture additionally fell during this period. Proof is found in unearthings of the western areas of the Mississippi Valley somewhere in the range of 1150 and 1350, which show durable examples of hotter, wetter winters and cooler, drier summers.

During this period, the Pueblo II turned out to be more independent, diminishing exchange and association with more far off networks. Southwest ranchers adjusted water system strategies to exploit occasional precipitation, including soil and water control highlights, for example, really look at dams and patios. The district's populace kept on being versatile, forsaking settlements and fields when essential. Alongside the adjustment of precipitation designs, there was a fall in water table levels because of an alternate cycle disconnected to precipitation. This constrained the deserting of settlements in the more parched or over-cultivated locations.

There are indications of a significant change in religion during this period. Chacoan and different constructions fabricated initially along cosmic arrangements, and thought to have filled significant stylized needs, were efficiently destroyed. Entryways were fixed with rock and mortar. Kiva dividers show marks from incredible flames set inside them, which likely required evacuation of the monstrous rooftop - an assignment which would require critical exertion. In certain spots, homes were deserted, clans split and separated and resettled far away. This proposes the strict designs were purposely deserted gradually after some time. Puebloan custom holds that the progenitors had accomplished extraordinary otherworldly power and command over regular powers, and utilized their power in manners that made nature change, and prompted a progression of potentially negative side-effects. Potentially, the destroying of their strict constructions was a work to emblematically fix the progressions they believed they caused because of their maltreatment of their profound power, and in this manner set things straight with nature.

ost present day Pueblo people groups (regardless of whether Keresans, Hopi, or Tanoans) affirm the old Pueblo didn't "disappear", as is generally assumed, yet relocated to regions in the southwest with more ideal precipitation and trustworthy streams. Over the long haul, they converged into the different Pueblo people groups whose relatives actually live in Arizona and New Mexico. This viewpoint isn't new. It was communicated by mid twentieth century anthropologists, including Frank

Hamilton Cushing, J. Walter Fewkes and Alfred V. Comedian. Numerous cutting edge Pueblo clans follow their heredity from settlements. For instance, the San Ildefonso Pueblo individuals accept that their predecessors lived in both the Mesa Verde and the Bandelier regions. Proof likewise recommends that a significant change occurred in the Anasazi region and regions occupied by their social neighbors, the Mogollon. The contemporary history specialist James W. Loewen concurs with the oral customs in his book, Lies Across America: What Our Historic Markers and Monuments Get Wrong (1999), yet there is an absence of agreement inside the expert scholastic local area on the subject.

Environmental debasement might have been the reason for struggle and fighting. Close to Kayenta, Arizona, Jonathan Haas of the Field Museum in Chicago has been concentrating on a gathering of Ancient Pueblo towns whose occupants moved from the gulches to the high plateau tops during the late thirteenth century. The main explanation Haas can see for a move so distant from water and arable land is safeguard against adversaries. He declares disconnected networks relied upon assaulting for food and supplies, and that interior clash and fighting became normal in the thirteenth century. This contention might have been bothered by an inundation of less settled people groups, Numic-speakers like the Utes, Shoshones and Paiute individuals, who might have started in what is today California. Others recommend that more created towns, for example, that at Chaco Canyon overemphasized their current circumstance, bringing about inescapable deforestation and in the long run the fall of their civilisation through fighting over exhausted resources.

A 1997 removal at Cowboy Wash close to Dolores, Colorado, tracked down stays of something like 24 human skeletons that displayed proof of savagery and dismantling, with solid signs of barbarianism. This unobtrusive local area seems to have been deserted during a similar time period.
Other unearthings inside the Puebloan culture region and a similar period produce shifting quantities of unburied, and now and again eviscerated, bodies. This proof of fighting, struggle, and barbarianism is fervently bantered by certain researchers and vested parties. Recommended choices include: a local area under the tension of starvation or outrageous social pressure, dismantling and barbarianism directed as strict custom or in light of strict struggle, the activities of untouchables looking to drive out a settled agrarian local area through determined monstrosity, or an intrusion of a settled district by traveling thieves who rehearsed cannibalism.

Tiwanaku

Tiwanaku was the focal point of a significant South American culture for more than 1,000 years and is viewed as a significant antecedent to the Inca Empire. Situated on the eastern shore of Lake Titicaca, 45 miles/72 km west of La Paz in western Bolivia, thrived from around 300 BC to 800 AD. The city is accepted to have been something other than the capital of a sweeping realm, it likewise filled in as a cosmological focus and a position of moral importance, and in this way an objective for pilgrimages.

The public area map underneath provided by Wikimedia Commons shows the degree of the Tiwanaku domain:

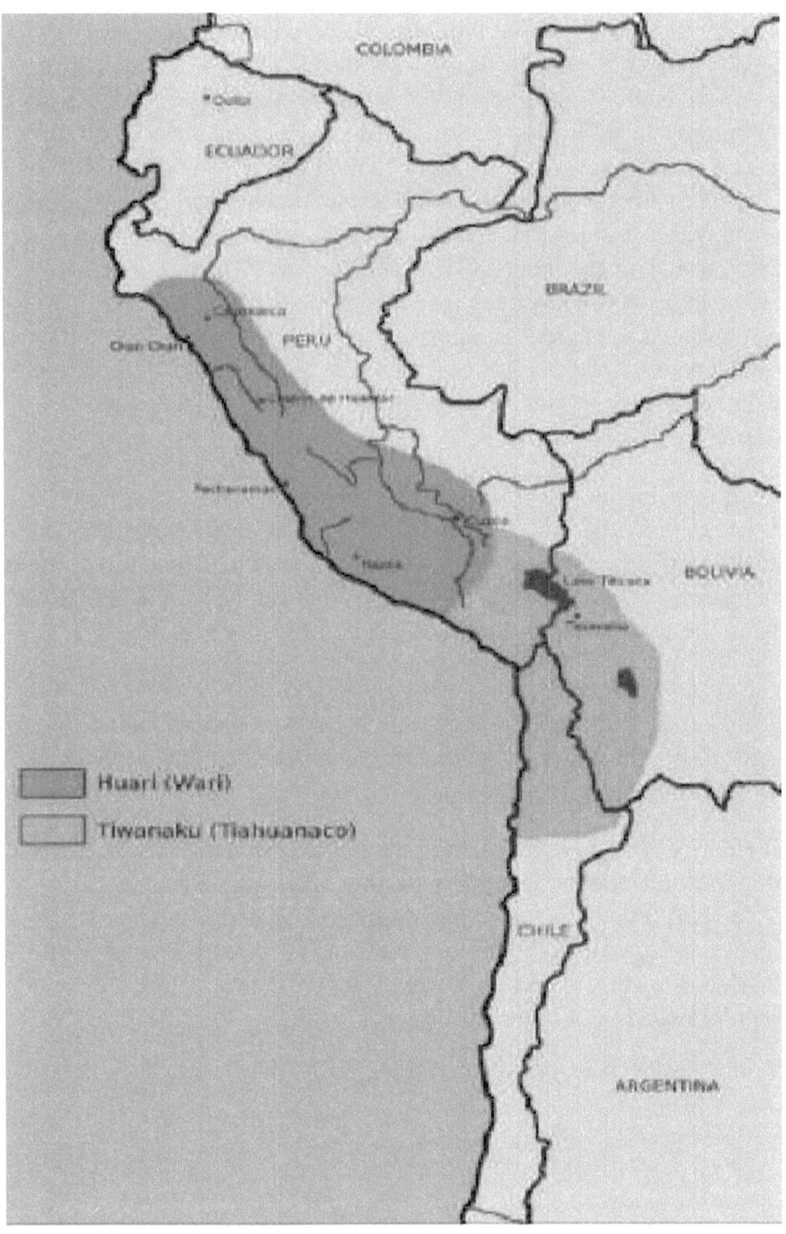

The city's area in the Titicaca Basin between the lake and dry high countries was obviously fit to particular agribusiness. It had plentiful, customary precipitation designs, while the lake was a wellspring of fish and wild birds. A portion of the land was utilized as field llamas while different plots of land were committed to a cultivating procedure called "overwhelmed raised field" farming. The nearby name for this sort of cultivating is "suka kollu". This strategy for cultivating requires the development of counterfeit stages to have the harvests, with the stages isolated by shallow trenches. These waterways accomplish more than just inundate the fields. As Lake Titicaca is 12,500 feet/3,800 m above ocean level, the region is presented to a lot more significant levels of sun based radiation than as a rule happens close to the ocean level. The waterways ingest heat from the radiation during the day and delivery it around evening time, protecting the fields and shielding them from extreme frosts.

The suka kollu technique is work escalated, yet all the same profoundly useful. Customary cultivating techniques in the Andes commonly yields 2.4 metric huge loads of potatoes per hectare contrasted with current horticultural works on utilizing fake compost and pesticides that can yield up to 14.5 tons per hectare. The suka kollus regularly produce 21 tons for every hectare.

individuals of Tiwanaku had no composed language, in spite of the fact that they utilized a means of recording data utilizing tied yarn called quipu. As archeologists have yet gain a lot of headway understanding quipos, there are significant holes in our insight about this civilisation.

Their religion seems to have involved numerous divine beings and focussed on farming usefulness. The main god was Viracocha – the divine force of activity. He was viewed as a maker and destroyer. Legend had it he rose from Lake Titicaca and gave us light, the sun, moon and stars and furthermore made individuals by breathing into stones. The public area picture underneath, provided by Wikimedia Commons, shows Viracocha in all his glory:

Archeological examination upholds a hypothesis that around 400 AD the city went through a critical change from a city state to an extensive realm that spread into parts of Bolivia, Peru and Chile. There is little proof to propose this development was accomplished principally from fighting, so it appears to be coherent Tiwanaku utilized its benefits in farming result, in addition to its status as a journey objective, to grow.

Force seems to have been utilized to curb obstruction from certain clans toward the north. There is proof the foundations of sculptures were taken from different clans and afterward positioned in subordinate situations to strict sculptures in Tiwanaku to mean the city's superiority.

The city developed from 600 – 800 AD, and its populace is accepted to have reached something like 15,000. Satellite imaging of suka kollus proposes the populace for the Titicaca Basin would have been somewhere in the range of 285,000 and 1,482,000 people.

Distribution of food, merchandise and the method for transport (principally llamas utilized similarly as ponies, jackasses and camels somewhere else) was concentrated heavily influenced by the Tiwanaku gentry. This framework functioned admirably until around 950 AD. As of now there was a huge change in the area's environment, with a relatively abrupt, sharp fall in precipitation in the Titicaca Basin.

owns and settlements on the edge of the Tiwanaku lands were quick to be impacted and they had no food excesses to ship off the capital. Cultivates near the middle held out a couple of years longer, on account of the suka kollus. Continuously 1000, even these homesteads were desolate. Inside 50 years, a flourishing society had been annihilated by environmental change. The Titicaca Basin was deserted for a long time until climatic conditions improved.

In 1445, the Incas ventured into the Titicaca Basin and accepted control of the clans that had moved once more into the space. Individuals turned out to be important for the Inca Empire until the appearance and success by the Spanish in the next century. There were such countless likenesses between the Tiwanaku and Inca lifestyle, that it appears to be plausible the previous enlivened the individuals who later turned into the Inca.

Archeologists have set up that the Wari – the realm toward the north of the Tiwanaku – utilized a similar iconography in their specialty. The Tiwanaku made mummies in a very much like style to the Incas and were frequently housed in internment loads over the ground. The Tiwanaku god Viracocha was additionally an Incan god. A few antiquarians have ventured to such an extreme as to accept the whole Inca culture started hundreds of years sooner on the shores of Lake Titicaca and that the Tiwanaku are the immediate progenitors of the Incas.

Doggerland

Thus far, we have introduced instances of civilisations/societies whose destruction was in some measure part of the way owing to environmental change, with human movement adding to the reason for that environmental change much of the time. Those progressions were adequately slow to have advanced without notice in the beginning phases. They were likewise sluggish enough for the principal individuals to find the environment changes to outlast the full impacts of the harm to the spot they possessed. This isn't true in Doggerland. The reason for its downfall – rising ocean levels because of environmental change – had infringed on the space over a time of a few centuries, yet the end arrived in a solitary day.

oggerland is a name given by archeologists and geologists to a previous landmass in the southern North Sea that associated the island of Great Britain to central area Europe during and after the last Ice Age. Geographical reviews have recommended that Doggerland was a huge space of dry land that extended from Britain's east coast across to the current shore of the Netherlands and the western shorelines of Germany and Denmark. Doggerland was likely a rich environment with human residence in the Mesolithic time frame.

he archeological capability of the space had first been examined in the mid twentieth century, however premium strengthened in 1931 when a business fishing vessel working between the shoals and transportation risks known as the Leman Bank and Ower Bank east of the Wash, hauled up a rich spiked horn point that dated to when the region it came from was tundra. Later vessels have hauled up mammoth and lion stays, among other remaining parts of land creatures, just as little quantities of ancient apparatuses and weapons which were utilized by the locale's inhabitants.

Before the principal frigid time of the momentum Pleistocene-Holocene Ice Age, the River Rhine streamed North through what is currently the bed of the North Sea. It is accepted a Cenozoic residue store in East Anglia is the bed of an old course of the Rhine. The Weald was twice the length it is currently and extended across the what has turned into the Strait of Dover; the advanced Boulonnais in North-eastern France is a remainder of its east end.

When the glaciations of northern Europe happened, when Scandinavian and Scottish ice sheets came into contact they framed a monster ice dam. Subsequently, a huge proglacial lake shaped behind this regular dam, which got stream seepage and ice soften from quite a bit of northern Europe and Baltic waste through the Baltic River System. The appropriated water ultimately flooded over the Weald into the English Channel and cut a profound chasm which ocean disintegration later extended continuously into the Strait of Dover.

uring the latest glaciation, the North Sea and practically each of the British Isles were covered with frosty ice and the ocean level was around 120 meters (390 feet) lower than as of now. A significant part of the land that was later submerged

by the North Sea and English Channel was a span of low-lying tundra, stretching out the extent that the northern place of what is currently Scotland.

Evidence including the forms of the current seabed, shows that after the primary fundamental Ice Age the watershed between North Sea seepage and English Channel waste expanded East from East Anglia then South-east to the Hook of Holland, not across the Strait of Dover, and that the Thames, Meuse, Scheldt and Rhine streams joined and streamed along the English Channel dry bed as a wide lethargic waterway which in the long run released into the Atlantic Ocean. At around 8000 BC, the north-bound waterfront region, presently called Doggerland, had a shore of tidal ponds, salt swamps, mudflats, and sea shores, and inland streams and waterways and bogs, and here and there lakes. It might have been the most extravagant hunting, fowling and fishing ground in Europe accessible to the Mesolithic culture of the time.

As ocean levels rose after the finish of the last cold time of the ebb and flow ice age (it could be said we are living in an "Ice Age" even in the mid 21st century in light of the fact that for a large portion of our planet's set of experiences there have been no polar ice covers), and the level of the land sank due to isostatic change, Doggerland became lowered underneath the North Sea, removing what was already the British landmass from the European central area by around 6500 BC. The Dogger Bank, which had been a moderately upland space of Doggerland, is accepted to have stayed as an island until no less than 5000 BC. Before it overflowed totally, Doggerland was a wide undulating plain holding back complex wandering waterway frameworks, with associating channels and lakes. Key stages are currently accepted to incorporate the steady advancement of a huge flowing embayment between eastern England and Dogger Bank by 7000 BC, and fast ocean level ascent from that point, prompting the Dogger Bank turning into an island and Great Britain being at last actually separated from the mainland of Europe.

The primary investigations of the remaining parts of plants brought to the surface from Dogger Bank had been directed as ahead of schedule as 1913 by palaeobiologist Clement Reid and the remaining parts of creatures and worked stones from the Neolithic time frame had been found around the

edges of the space. In his book The Antiquity of Man, distributed in 1915, anatomist Sir Arthur Keith had examined the archeological capability of the space. Then, at that point, in 1931, the fishing boat Colinda pulled up a piece of peat while fishing close to the Ower Bank, 25 miles
(40 km) East of Norfolk. The peat contained a thorned prong point, perhaps utilized as a spear or fish skewer, 8.5 inches (220 mm) long, later recognized to
date from somewhere in the range of 4,000 and 10,000 years prior, when the region was tundra. The device was shown in the Castle Museum in Norwich.

Interest in the space was restored during the 1990s on account of crafted by Prof. Bryony Coles, who named the region "Doggerland" ("after the extraordinary banks in the southern North Sea") and made a progression of speculative guides of the space. Despite the fact that Prof. Coles perceived the momentum alleviation of the southern North Sea seabed is certifiably not a sound manual for the geography of Doggerland 10,000 years sooner, the geology of the space has all the more as of late been remade all the more definitively utilizing seismic study information acquired through petrochemical investigation surveys.

skull section of a Neanderthal, dated at more than 40,000 years of age, was recuperated from material dug from the Middeldiep, a district of the North Sea exactly 10 miles (16 km) off the shore of Zeeland, and was shown in Leiden in 2009.

In March 2010, it was accounted for that acknowledgment of the expected archeological significance of the space could influence the future improvement of seaward wind ranches in the North Sea.

While it is clear individuals possessed Doggerland and may even have had a particular stone age culture, this was not really a "civilisation". Likewise, these individuals were not liable for the environmental change that suffocated their property. So what environment actuated power of nature was so incredible it could eradicate a land covering large number of square miles in under a day?

The researchers Bernhard Weninger, Rick Schulting, Marcel Bradtmöller, Lee Clare, Mark Collard, Kevan Edinborough, Johanna Hilpert, Olaf Jöris, Marcel Niekus, Eelco J. Rohling and Bernd Wagner accumulated a complete report named "The calamitous last flooding of Doggerland by the Storegga Slide tidal wave". I will draw on the substance of this report to clarify what occurred at Doggerland on the grounds that it is imperative with regards to the second 50% of this book to have legitimate, authorize researchers disclose the what befell Doggerland and why. One significant highlight note: "the Storegga Slide" was really a progression of no less than three comparable occasions isolated by millennia. It is the last emission that is the subject of the report below.

"Theoretical – Around 8200 calBP, enormous pieces of the now lowered North

Sea mainland rack ('Doggerland') were disastrously overflowed by the Storegga Slide tidal wave, probably the biggest torrent known for the Holocene, which was created on the Norwegian waterfront edge by a submarine avalanche. In the current paper, we infer an exact calendric date for the Storegga Slide torrent, utilize this date for recreation of contemporary shorelines in the North Sea corresponding to quickly rising ocean levels, and examine the expected impacts of the wave on the contemporaneous Mesolithic populace. One principle consequence of this review is an out of the blue high wave sway relegated toward the western locales of Jutland…

a nearly huge number of stores on the shores of Norway and eastern Scotland would now be able to be securely ascribed to the Second Storegga Slide torrent. The age of the tidal wave clearly elaborate some 2400–3200km3 of material that spread across the North Atlantic ocean bottom, out and out covering a space of around 95 000km2 (Haflidason et al. 2005) – that is about the size of Scotland. Bryn et al. (2005) propose the reason for the Storegga slide was a solid quake in the North Atlantic, yet further examinations are important to validate this speculation. ..

Traces of the relating Second Storegga Slide torrent have been recognized in numerous locales of the North Atlantic, with the best-concentrated on areas on the bank of Norway and eastern Scotland. On the Norwegian coast, at areas straightforwardly inverse to the sub-marine avalanche district, the tidal wave had a greatest runup of 10–12m. Further north, a runup of 6–7m is recreated. On the eastern bank of Scotland average runup statures surpass 3–5m (Smith et al. 2004). Storegga stores are additionally known from the Faroes (Grauert et al. 2001) and the Shetland Islands, where runup surpasses 20m (Bondevik et al. 2005). Late examinations show that the tidal wave most likely even arrived at the east shore of Greenland (Wagner et al. 2007). This would concur with displaying studies (Bondevik et al. 2005), as indicated by which the wave front would have crossed the North Atlantic inside 3 hours, with maximal height on the untamed expanse of 3m. The size of these waves, and their spread over such an enormous region, demonstrate that a large portion of the volume of the slide was engaged with the age of the torrent (Bondevik et al. 2005). On the Norwegian coast, the appearance of the main wave would have been related with a significant water withdrawal, comparing to an anticipated beginning ocean

level drop of 20m. The model likewise predicts that different waves ought to happen. This is affirmed for stores presumably set somewhere around the Storegga slide tidal wave on the east bank of Greenland, where the grain-size arrangement, biogeochemical and macrofossil information demonstrate that the Loon Lake bowl was immersed by something like four waves (Wagner et al. 2007). The impacts of the wave on other North Sea coasts – and remarkably on Mesolithic Doggerland (Coles 1998) – have not yet been demonstrated. As a beginning stage for our investigations towards the expected impacts of the Storegga Slide wave in the southern North Sea, we accept that runup in this district is probably going to have been around 3m (pers. comm. Bondevik 2007).

Due to rising ocean levels in the ninth thousand years calBP, the specific planning of the Storegga Slide wave comparative with contemporaneous ocean levels in the North Sea is vital for the recreation of the torrent's ecological effect. Right now the North Sea locale was encountering a period of most quick early Holocene ocean level change (Lambeck 1995; Shennan et al. 2000; Behre 2003), in blend with similarly huge glacio-and hydro-isostatic land-level changes, for example shifting of Scotland and Norway (Lambeck 1995; Dawson and Smith 1997; Gyllencreutz 2005b). To additionally entangle matters, because of quickly rising ocean levels during the ninth thousand years, an ever increasing number of areas of Doggerland – a now lowered land-region arranged among Britain and the mainland (Coles 1998) – were becoming lowered. Remittance additionally must be made for the flowing system at the time.

To work with investigation of the ecological effect of the Storegga Slide wave in the southern pieces of Doggerland (where we anticipate the most elevated thickness of Mesolithic occupation, see beneath), we would now be able to depend on an exceptionally exact date for the tidal wave occasion available to us: 7300 ± 30 14C-BP (95%-certainty), or 8100 ± 100 calBP (95%-certainty). The significance of utilizing a proper territorial ocean level worth in any examination of the effect of the Storegga slide wave is exemplified by information from the Shetland Islands.

There, the torrent seems to have attacked beach front lakes and have run up peaty slopes to a most extreme stature of 9.2m over the current elevated tide level (Bondevik et al. 2005). In any case, around 7300 14C-BP, ocean levels around the Shetland Islands and the Faroes remained at 10–15m underneath the

present level (Lambeck 1995), so the remade runup tallness truly probably been inside a reach around 19–25m over the ocean level of that time.

Within certainty restricts, this would be the biggest runup recreated anyplace for the Storegga Slide torrent (Bondevik et al. 2005). Concerning level and wave impacts on our review district – Doggerland (Coles 1998) – various geographical and geomorphological limit conditions should be thought about. First is the fast ascent of ocean levels in the early Holocene. For instance, in the southern North Sea (an area with negligible isostasy), ocean level ascent between 9000 calBP and 7000 calBP adds up to a normal worth of 1.25m/100 yrs (Behre 2003). Furthermore, a few superimposed geomorphological and climatic cycles (with their own time-scales) have contributed and muddled the ocean level changes during the time period (Tab. 4)…

Key Event or Process	Duration	Affected Region	Date	Reference
Abrupt Drainage of Lake Agassiz	Months	North Atlantic	8470 ± 300 calBP	Barber et al. 1999
Rapid rise in global sea-level by 0.2–0.5 m	Months	Global	~ 8200 calBP	Bauer et al. 2004
Reduced North Atlantic Deep Water Formation	Two Centuries	Global	8290–8060 calBP	Thornalley et al. 200?
Storegga Slide Tsunami	Hours	North Sea	8100 calBP	Bondevik 1997
Eustatic Sea Level Rise	Millennia	Northwest Europe	Continuous	Lambeck 1995
Slow Flooding of Doggerland	Centuries	North Sea	~8000 calBP	Behre 2003
Slow Final Flooding of Doggerland	Centuries	North Sea	~7000 14C-BP	Shennan et al. 2000
Rapid Final Flooding of Doggerland	Hours	North Sea	8100 ± 300 calBP	this paper

Tab. 4. Key events, processes, time scales, dates, and geographic regions.

… Two key perceptions can be produced using Figure 2…

… The connection of the 14C-age for the Storegga Slide and Tsunami with this ocean level bend (Fig. 2) shows that the Storegga Slide happened when the ocean level in the southern North Sea remained at around 17m higher than the present level.

Secondly, Figure 2 proposes that the Storegga Slide happened during the time of the notable '8200 calBP' environment occasion. The ramifications of this perception will be concentrated further below.

Following Barber et al. (1997), the grouping of occasions related with the '8200 calBP' occasion is as per the following: during deglaciation, a leftover ice mass impeded the toward the north waste of the enormous chilly lakes Agassiz and Ojibway, which recently released south-toward the east over ledges into the St Lawrence waterway. Around 8500 calBP (8470±300 calBP as per Barber et al. 1997), the ice dam fell, permitting the lakes to deplete quickly northwards into the Labrador Sea.

The arrival of an expected 1.6 x 1014 m3 of new water (Teller et al. 2002) from the proglacial lakes through the Hudson Strait would have significantly debilitated profound water arrangement in the North Atlantic (e.g., LeGrande 2006). Temperatures in the North Atlantic district diminished unexpectedly, with resulting recuperation over the accompanying 200 years or thereabouts (for example LeGrande et al. 2006; Thomas et al. 2007). In focal Greenland the surface air temperature dropped by 3–6°C (for example Johnsen et al. 2001), and maybe up to 7.4°C (Leuenberger et al. 1999). A decrease in air temperature of this extent is probably going to be connected with drier conditions and more grounded twists over the North Atlantic and the encompassing area (Alley et al. 1997; Bauer et al. 2004; LeGrande 2006).

The freshwater discharge gauges are of significance for the current examinations, since this water would prompt an unexpected ascent of worldwide mean ocean level. The assessments range from around 0.25 to 0.5m, with time sizes of the delivery thought to be in the request for a while to a year (for example Bauer et al. 2004; LeGrande 2006)…

… Of unique interest to our review, the worldly construction of the '8200 calBP' cooling occasion has been contemplated exhaustively by Thomas et al. (2007), who infer that the occasion had a general term of 220 ± 2 years and a focal, 4-drawn out spike at 8222 calBP, during which Greenland ice surface temperatures came around up to 13 ± 2 °C (for correlation: cooling during the Younger Dryas adds up to approx. 15 °C). We utilize these outcomes in assessing the transient connection between the 8200 calBP environment occasion and the Storegga Slide tidal wave, as follows.

Figure 3 represents that the Storegga Slide torrent happened, with 95% certainty, sooner or later during the span 8200–8000 calBP. We can state

this is certainly inside the time of decreased North Atlantic Deep Water (NADW) arrangement and specialist circum-Atlantic cooling (8247–8086 calBP, as per Thomas et al. 2007). Dating imperatives are additionally adequate to express that it is far-fetched that the torrent happened close to the beginning of the 8200 calBP environment occasion, or, all in all, the Storegga Slide was not coordinated with the Hudson Bay flood, however post-dated it. Therefore, the wave seems to have affected the southern North Sea sooner or later throughout the 8200 calBP environment occasion. Further accuracy is blocked by the way that the wave's 14C-age of 7300 ± 30 14C-BP (95%) falls into a level district of the tree-ring alignment bend (Fig. 3). Considering that diminished North Atlantic Deep Water (NADW) development might cause changes in the carbon cycle that might prompt such supposed radiocarbon plateaux in the alignment bend (as displayed for the Younger Dryas, Hughen et al.
2006), this gives additional certification to the idea that the Storegga Slide happened eventually inside the 8200 calBP environment occasion. To close, the Storegga tidal wave occasion happened inside one to two centuries after the worldwide ocean level leap of 0.25–0.5m that was related with the Hudson Bay flood. This juxtaposition would have assisted with expanding the flooding effect of the torrent in low-lying seaside regions.

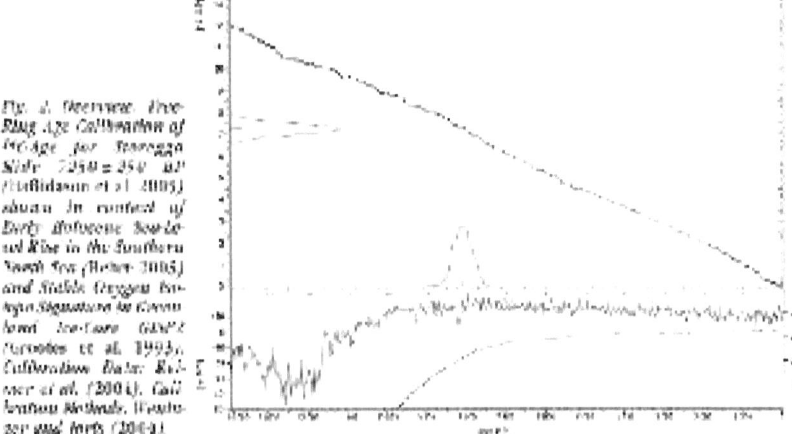

Fig. 4. Dendro-Tree-Ring Age Calibration of ^{14}C-Age for Storegga Slide 7250 ± 250 ^{14}C BP (Haflidason et al. 2005) shown in context of Early Holocene Sea-Level Rise in the Southern North Sea (Behre 2005) and Stable Oxygen Isotope Signature in Greenland Ice-Core GRIP (Grootes et al. 1993). Calibration Data: Reimer et al. (2004). Calibration Methods: Weninger and Jöris (2004).

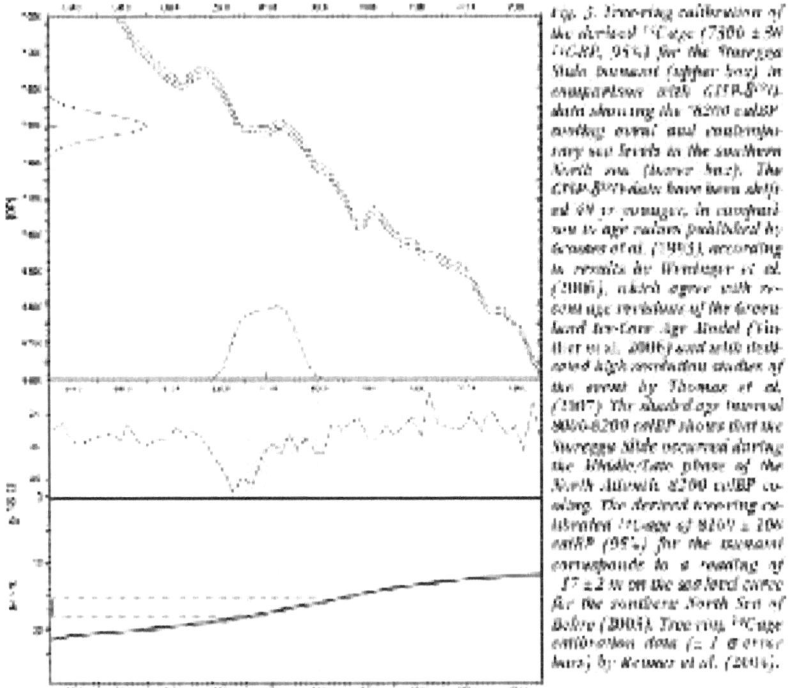

Fig. 5. Tree-ring calibration of the derived ^{14}C age (7300 ± 80 ^{14}C BP, 95%) for the Storegga Slide tsunami (upper box) in comparison with GRIP-δ^{18}O data showing the 8200 calBP cooling event and contemporary sea levels in the southern North sea (lower box). The GRIP-δ^{18}O data have been shifted by 42 ss younger, in comparison to age values published by Grootes et al. (1993), according to results by Weninger et al. (2006), which agree with recent age revisions of the Greenland Ice-Core Age Model (Vinther et al. 2006) and with dedicated high-resolution studies of the event by Thomas et al. (2007) The shaded age interval 8050-8200 calBP shows that the Storegga Slide occurred during the Middle/Late phase of the North Atlantic 8200 calBP cooling. The derived tree-ring calibrated ^{14}C-age of 8200 ± 200 calBP (95%) for the tsunami corresponds to a reading of 17 ± 2 m on the sea level curve for the southern North Sea of Behre (2005). Tree-ring ^{14}C-age calibration data (± 1 σ error bars) by Reimer et al. (2004).

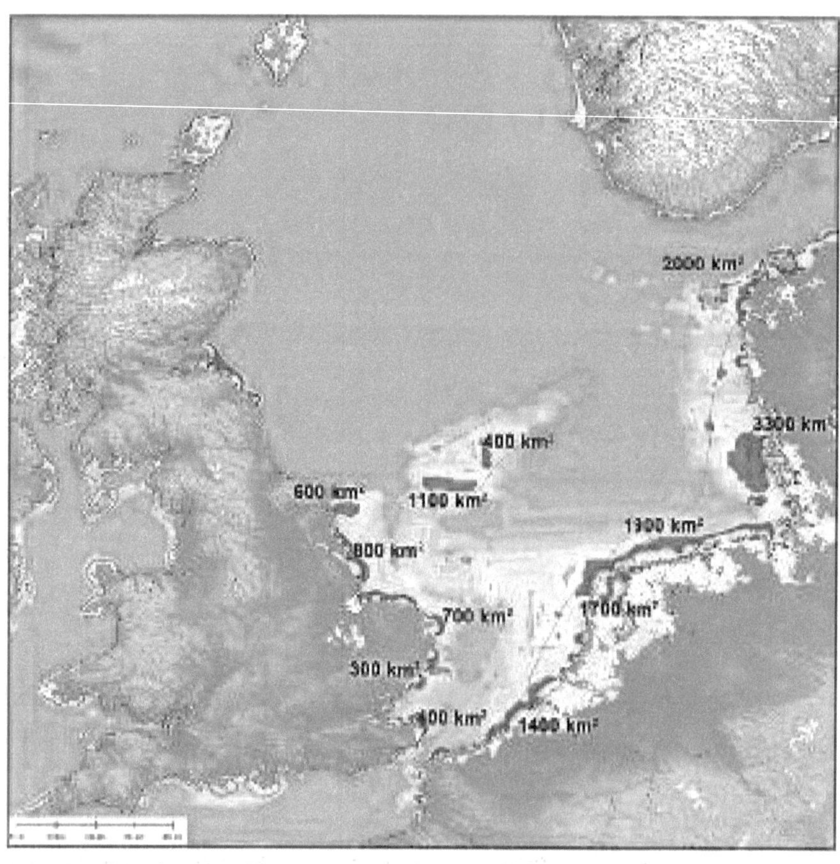

Fig. 4. Hypothetical regions with major impact by the Storegga Slide tsunami. Ocean colour shading is based on SRTM bathymetric data (United States Geological Survey 2006; cf. text). Major individual hypothetical tsunami impact areas, represented by the SRTM-bathymetric depth interval −17 ±5 m, are shaded red. Due to applied reconstruction and specific colour shading approach, red shaded areas represent hypothetical 'run-in' areas. These are not identical to potentially even more dangerous 'run-up' areas (cf. text). Thin brown lines represent digitized palaeogeographic coastlines according to Shennan et al. (2000), but slightly changed to allow for minor differences in the reconstructions given by Behre (2003). Together, these two coastlines approximate Doggerland some 200 ¹⁴C yrs 'before' and 'after' the tsunami event. For simplicity, the Doggerbank 'island' is only shown for the date c. 7500 ¹⁴C BP. Whether this 'island' was really subaerial, or not, at the time of the tsunami, cannot be decided with given data.

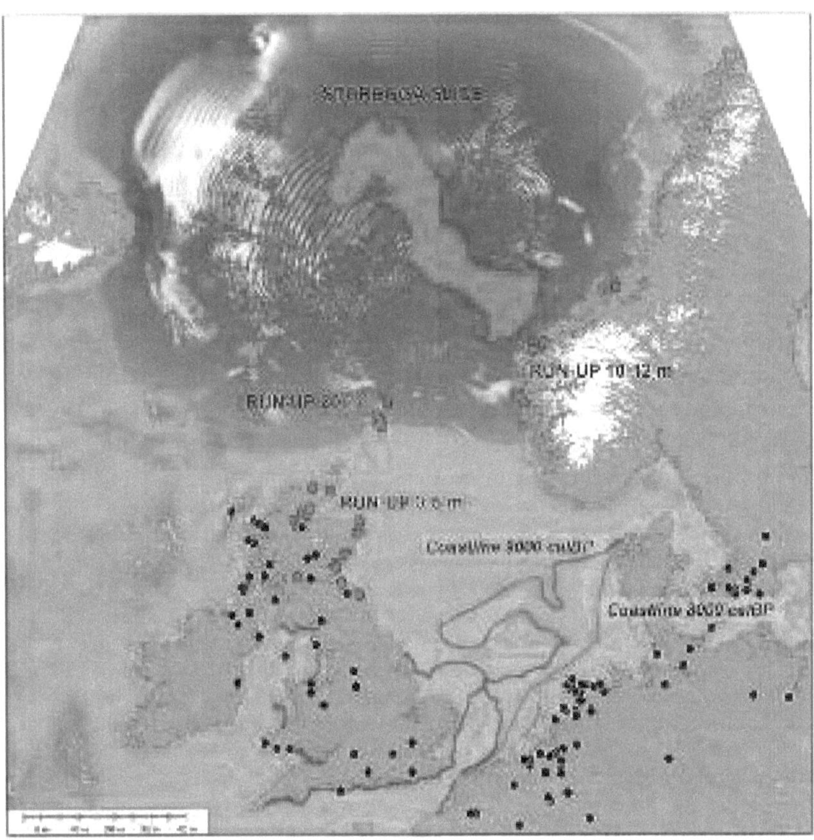

Fig. 5. Early Holocene palaeogeography of the Northwest European continental shelf ('Doggerland') and geographic distribution of ^{14}C-dated Mesolithic sites in Northwest Europe for the time-window 7600–7000 [14]CBP. Palaeogeographic coastlines according to Shennan et al. (2000) and Behre (2003), with colour shading on the base of SRTM bathymetric data (cf. text). Radiocarbon-dated Mesolithic sites according to Weninger et al. in press, shown as black dots. Red dots indicate sites with radiocarbon-dated tsunami deposits (cf. Appendix, Tab. 8). Area of the submarine Storegga Slide digitized and georeferenced according to Bondevik et al. (2003), shown red. Modelled wave for the Storegga tsunami taken from Bondevik et al. (2005), adapted and projected onto the map graphically, with no vertical scaling. The modelled tsunami wave has a height of 3 m on the open ocean (Bondevik et al. 2005) and is likely to have reached the southern North Sea with this height (Bondevik, pers. comm. 2007).

Since the spearheading investigations of Coles (1998), it is past confidence that Doggerland was an occupied scene during the Late Paleolithic and prior Mesolithic periods. As far as assessing the effect of the Storegga

slide occasion on contemporary human populaces, results will rely firmly

upon the degree of the space affected, the seriousness of the tidal wave over this space, and the thickness and conveyance of human settlement (Fig. 5).
Average populace densities for Mesolithic northwest Europe, in light of on ethnographic similarity, have been assessed on the request for 0.05 to

0.10 individual/km2 (Binford 2001; Constandse-Westermann and Newell 1989; Rozoy 1978). In any case, the populace would not have been equally conveyed over Doggerland, and we can propose most assuredly that beach front, lacustrine and riverine regions would have encountered significantly higher populace densities (Fischer 1997; Paludan-Müller 1978), maybe to the request for 0.50 to 1.0 individual/km2 (cf. Schulting in press), while regions further inland (away from assets) would have been moderately inadequately populated. There exists some steady isotope and archeological proof on the side of these ideas (Schulting in press; Schulting and Richards 2001). Since it is definitively the seaside and close shore riverine regions (the last due to a channeling impact up beach front waterway valleys) that would have been generally impacted by the Storegga tidal wave, there may impressively affect the contemporary populace. For instance, one of the most outstanding geo morphological highlights in a new 3D-seismic planning activity of the southern North Sea is the presence of a focal lake known as the 'External Silver Pit' (Gaffney et al. 2007). Briggs et al. (2007) decipher two extend edges inside the Pit as shoals that framed in an estuarine climate during the Early Holocene offense, construing from this the presence of solid flowing flows in the north-bound estuary. Following Donovan (1975), these flowing flows might have been to some extent answerable for the arrangement of the Outer Silver Pit melancholy itself. Comparative estuarine highlights are notable from the ocean bottom in the Danish archipelago, where they support various Mesolithic settlements (Fischer 2004).

They would have, (I) pulled in a grouping of Mesolithic settlements (Fischer 1997; 2004) and (ii), been vigorously affected by a diverting of energy during the effect of the Storegga tsunami.

Table 7 presents different potential situations for the quantity of people impacted by the Storegga tidal wave, in view of the 'peril regions' displayed in

red in Figure 4. As a first estimate, and accepting that portion of the space under danger was seriously affected, it tends to be proposed that exactly 700 to 3000 people were impacted. This number is adequately enormous to have conceivably brought about the eradication of various nearby groups, or potentially even a local persuasive clan (cf. Newell et al. 1990.table 13). This doesn't really suggest that all were killed quickly, albeit given the probable velocity and size of the occasion, countless individuals would more likely than not have been gotten and suffocated by the unavoidably rising waters, while numerous others would have been uprooted. Nor would the results be restricted to the wave's prompt effect, as useful beach front regions might have been crushed, shellfish beds annihilated and covered by sands, along with any proper fishing offices, very much bore witness to for the Late Mesolithic Ertebølle period (Pedersen 1997), yet in addition known from the early Kongemose (c. 8300 calBP) in Denmark (Fischer 2004). Besides, contingent upon the season that the wave hit, any put away food varieties intended to endure over the colder time of year may likewise have been lost (cf. Spikins 2008), with resulting starvation among survivors. Without a doubt, macrofossil investigation of fish bone and twigs from stores in Norway has shown that the torrent presumably happened during late fall (Bondevik et al. 1997). It is possible, especially with regards to keeping rising ocean levels as of now, that the last relinquishment of the excess leftovers of Doggerland as a position of extremely durable residence by Mesolithic populaces was achieved by the Storegga tsunami.

Thus, both the quick and longer-term influences of this occasion, as far as populace rearrangement and social memory would have been extensive, in spite of the fact that it stays hard to give more explicit subtleties at this stage (cf. Coles 1998; Waddington 2007; Ward et al. 2006). One clear impact of the last division of Britain and the landmass is a solid impression of insularity in the previous, seen most obviously in the nonappearance in Britain of the acrobat armatures that rule later Mesolithic microlith businesses on the contiguous mainland from c. 8500 calBP (Jacobi 1976). It just so happens, this date is predictable with a portion of the later gauges given by palaeo-natural analysts for the development of the English Channel (see Tab. 5), and could even be deciphered as giving autonomous corroboration.
While the interaction subsequently seems to have effectively been well in progress, the

Storegga tidal wave might have at long last cut off any excess (for example flowing) interface among England and the continent."

	area (km²)	Population density (person/km²)			
		0.05	0.10	0.50	1.00
Total area under threat	13 600	680	1360	6800	13 600
1/2 area	6800	340	680	3400	6800
1/4 area	3400	170	340	1700	3400

Tab. 7. Estimated population sizes in the study area affected by the Storegga tsunami at various population densities. The most likely scenario may be a population density of 0.10 to 0.50 person/km² over an impacted area of some 6800km², affecting some 700 to 3000 people, both directly and indirectly (see text).

So presently we have extremely impressive proof that occasions brought about by environmental change can prompt the all out obliteration of a huge region in a period as short as only one day and that the region's populace can die subsequently, leaving scarcely a hint of their reality for posterity.

Atlantis

This carries us to the subject of the legendary Atlantis – an old, legendary realm that, probably, was annihilated in a solitary day. Genuine proof the spot existed is very restricted. The most solid references we have are the compositions of the Greek scholar Plato north of 9,000 years after the obliteration of Atlantis and a couple of legends of the Mayan and Aztec cultures.

The word Atlantis is gotten from the Greek Ἀτλαντὶς νῆσος which signifies "Island of Atlas". As per Plato, Atlantis was an island with an amazing naval force that set up a huge domain in northern Africa and attempted to overcome Greece. His depiction of its area has been interpreted as "before the Pillars of Hercules" by a few and "past the Pillars of Hercules" by others.

There is some discussion with respect to where the Pillars of Hercules really were, however standard assessment puts this milestone at where the Atlantic Ocean meets the Mediterranean. For the individuals who accept Atlantis might have been around here, there is a lot of fortuitous proof. Due South of this point, in Morocco, lie the Atlas Mountains. Atlantic, Atlas, Atlantis. Is it an incident the names are so comparable? There is even a lowered island close to the Strait of Gibraltar – Spartel – which became lowered around 12,000 years ago.

Much of what Plato expounded on Atlantis is unlikely or even tremendously inconceivable, particularly his attestation that Atlantis was at battle with the Athenians around 9,600 BC. Whatever is expounded on the sanctuaries, religion, domains and regal line of Atlantis isn't significant for this situation on the grounds that there is zero proof to demonstrate these parts of Plato's story.

Göbekli Tepe and Tell Qaramel are the benchmarks for "civilisation" now, and as the previous was the inexact site of the improvement of arable agribusiness and the last option seems to have spearheaded domesticated animals cultivating and perhaps the utilization of pack animals, it shows up improbable a culture more than 2,500 miles/4,000 km away was better at taking care of its own kin, which thusly makes it hard to envision Atlantis would have been more evolved. What makes a difference about Plato's record is the physical description.
Luckily this is the primary part of his composing that sounds accurate, albeit even there he in all likelihood overstates its size.

tlantis is portrayed as a round island with a progression of three roundabout channels or canals. The round, ordinary element infers an absence of rock that would give the base material to slopes – higher ground. The trenches or canals additionally infer the island is just barely above ocean level. Consider Venice, Amsterdam or Bangkok and their arrangement of trenches that go about as seepage channels for rising water. These spots are dangerously near, or even underneath, ocean level.
Without different man-made protections, each of the three urban areas would have been lowered by now.

ccording to Plato, Atlantis met its end around 9,600 BC. As he additionally expresses this occurred subsequent to losing a conflict to Athens, we know in some measure a piece of his story should be erroneous. Then again, as there are various stories from societies as various as the Mayans, the Aztecs, the Celts, the Egyptians and the Greeks that a civilisation some place out in the

Atlantic died in the

faint and far off past in a solitary day because of a characteristic disaster, maybe some of what Plato composed was right. He depicted precisely the sort of country generally powerless against being crushed in a solitary day by a torrent. Furthermore we realize this is what befallen Doggerland.

s it conceivable the tidal wave released by the Storegga Slide – or a comparative occasion in ancient times (like one of the prior ejections at Storegga) – wrecked a low-lying island in the North-west Atlantic close to the shoreline of Spain and additionally Morocco? Is it further conceivable this island was home to a somewhat progressed civilisation that had formed into what might be compared to a maritime superpower?

Certainly, an islanders would have a lot of motivating force for being great shipbuilders. They may likewise have acquired comprehension of how things work by social event data from various pieces of Europe, Africa and conceivably even the Americas. As we have proof a portion of individuals at Tell Qaramel had made a trip west to the Mediterranean, is it so awesome to assume some daring men from just past the Strait of Gibraltar may have made a journey toward the eastern shores of that ocean around a similar time? Could a progression of bold adventurers/dealers be the premise of the legend?

The time frame from 13000 - 10000 BC denotes various gigantic changes in mankind. Moreover, these advances were not bound to one settlement or clan. Coordinated religion, cultivating and constructing super durable settlements were completely accomplished in this period (and perhaps prior), so may conditions have been ideal for individuals of Atlantis to add their commitment to our general turn of events? A specific measure of disengagement at home, and thusly security from trespassers and different carnivores, may likewise have permitted Atlanteans to flourish.

hile this does rather go against my previous statement that Atlantis presumably would not have been further developed than Göbekli Tepe and Tell Qaramel, this attestation isn't outlandish. Assuming the Neolithic individuals in the Levant had the option to fabricate stone pinnacles and segments, is it doubtful to the point that individuals on the Moroccan coast

had the option to transform trees into secure boats? Could they not have
burrowed waste channels/trenches to shield settlements from flooding?
ould individuals of Atlantis have been profoundly coordinated tracker finders
who exploited plentiful game on the savannah that is presently the

Sahara Desert and the products of the soil filling wild in the Atlas Mountains
and beach front districts? Could they not have formed fishing into a method
for taking care of enormous networks? At last, could they not have been
adventurers who came into contact with our societies along the
Mediterranean coast and beyond?

Without hard proof, the best anyone can hope for at this point is to guess.
Doggerland has given outright evidence of the sort of harm that can be
caused for a land and its occupants in a solitary day as an outrageous
consequence of environmental change. Atlantis likely could be another
such model. More on that point later.

Storegga Slide Revisited

Thus far, this book has worried about instances of societies being finished
because of environmental change. Human movement was a contributing
element to that environmental change in most of cases. By and large, the end
was steady, permitting individuals to continue on and start once more.
Millennia prior, it was a lot more straightforward for a dislodged country or
clan to observe another home, so the cycle was normally genuinely straight
forward. As the total populace extended, the quest for new fields by
individuals who had to move from their countries definitely implied the new
domain they needed had as of now been settled.

Invariably, this prompted wars. The fresh introductions would either
overcome individuals whose land they attacked or be crushed and the
survivors ingested into the current populace. Sometimes, trespassers would be
crushed, however would hold sufficient military power to stay a strong
gathering and would move somewhere else to attempt their luck.

We have likewise perused of something like one recorded instance of a
considerable region being annihilated in a solitary day because of a
cataclysmic event brought about by environmental change. There is
additionally a collection of proof that recommends it may have happened at

least a time or two. This assumption expects perusers to accept a spot Plato called Atlantis truly existed, regardless of whether a significant part of the depiction of this legendary realm is the consequence of creative mind and mystery rather than certain knowledge.

As we probably are aware, urban areas and little realms have been annihilated in a solitary day by seismic tremors and tidal waves, clearly it isn't excessively far-brought to accept a bigger domain could experience a similar destiny. A progression of cataclysmic events in the mid 21st century ought to help us all to remember the unexpected, annihilating powers that can be released and how even the most mechanically progressed countries are weak to forestall them.

The focal point of this book presently changes from the past to the future, maybe the exceptionally not so distant future. The normal reason for the annihilation of Doggerland, and maybe Atlantis, is with us still and represents an immediate danger to pretty much every country on the planet. A power of nature, released by rising worldwide temperatures, lies lethargic. At some at this point dubious point, a basic edge will be reached. There will be no guard when that second shows up. All that we can expect is adequate admonition for at minimum a portion of those in its way to escape.

To comprehend the idea of the danger we are confronting it is important to reevaluate what befallen Doggerland. The article by Bernhard Weninger, Rick Schulting, Marcel Bradtmöller, Lee Clare, Mark Collard, Kevan Edinborough, Johanna Hilpert, Olaf Jöris, Marcel Niekus, Eelco J. Rohling and Bernd Wagner essentially worried about demonstrating when the Storegga Slide(s) happened and the resulting impacts of the tidal waves released by the occasion. The article is somewhat unclear with regards to the causes. The time has come to give more details.

The Storegga Slide was the biggest known submarine slide on a mainland edge, with an absolute space of around 95,000 km² (roughly the size of Scotland) of the seabed falling. There is exceptionally solid proof the chief justification for this monstrous breakdown was that the strong material underneath the seabed in the slide region was methane hydrate (otherwise called methane clathrate). Methane hydrate is a substance where a lot of methane gas is frozen inside water ice.

During the last ice age, submarine stores of methane hydrate would have been as strong an establishment for the seabed as most types of rock, and the seabed's solidness would not have been undermined by the presence of generous stores of methane hydrates. The continuous change in environment that started around 18,000 years prior would have changed this.

As each peruser should know, expanding the temperature of a material containing a high volume of gas will prompt that substance extending. This development of a substance in a restricted space will weaken encompassing regions that keep it. Just, something needs to give.

or the situation of submarine methane hydrate stores, the easy way out for such a development is the genuine ocean bed. When the ocean bed has been cracked by the vertical strain of dissolving methane hydrate, methane gas and surprisingly still-frozen methane hydrate can get away. Assuming adequate amounts of methane hydrates escape from a submarine store, the region underneath the ocean bottom is burrowed out and a breakdown of that space is inevitable.

It is critical to push the reasons for the Storegga Slide were more mind boggling than the situation depicted previously. As its name recommends, the Storegga Slide included the development of ocean bottom garbage saved during the as of late finished ice age down the incline of the mainland rack . This development of trash acquired minimum amount and set off an extremely amazing quake. This quake would presumably have been adequate without help from anyone else to trigger a wave, potentially one incredible enough to convey the deathblow to Doggerland. The extra interruption brought about by the close synchronous ejection of gigantic methane hydrate stores over a space of 95,000 km² made what has been portrayed as a megatsunami.

n assessment of environment information for the time of the Storegga Slide uncovers information that may seem to go against the thought that rising temperatures were an essential variable in this cataclysmic event. The world had experienced a nearly cool stage for a few centuries preceding the Storegga Slide. Such an investigation overlooks the way that the development to the occasion had been occurring over a time of millennia.

The methane hydrate stores off the bank of Norway were a sort of underground ice sheet. Ice sheets will generally move or create at an apparently extremely sluggish (yet unyielding) pace, consequently the expression "cold" to portray something moving at such low rates. It required millennia of continuous warming to begin the interaction that prompted the Storegga Slide, and a slight cooling for years and years would not have

made much difference.

The slide of garbage on the slant over the methane hydrate was the impetus for the emission. When might the gas have been delivered if there had been no slide? The short answer is I don't have the foggiest idea, and I presume no other person has made a logical report that could give a conclusive answer.

There are several things I can say with certainty. Initially, the idea of the seabed around Storegga permitted methane hydrate to escape preceding and after the Storegga Slide. Without a doubt, gas is getting away from the seabed even in the 21st century. It appears to be conceivable that had the slide not happened, gas would have avoided leaving an expanding number of pockets of empty space straightforwardly underneath the seabed. In the end, spaces of that seabed would fall, perhaps setting off waves. We may have had a progression of generally minor calamities in absolutely normal terms, however they would have occurred now and again when the land encompassing them was populated by further developed societies that might have been crushed by even a "standard" tsunami.

The subsequent truth is the Storegga Slide concurred with an unexpected finish to a cool period in worldwide environment. It has been assessed that a sizable level of the world's barometrical methane was presented by the ejection brought about by the Storegga Slide. As methane is an exceptionally intense ozone depleting substance, this data has extremely significant ramifications for our normal future.
As the world has seen two submarine seismic tremors in the mid 21st century that set off enormous tidal waves that caused a path of annihilation and death toll, I feel it would extraordinarily help our comprehension of previous occasions assuming we investigate what really occurred in the two later regular disasters.

The 2004 Boxing Day Tsunami

On Sunday, December 26, 2004 at 00:58:53 UTC, an undersea megathrust quake happened with its focal point off the west shore of Sumatra, Indonesia. The actual tremor is referred to by mainstream researchers as the Sumatra-Andaman quake. The subsequent torrent is given different names, including the 2004 Indian Ocean Tsunami and the Boxing Day Tsunami.

The quake was brought about by subduction and set off a progression of obliterating waves along the banks of most landmasses lining the Indian Ocean, killing north of 230,000 individuals in 14 nations, and immersing beach front networks with waves up to 30 m (98 feet) high. It was one of the deadliest cataclysmic events in written history. Indonesia was the most exceedingly awful impacted, trailed by Sri Lanka, India, and Thailand.

With an extent of somewhere in the range of 9.1 and 9.3, this was the third biggest tremor at any point recorded on a seismograph. The seismic tremor had the longest span of blaming at any point noticed: somewhere in the range of 8.3 and 10 minutes. It made the whole planet vibrate as much as 1 cm (0.4 inches) and set off different tremors as distant as Alaska.

The hypocentre of the primary quake was roughly 160 km (100 miles), in the Indian Ocean a little toward the north of Simeulue island, off the western shore of northern Sumatra, at a profundity of 30 km (19 miles) beneath mean ocean level. The northern segment of a component known as the Sunda megathrust, which had been expected to be torpid, burst. This crack was 1,300 km/810 miles in length. The seismic tremor was felt all the while as distant as Bangladesh, India, Malaysia, Myanmar, Thailand, Singapore and the Maldives. Spread shortcomings, or auxiliary "spring up deficiencies", caused long, slender pieces of the seabed to spring up right away. Maybe like a goliath clench hand pushing upwards, the unexpected rise of the seabed additionally expanded the tallness and speed of waves, causing the total annihilation of the close by Indonesian town of Lhoknga.

he accompanying guide given by the United States Geological Survey shows the wave construction of the wave. The red piece addresses a "positive" wave and the blue a "negative" wave.

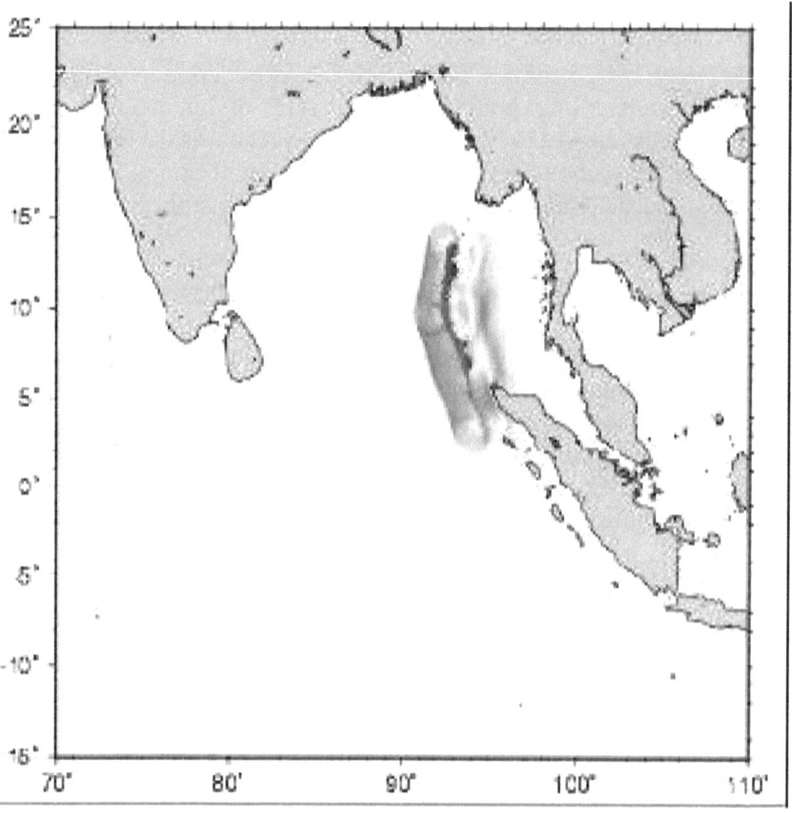

Indonesia lies between the seismic separation point known as the Pacific Ring of Fire along the north-eastern islands contiguous and including New Guinea and another separation point called the Alpide belt along the south and west from Sumatra, Java, Bali, Flores, and Timor.

The Sumatra-Andaman tremor was the biggest quake starting around 1964, and the second biggest since the Kamchatka quake of October 16, 1737.

The megathrust tremor was bizarrely enormous in topographical and geographical degree. An expected 1,600 kilometers (1,000 miles) of shortcoming zone surface slipped (or burst) around 15 meters (50 feet) along the subduction zone where the India Plate slides (or subducts) under the abrogating Burma Plate. The slip didn't occur momentarily however occurred in two phases over a time of a few minutes:

- Seismographic and acoustic information show the main stage highlighted a break around 400 km (250 miles) in length and 100 km (62 miles) wide, found 30 km (19 miles) underneath the ocean bed – the biggest burst at any point known to have been brought about by a tremor. The burst continued at a speed of around 2.8 km each second (1.7 miles each second) (10,000 km/h or 6,200 mph), starting off the shoreline of Aceh and continuing north-westerly for around 100 seconds.
  - A delay of about an additional 100 seconds happened before the break proceeded with northwards towards the Andaman and Nicobar Islands. Notwithstanding, the northern burst happened more leisurely than in the south, at around 2.1 km each second (1.3 miles each second) (7,500 km/h or 4,700 mph), proceeding with north for an additional five minutes to a plate limit where the shortcoming type changes from subduction to strike-slip (the two plates slide past each other in inverse directions). The India Plate is essential for the incomparable Indo-Australian Plate, which underlies the Indian Ocean and Bay of Bengal, and is floating north-east at a normal of 6 cm each year (2.4 inches each year). The India Plate meets the Burma Plate (which is viewed as a part of the incomparable Eurasian Plate) at the Sunda Trench. Now the India Plate subducts underneath the Burma Plate, which conveys the Nicobar Islands, the Andaman Islands, and northern Sumatra. The India Plate sinks progressively deep underneath the Burma Plate until the rising temperature and tension drive unstable materials out of the subducting plate. These unpredictable materials ascend into the overlying plate causing incomplete dissolving and the development of magma. The rising magma interrupts into the outside above and exits the Earth's covering through volcanoes as a volcanic arc.

he volcanic action that outcomes as the Indo-Australian Plate subducts the Eurasian Plate has made the Sunda Arc.

As well as the sideways development between the plates, the ocean bottom is assessed to have ascended by a few meters, uprooting an expected 30 cubic km (7.2 cu miles) of water and setting off annihilating tidal wave waves. The waves didn't start from a solitary point source, as was incorrectly portrayed in certain delineations of their ways of movement, but instead transmitted outwards along the whole 1,600 km (1,000 miles) length of the break (going about as a line source). This extraordinarily expanded the geological region over

which the waves were noticed, coming to the extent Mexico, Chile, and the Arctic. The raising of the ocean bottom altogether decreased the general limit of the Indian Ocean, creating a super durable ascent in the worldwide ocean level by an expected 0.1 millimeters (0.004 inches).

he energy delivered on the Earth's surface just (ME, which is the seismic potential for harm) by the 2004 Indian Ocean quake and tidal wave was assessed at 1.1×1017 joules, or what could be compared to 26.3 megatons of TNT. This energy is comparable to north of 1,502 times that of the nuclear bomb dropped on Hiroshima, yet not exactly that of Tsar Bomba, the biggest atomic weapon at any point exploded. Notwithstanding, this energy figure is nevertheless a little part of the outright energy discharge by this shake, as there were 4.0×1022 joules (4.0×1029 ergs) altogether, by far most of it underground. This likens to 4.0×1022 J, north of 363,000 times more than its ME. This is a genuinely huge figure, identical to 9,560 gigatons of TNT same (550 million times that of the Hiroshima bomb), or around 370 years of energy use in the United States at 2005 degrees of 1.08×1020 J.

The main recorded tremors with a bigger result as far as MW were the 1960 Chilean and 1964 Alaskan shudders, with 2.5×1023 joules (250 ZJ) and 7.5×1022 joules (75 ZJ) respectively.

The quake produced a seismic swaying of the Earth's surface of up to 20–30 cm (8–12 inches), comparable with the impact of the flowing powers brought about by the Sun and Moon. The shock rushes of the tremor were felt across the planet; as distant as the U.S. province of Oklahoma, where vertical developments of 3 mm (0.12 in) were recorded. By February 2005, the quake's belongings were as yet recognizable as a 20 μm (0.02 mm; 0.0008 in) complex consonant swaying of the Earth's surface, which bit by bit reduced and converged with the relentless free wavering of the Earth over four months after the earthquake.

The shift of mass and the gigantic arrival of energy caused a marginally change in the Earth's pivot. The specific sum isn't yet known, yet hypothetical models recommend the seismic tremor abbreviated the length of a day by
2.68 microseconds, because of an abatement in the oblateness of the Earth. It likewise made the Earth minutely "wobble" on its hub by up to 2.5 cm (1 inch) toward 145° East longitude, or maybe by up to 5 or 6 cm (2.0 or 2.4 inches). As the flowing impacts of the Moon increment the length of a day by an

normal of 15 μs each year, any rotational change because of the quake will be lost in a genuinely brief period. Essentially, the regular Chandler wobble of the Earth, which at times can be up to 15 m (50 feet), will ultimately counterbalance the minor wobble created by the earthquake.

The abrupt vertical ascent of the seabed by a few meters brought about by the tremor dislodged gigantic volumes of water, prompting a torrent that struck the coasts along the Indian Ocean. A tidal wave which causes harm far away from its source is in some cases called a teletsunami and is considerably more liable to be delivered by vertical disturbance of the seabed than by even motion.

The wave acted distinctively in profound water than in shallow water. In profound sea water, tidal wave waves structure just a little protuberance, scarcely observable and innocuous, which for the most part goes at an exceptionally rapid of 500 to 1,000 km/h (310 to 620 mph); in shallow water close to shorelines, a tidal wave dials back to just many km each hour, however in doing as such structures enormous damaging waves, chiefly on the grounds that the tallness of the wave rises impressively. It is the stature and mass of the wave that causes such a lot of obliteration. Researchers examining the harm in Aceh (in Sumatra) found proof that the wave arrived at a stature of 24 meters (80 feet) when coming shorewards along enormous stretches of the shoreline, ascending to 30 meters (100 feet) in certain spaces while infiltrating inland.

Radar satellites recorded the statures of wave waves in profound water: at two hours after the quake, the most extreme tallness was 60 cm (2 feet). These were the very first such perceptions made. Sadly, these perceptions couldn't be utilized to give a notice, since the satellites were not worked for that reason and the information required hours to analyse.

According to Tsunami Society VP Tad Murty, the complete energy of the tidal wave waves on that day was comparable to around five megatons of TNT (20 petajoules). This is over two times the complete touchy energy delivered during all of World War II (counting the two nuclear bombs), yet several significant degrees not exactly the energy delivered in the seismic tremor itself. In many spots the waves went similar to 2 km (1.2 miles) inland.

Because the 1,600 km (1,000 mi) shortcoming impacted by the tremor was in an almost north-south direction, the best strength of the tidal wave waves was an east-west way. Bangladesh, which lies at the northern finish of the

Bay of Bengal, had not many losses regardless of being a low-lying nation moderately close to the focal point. It likewise profited from the way that the tremor continued all the more leisurely in the northern crack zone, incredibly lessening the energy of the water removals in that region.

Coasts that have a landmass among them and the torrent's source are generally protected; nonetheless, wave waves can now and then diffract around such landmasses. This is the reason the Indian province of Kerala was hit by the tidal wave in spite of being on the western bank of India, and the western shoreline of Sri Lanka likewise experienced considerable effects. Likewise distance from the beginning stage was no assurance of wellbeing: Somalia was hit more diligently than Bangladesh in spite of being a lot farther away.

Because of the distances in question, the torrent took somewhere in the range of fifteen minutes to seven hours (on account of Somalia) to arrive at the different shores. The northern areas of the Indonesian island of Sumatra were hit rapidly, while waves struck Sri Lanka and the east shore of India around an hour and a half to two hours after the fact. Thailand was likewise struck around two hours after the fact regardless of being nearer to the focal point, on the grounds that the wave voyaged all the more leisurely in the relatively shallow Andaman Sea off its western coast.

The wave was seen similar to Struisbaai in South Africa, exactly 8,500 km (5,300 mi) away, where a 1.5 m (5 ft) elevated tide arrived at the shore around 16 hours after the tremor. The moderately prolonged stretch of time it took to arrive at this spot at the southernmost place of Africa was most likely because of the expansive mainland rack off South Africa blocking the entry of the waves and in light of the fact that the torrent would have followed the South African coast from east to west. The torrent additionally arrived at Antarctica, where flowing checks at Japan's Showa Base recorded motions of up to a meter (3 feet 3 inches), with unsettling influences enduring two or three days.

ome of the tidal wave's energy got away into the Pacific Ocean, where it created little yet quantifiable waves along the western banks of North and South America, normally around 20 to 40 cm (7.9 to 16 in). At Manzanillo, Mexico, a 2.6 m (8 feet 6 inches) peak to-box wave was recorded. The wave was adequately enormous to be recognized in Vancouver, Canada. This brought up new issues for mainstream researchers on the grounds that the tidal waves estimated in certain pieces of South America were bigger than those deliberate in certain pieces of the Indian Ocean. One hypothesis is that the tidal waves were engaged and aimed at long ranges by mid-sea edges that run along the edges of the mainland plates.

According to the U.S. Topographical Survey an aggregate of 227,898 individuals all over the planet kicked the bucket as an immediate consequence of the seismic tremors and resulting tsunamis(see table beneath for subtleties). As far as fatalities, this was one of the ten most exceedingly awful seismic tremors in written history, just as the single most noticeably terrible torrent ever. Indonesia was the most exceedingly awful impacted region, with most loss of life gauges at around 170,000. Nonetheless, one more report by Indonesian wellbeing clergyman Fadilah Supari has assessed the demise complete to be pretty much as high as 220,000 in Indonesia alone, which would build the general absolute to around 280,000 casualties.

The tidal wave caused genuine harm and passings to the extent the east shoreline of Africa, with the farthest recorded passing because of the tidal wave happening at Rooi Els in South Africa, 8,000 km (5,000 miles) away from the focal point. Altogether, eight individuals in South Africa passed on due to unusually high ocean levels and waves.

In reports by different help organizations, it is assessed that 33% of the dead seem, by all accounts, to be kids. This is an impression of the extent of kids in the populaces of a significant number of the impacted districts and furthermore in light of the fact that kids were the most un-ready to oppose being overwhelmed by the flooding waves. Oxfam proceeded to report that upwards of multiple times a greater number of ladies than men were killed in certain areas since they part of fishing networks and were looking out for the ocean side for the anglers to return and taking care of their youngsters in homes exceptionally near the shore.

In an expansion to the huge number of neighborhood inhabitants, up to 9,000 unfamiliar vacationers (for the most part Europeans) partaking in the pinnacle occasion travel season were among the dead or missing, particularly individuals from Scandinavia. The European country most noticeably terrible impacted may have been Sweden, whose official loss of life was 543.

A highly sensitive situation was pronounced in Sri Lanka, Indonesia, and the Maldives. In the repercussions of the twin catastrophes, the United Nations accepted the help activity would be the costliest in mankind's set of experiences. Then, at that point, UN Secretary-General Kofi Annan expressed recreation would most likely take somewhere in the range of five and ten years. State run administrations and NGOs dreaded the last loss of life could serve because of illnesses and starvation. Allures for help provoked a monstrous philanthropic reaction from around the world. Luckily, numerous of

the most exceedingly awful apprehensions didn't become reality.

or reasons for setting up timetables of nearby occasions, the time regions of impacted regions are: UTC+3: (Kenya, Madagascar, Somalia, Tanzania); UTC+4: (Mauritius, Réunion, Seychelles); UTC+5: (Maldives); UTC+5:30: (India, Sri Lanka); UTC+6: (Bangladesh); UTC+6:30: (Cocos Islands, Myanmar); UTC+7: ((western) Indonesia, Thailand); UTC+8: (Malaysia, Singapore). Since the tremor happened at 00:58:53 UTC, utilize the above balances to carve out the neighborhood opportunity of the earthquake.

he accompanying table gives subtleties of passings and wounds for the most noticeably terrible impacted countries:

Country where passings occurred

	Confirmed	Estimated	Injured	Missing	Displaced
Indonesia	130,736	167,799	n/a	37,063	500,000+
Sri Lanka*	35,322	35,322	21,411	n/a	516,150
India	12,405	18,045	n/a	5,640	647,599
Thailand	5,395	8,212	8,457	2,817	7,000
Somalia	78	289	n/a	n/a	5,000
Myanmar (Burma)	61	400-600	45	200	3,200
Maldives	82	108	n/a	26	15,000+
Malaysia	68	75	299	6	n/a
Tanzania	10	13	n/a	n/a	n/a
Seychelles	3	3	57	n/a	200
Bangladesh	2	2	n/a	n/a	n/a
South Africa	2	2	n/a	n/a	n/a
Yemen	2	2	n/a	n/a	n/a
Kenya	1	1	2	n/a	n/a
Madagascar	n/a	n/a	n/a	n/a	1,000+
Total	184,167	230,273	c.125,000	45,752	1,690,000

*Note: Figures for Sri Lanka do exclude roughly 19,000 missing individuals at first announced by Tamil Tiger specialists from locales under their control.

This quake was the greatest in the Indian Ocean for maybe 700 years. In 2008, a group of researchers working at Phra Thong, a hindrance island along the hard-hit western shoreline of Thailand, uncovered proof of no less than three past significant tidal waves at similar spot in the first 2,800 years with the latest accepted to have happened around 550 to 700 years prior. A second logical group tracked down comparable proof of past waves during the past 1,200 years in Aceh, an area at the northern tip of Sumatra. adiocarbon dating of bark sections in soil quickly underneath the subsequent sand layer drove the researchers to reason that the latest archetype to the 2004 tidal wave likely happened between A.D. 1300 and 1450.

The 2004 torrent was the deadliest in written history. Preceding 2004, the deadliest recorded torrent in the Pacific Ocean happened in 1782, when roughly 40,000 individuals were killed by a tidal wave in the South China Sea. The torrent made by the 1883 emission of Krakatoa is thought to have caused around 36,000 passings. The most lethal torrent somewhere in the range of 1900 and 2004 happened in 1908 in Messina, Italy, on the Mediterranean Sea, where a tremor and ensuing tidal wave killed 70,000. The most lethal torrent recorded in the Atlantic Ocean came about because of the 1755 Lisbon quake, which had a loss of life joined from the real tremor and coming about flames of over 100,000.

The 2004 tremor and wave have been portrayed as the deadliest cataclysmic event since either the 1976 Tangshan tremor or the 1970 Bhola twister. It may have been much more dreadful than both of these debacles yet vulnerabilities over losses of life make it difficult to state without any hesitation concerning which of these cataclysmic events was the deadliest.

The Boxing Day Tsunami crushed various nations around the Indian Ocean, yet it was by all account not the only exceptionally ruinous tidal wave of the mid 21st century. In March 2011, one more misfortune unfurled off the bank of Japan.

The March 2011 Tohoku Tsunami

The 2011 Tōhoku seismic tremor, otherwise called the Great East Japan Earthquake, was a greatness 9.0 undersea megathrust quake off the eastern shore of Japan that happened at 14:46 JST (05:46 UTC) on March 11, 2011. Its focal point was roughly 70 km (43 miles) east of the Oshika Peninsula of Tōhoku and the hypocentre around 32 km (20 miles) profound. It was the most impressive tremor known to have hit Japan, and one of the world's five by and large since present day record keeping started in 1900. The tremor set off incredibly damaging wave waves up to 40.5 meters (133 feet) in Miyako, Iwate, Tōhoku. There were recorded instances of the waves making a trip up to 10 km (6.2 miles) inland. The torrents accomplished more than cause the passings of thousands of individuals and annihilate a wide scope of framework: immense waves were answerable for various very genuine atomic mishaps, explicitly a progression of Level 7 emergencies at three reactors in the Fukushima I Nuclear Power Plant complex, and the related clearing zones influencing countless residents.

This seismic tremor happened where the Pacific Plate is subducting under the plate underneath northern Honshu. The Pacific plate, which moves at a pace of 8 to 9 cm (3.1 to 3.5 inches) each year, plunges under Honshu's hidden plate delivering a lot of energy simultaneously. This movement pulls the upper plate down until the pressure develops enough to cause a seismic occasion. The break constrained the ocean bottom to rise a few meters. A shake of this greatness typically has a break length of somewhere around 480 km (300 miles) and by and large requires a long, generally straight issue surface. Since the plate limit and subduction zone in the space of the burst isn't extremely straight, it is surprising for the extent of a tremor to surpass 8.5 under those conditions. The greatness of this quake astonished a few seismologists. The hypocentral locale of this seismic tremor reached out from seaward Iwate Prefecture to seaward Ibaraki Prefecture.

he Japanese Meteorological Agency announced that the quake might have cracked the issue zone from Iwate to Ibaraki with a general length of 500 km (312 miles) and a width of 200 km (120 miles). Ensuing examination uncovered this tremor comprised of a bunch of three events.

This quake delivered a surface energy (Me) of $1.9\pm0.5\times1017$ joules,[48] disseminated as shaking and tsunamic energy, which is almost twofold that of the 9.1-size 2004 Indian Ocean quake and tidal wave that killed 230,000 individuals. As a main researcher brought up - assuming that it were feasible to outfit simply the surface energy from this quake, it would control a city the size of Los Angeles for a whole year. The complete energy delivered, otherwise called the seismic second (M0), was in excess of multiple times the surface energy and

was determined by the USGS at 3.9×1022 joules, which is somewhat not exactly the 2004 Indian Ocean tremor. This is comparable to 9,320 gigatons of TNT, or around 600 million times the energy of the Hiroshima nuclear bomb.

The seismic tremor was brought about by 5 to 8 meters up push on a 180-km wide stretch of seabed around 60 km seaward from the east bank of Tōhoku. The outcomes of this push were basically the same as that of the 2004 Indian Ocean tremor to the extent that it additionally prompted a significant wave which brought obliteration along the Pacific shore of Japan's northern islands and brought about the deficiency of thousands of lives and crushed whole towns. The torrent proliferated across the Pacific, and admonitions were given and departures completed. In numerous nations lining the Pacific, including the whole Pacific shoreline of North and South America from Alaska to Chile. Luckily, while the torrent was recorded in large numbers of these spots, it had a generally minor effect. Indeed, even Chile's part of Pacific coast, which is about

17,000 km (11,000 miles) from Japan, was struck by torrent waves 2 m (6.6 feet) high. A wave stature of 38.9 meters (128 feet) was recorded at

Omoe promontory, Miyako city, Iwate prefecture.

The wave cautioning gave by the Japan Meteorological Agency was the most genuine on its notice scale: it appraised the danger as a "significant tidal wave", with waves somewhere around 3 m (9.8 feet) high. The genuine tallness anticipated for different piece's of the shoreline shifted with the best being for Miyagi at 6 m (20 feet) high. The wave immersed an all out space of roughly 561 km2 (217 sq miles) in Japan.

The tremor occurred around 67 km (42 miles) from the closest point on Honshu's coast, and beginning appraisals showed the torrent would have required 10 to 30 minutes to arrive at the spaces originally impacted, and afterward regions farther north and south dependent on the topography of the coastline.

Just more than an hour after the quake, at 15:55 JST, a tidal wave was noticed flooding Sendai Airport, which is close to the shoreline of Miyagi Prefecture, with waves clearing away vehicles and planes and flooding different structures as they voyaged inland. The effect of the wave in and around Sendai Airport was recorded by a NHK News helicopter, and the subsequent video showed various vehicles on nearby streets attempting to get away from a moving toward wave and being overwhelmed by it. A four meter-high wave hit Iwate Prefecture. Wakabayashi Ward in Sendai was likewise especially hard hit. Somewhere around 101 assigned torrent clearing destinations were struck by the waves.

Similarities with the 2004 Indian Ocean seismic tremor and tidal wave proceed with regards to the harm caused by flooding water, however substantially more limited, was definitely more lethal and dangerous than the real shudder. There were reports of whole towns obliterated from wave hit regions in Japan, incorporating 9,500 missing in Minamisanriku.

One of the critical elements behind the high loss of life from the wave was the size of the water flood was a lot bigger than expected. The tidal wave dividers at a few of the impacted urban communities were intended to adapt to a lot more modest torrent statures. Additionally, many individuals trapped in the torrent imagined that they were situated on ground sufficiently high to be safe.

The towns of Kuji and Ōfunato were as a rule obliterated. Likewise obliterated was Rikuzentakata, where the tidal wave was recorded as three stories high. Different urban communities obliterated or seriously harmed by the tidal wave incorporate Kamaishi, Miyako, Ōtsuchi, and Yamada (in Iwate Prefecture), Namie, Sōma and Minamisōma (in Fukushima Prefecture) and Shichigahama, Higashimatsushima, Onagawa, Natori, Ishinomaki, and Kesennuma (in Miyagi Prefecture). The most serious impacts of the wave were felt along a 670-km (420 miles)- extended length of shoreline from Erimo in the north to Ōarai in the south, with the vast majority of the obliteration in that space happening soon after the quake. The torrent washed away the sole extension to Miyatojima, Miyagi, detaching the island's 900 inhabitants. A two meter high torrent struck Chiba Prefecture around 2 ½ hours after the shake, making substantial harm urban areas, for example, Asahi.

On March 13, 2011, the Japan Meteorological Agency (JMA) delivered subtleties of tidal wave perceptions recorded around the shore of Japan following the tremor. These perceptions included torrent greatest readings of more than 3 m (9.8 feet) at the accompanying areas and times on March 11, 2011, following the tremor at 14:46 JST:

- 15:12 JST – off Kamaishi – 6.8 m (22 feet)

- 5:15 JST – Ōfunato – 3.2 m (10 feet) or higher

- 15:20 JST – Ishinomaki-shi Ayukawa – 3.3 m (11 feet) or higher

- 15:21 JST – Miyako – 4.0 m (13.1 feet) or higher

- 15:21 JST – Kamaishi – 4.1 m (13 feet) or higher

- 15:44 JST – Erimo-cho Shoya – 3.5 m (11 feet)

-

-

- 15:50 JST – Sōma – 7.3 m (24 feet) or higher• 16:52 JST – Ōarai – 4.2 m (14 feet)

On March 23, 2011, the Port and Airport Research Institute declared their own wave stature accounts which were acquired from different port destinations or by telemetry from seaward as follows:

- Port of Hachinohe – 5–6 m (16–19 feet)

- Port of Hachinohe region – 8–9 m (26–29 feet)

- Port of Kuji – 8–9 m (26–29 feet)

- Mooring GPS wave tallness meter at seaward of focal Iwate (Miyako) – 6 m (20 feet)

- Port of Kamaishi – 7–9 m (23–30 feet)
- Mooring GPS wave stature meter at seaward of southern Iwate (Kamaishi) – 6.5 m (22 feet)
- Port of Ōfunato – 9.5 m (31 feet)
- un up tallness, port of Ōfunato region – 24 m (79 feet)
- Mooring GPS wave tallness meter at seaward of northern Miyagi – 5.6 m (18 feet)
- Fishery port of Onagawa – 15 m (50 feet)
- ort of Ishinomaki – 5 m (16 feet)
- Mooring GPS wave tallness meter at seaward of focal Miyagi – couldn't measure
- Shiogama part of Shiogama-Sendai port – 4 m (13 feet)
- Sendai segment of Shiogama-Sendai port – 8 m (26 feet)
- Sendai Airport region – 12 m (39 feet)The accompanying guide given by Pekachu of Wikipedia substantiates the information above:

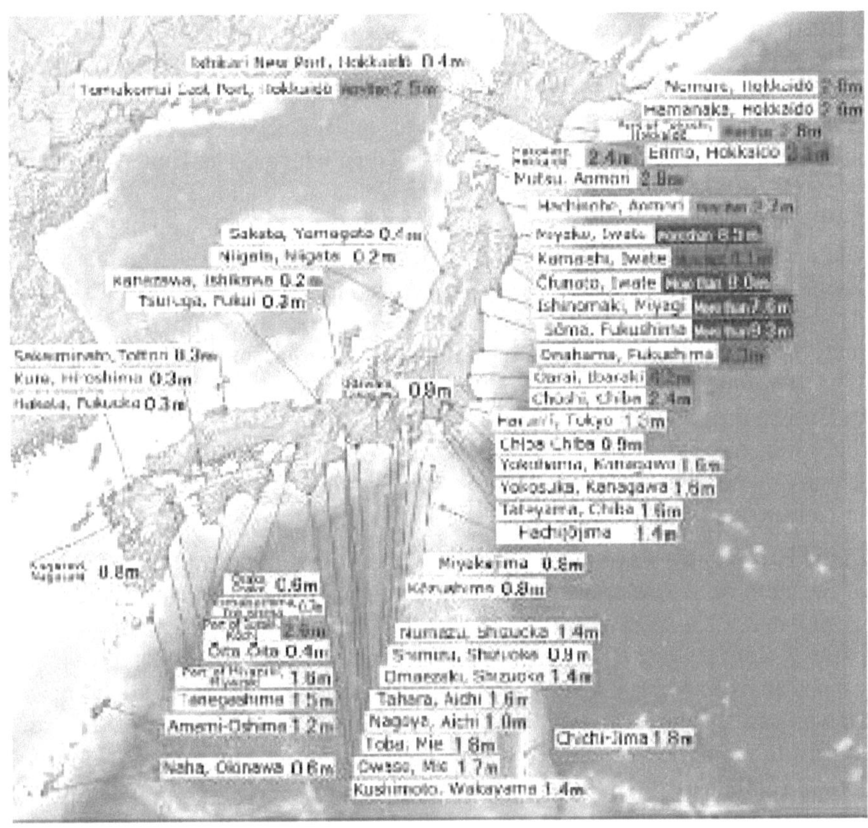

A joint examination group from Yokohama National University and the University of Tokyo additionally announced that the tidal wave at Ryōri Bay, Ōfunato was around 30 m high. They found fishing gear dispersed on the high precipice over the straight. At Tarō, Iwate, a University of Tokyo scientist announced an expected torrent stature of 37.9 m (124 feet) that arrived at the incline of a mountain around 200 m (656 feet) away from the coastline. Additionally, along the edge of a mountain 400 m (1,312 feet) from Aneyoshi fishery port in Omoe promontory in Miyako, Iwate, Tokyo University of Marine Science and Technology analysts recorded proof a tidal wave came to 38.9 m
(127 feet) up the incline. This is authoritatively perceived as the most elevated flood point for a wave in Japan, beating the past record of 38.2 m (125 feet) from the 1896 Meiji-Sanriku earthquake.

Shortly after the seismic tremor, the Pacific Tsunami Warning Center (PTWC) in Hawaii gave wave watches and alarms for chosen areas in the Pacific. At 07:30 UTC, PTWC gave an exhaustive torrent cautioning covering the whole Pacific Ocean. Russian specialists cleared 11,000 inhabitants from beach front spaces of the Kuril Islands. The United States West Coast and Alaska Tsunami Warning Center gave a torrent cautioning for the waterfront regions covering the majority of California, all of Oregon, and the western piece of Alaska, and a tidal wave warning covering the Pacific shores of the greater part of Alaska, and all of Washington and British Columbia, Canada. In California and Oregon, waves up to 2.4 m (8 feet) high struck a few regions, harming docks and harbors and causing over US$10 million in harm. Floods of up to 1 m (3.3 feet) hit Vancouver Island in Canada provoking a few clearings, and making boats be prohibited from the waters encompassing the island for 12 hours following the wave strike, leaving numerous island inhabitants nearby without the method for getting to or from work.

In the Philippines, waves up to 0.5 m (1.6 feet) high hit the eastern seaboard of the country. A few houses along the coast in Jayapura, Indonesia were annihilated. Experts in Wewak, East Sepik, Papua New Guinea emptied 100 patients from the city's Boram Hospital before it was hit by the waves that caused an expected US$4 million in harms. Neighborhood government in Hawaii assessed harm to public foundation alone at US$3 million, with harm to private properties, including resort inns, for example, the Four Seasons Resort Hualalai, assessed at a huge number of dollars. It was accounted for that a
1.5 m (5 feet) high wave totally lowered Midway Atoll's reef bays and Spit Island, killing more than 110,000 settling seabirds at the Midway Atoll National Wildlife Refuge. Other South Pacific nations, including Tonga and New Zealand and American Samoa and Guam, experienced bigger than ordinary waves, yet didn't report any significant harm. In Guam, a few streets were shut down off and individuals were emptied from low-lying regions. In Curry County, Oregon $7 million in harms happened, including the obliteration of 3,600 feet of dock space at the Brookings harbour.

Along the Pacific shore of Mexico and South America, tidal wave floods were recorded, yet there were not very many occurrences of genuine harm. Peru revealed a flood of 1.5 m (5 feet) and in excess of 300 homes harmed. The flood in Chile was sufficiently huge to harm in excess of 200 houses, with influxes of up to 3 m (9.8 feet). In the Galapagos Islands, a 3 m (9.8 feet) flood showed up 20 hours after the tremor, and furthermore after the torrent notice had been lifted. There was broad harm to structures on the islands and one man was harmed however there were no revealed fatalities.

he scale and degree of harm brought about by the tremor and coming about wave were huge, with the greater part of the harm being brought about by the wave. Video film of the towns that were most noticeably awful impacted show the number of were decreased to minimal more than heaps of rubble, with practically no pieces of any structures left standing. Appraisals of the expense of fixing the harm range all the way into the huge number of US dollars. A progression of "previously, then after the fact" satellite photos of crushed areas show enormous harm to numerous districts. In spite of the fact that Japan has contributed what might be compared to billions of dollars on enemy of tidal wave seawalls which line basically 40% of its 34,751 km (21,593 miles) shoreline and confront 12 m (39 feet) high, on this event the tidal waves just washed over the highest point of certain seawalls, and fell some in the process.

Japan's National Police Agency revealed on April 3, 2011, that 45,700 structures were obliterated and 144,300 were harmed by the tremor and torrent. The harmed structures remembered 29,500 constructions for Miyagi Prefecture, 12,500 in Iwate Prefecture and 2,400 in Fukushima Prefecture. 300 emergency clinics with 20 beds or more in Tōhoku were harmed by the fiasco, with 11 being totally annihilated. The quake and torrent made an expected 24-25 million tons of rubble and garbage in Japan.

It is assessed 230,000 vehicles and trucks were harmed or obliterated in the calamity. As of the finish of May 2011, occupants of Iwate, Miyagi, and Fukushima prefectures had mentioned the deregistration of 15,000 vehicles, which means the proprietors of those vehicles were thinking of them off as unrepairable or unsalvageable.

any thermal energy plants all over the planet are purposely fabricated exceptionally near the ocean in light of the fact that the ocean gives an ample and dependable wellspring of water and a spot to release squander. Japan is no exemption. The Fukushima I, Fukushima II, Onagawa Nuclear Power Plant and Tōkai thermal energy plants, comprising of eleven reactors, were closed down consequently following the tremor. Higashidōri, likewise on the upper east coast, had effectively been closed down for an intermittent review. Indeed, even after an atomic reactor is closed down, its cooling offices should stay functional to eliminate rot heat and to keep up with spent fuel pools. At Fukushima, the backup cooling process is controlled by crisis diesel generators at the plants and there is a further reinforcement provided by the close by Rokkasho atomic reprocessing plant. At Fukushima I and II wave waves flooded over seawall protections and annihilated diesel reinforcement power frameworks, prompting serious issues at Fukushima I, including three huge blasts and ensuing radioactive spillage. More than 200,000 individuals were cleared from the area.

post-quake tremor on April 7, 2011 brought about the deficiency of outside capacity to Rokkasho Reprocessing Plant and Higashidori Nuclear Power Plant however reinforcement generators stayed practical. Onagawa Nuclear Power Plant lost three of its four outside electrical cables and lost cooling capacity for as much as 80 minutes. A spill several liters of radioactive water happened at Onagawa.

Europe's Energy Commissioner Günther Oettinger tended to the European Parliament on March 15 and depicted the atomic mishap as an "end of the world". As the atomic emergency entered a subsequent month, specialists recognized Fukushima I was not the most exceedingly terrible atomic mishap ever, but rather may be considered the most complicated.

ater investigation showed three reactors (Units 1, 2, and 3) had endured emergencies and kept on spilling coolant water.

According to the Japanese government, the aggregate sum of radioactivity delivered into the air because of the mishaps to its thermal energy plants was around one-10th as much as was delivered during the Chernobyl calamity. Huge measures of radioactive material were likewise delivered into ground and sea waters. Accounts taken by the Japanese government 30 - 50 km (19 - 31 miles) from the plant showed radioactive caesium levels sufficiently high to cause concern, prompting an administration restriction on the offer of food filled in the area.

On December 16, 2011, Japanese specialists at long last proclaimed the plant to be steady, despite the fact that they had to recognize it would require a long time to disinfect the encompassing regions and to decommission the plant by and large. There were not many passings coming about because of the blast at the thermal energy stations, however various laborers forfeited themselves by being presented to deadly degrees of radiation while participating in the recuperation and cleanup operations.

apan is inclined to the two quakes and tidal waves and its guards against these catastrophic events is the most incredible on the planet. The country's foundation is intended to withstand such mishaps and government offices are prepared to adapt to the result. All things considered, the public authority and regular citizen populace was overpowered on March 11, 2011 and the episode was a public tragedy.

One year after the wave struck, the Japanese Red Cross declared there were as yet 260,000 uprooted individuals who needed long-lasting lodging and that these individuals could hope to stay in "brief" covers for a further five years. Garbage from the twin debacles has not been eliminated and neighborhood states in different pieces of Japan have reneged on vows to store part of the loss out of dread it very well may be defiled by radiation.

Imagine the results of a comparable occasion in a country not really good to go in this large number of regards and with a populace with less aggregate self-restraint. Envision a frightfully comparable debacle brought about by environmental change striking a country totally caught off guard for such a calamity. Later in this book, the situation will be clarified in considerably more detail.

Up to this point, the book has zeroed in on how environmental change plays had a definitive influence in the destruction of past civilisations. As the world's environment is continually changing – with or without input from human movement – it makes sense environmental change undermines areas of the planet in the 21st century and past in various ways.

The European Commission's broad, 142-page Technical Report on Water Scarcity and Drought Management in the Mediterranean and the Water Framework Directive which was distributed in 2007 addresses the subject with commendable lucidity. Central issues in its report are as per the following:-

"In the Mediterranean, the circumstances or the dangers of water lack are by and large ascribable at undeniable level and the development of interest notwithstanding restricted sustainable water assets and basically unpredictable and inconsistent characteristics consequently with availabilities that rarefy.

because of the expanded disseminations of the water assets and utilizations overall of the Mediterranean region, it is by looking at the particular geologies of the ones and others, through the previously mentioned pointers, that one can feature strain circumstances or present or future deficiency, while continuing at first, more helpfully, by country (Figures 1 and 2), disregarding the stores indicated.

Figure 1: Renewable regular assets per capita each year in Mediterranean

countries 2000-2025

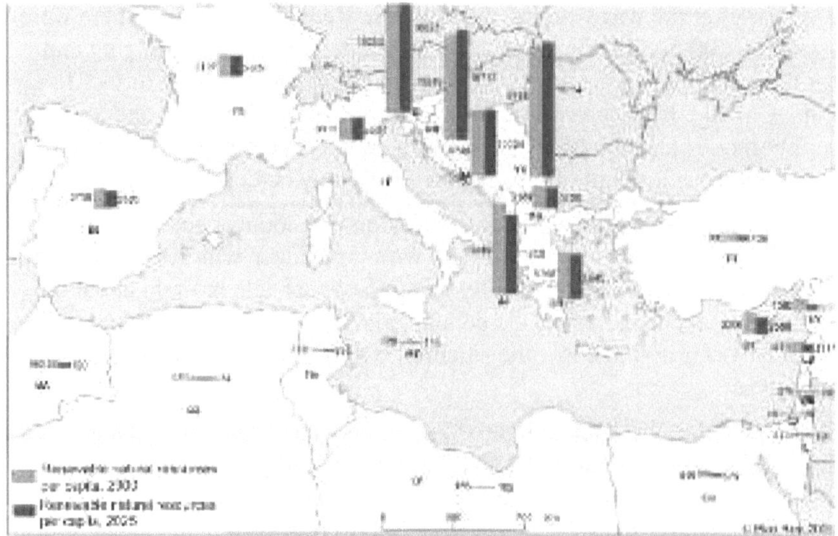

Figure 2: Exploitation file for inexhaustible normal assets per country, 2000-2025

Figures are introduced in informative supplement (table 17), which makes it conceivable to think about the circumstances of every Mediterranean country in 2000 and 2025 (as per populace projections "variable medium" of the United Nations (2003) and pursuing requests direction projections) on the consistency presumption of the reference inexhaustible regular water resources.

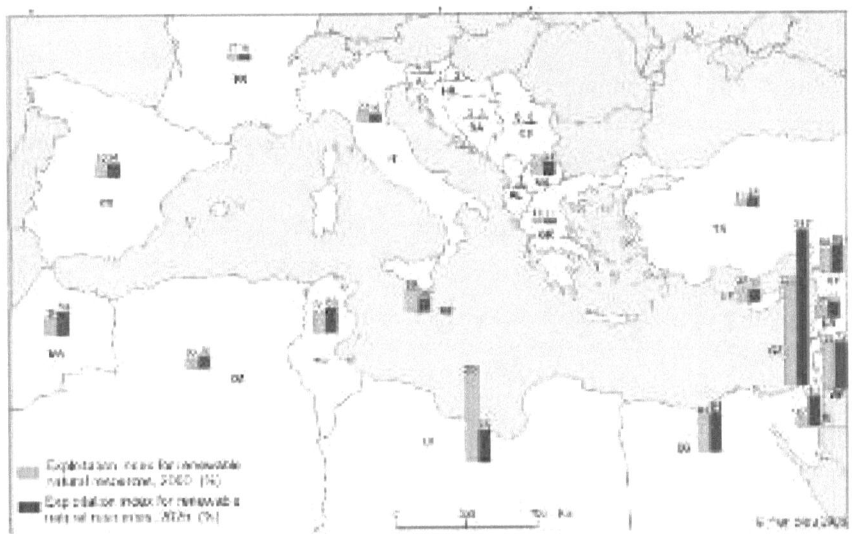

a similar abuse file of the inexhaustible regular assets determined for the Mediterranean catchment bowl for 2000 and 2025 as displayed in figure 3 features the assortment of situations:

• A first gathering of nations, where water withdrawals are near or surpass the normal yearly volume of inexhaustible regular assets (double-dealing file equivalent to or more prominent than 75 %), for example in 2000 Egypt, Israel and Libya, to be joined by 2025 by the Palestinian Territories and Spain's Mediterranean bowls. The regular assets in this large number of nations are now profoundly focused and they should meet a developing piece of their interest from other "unusual" sources.

• A second gathering of nations where all out request addresses a developing portion of the normal yearly volume of inexhaustible normal assets, however where the abuse record will remain somewhere in the range of 50 and 75 % until 2025: Malta, Syria and Tunisia.

• A third gathering of nations, where the double-dealing file lies somewhere in the range of 25 and 50 %, may by the by experience neighborhood or uncommon pressure: Lebanon, Cyprus, Morocco, joined by Turkey and Algeria by 2025.

• A fourth gathering of nations where the double-dealing file is under 25 %: Greece and the Eastern Adriatic, France and Italy, where all out request is

•

•

dropping.

Figure 3: Exploitation indices per basin, 2000-2025

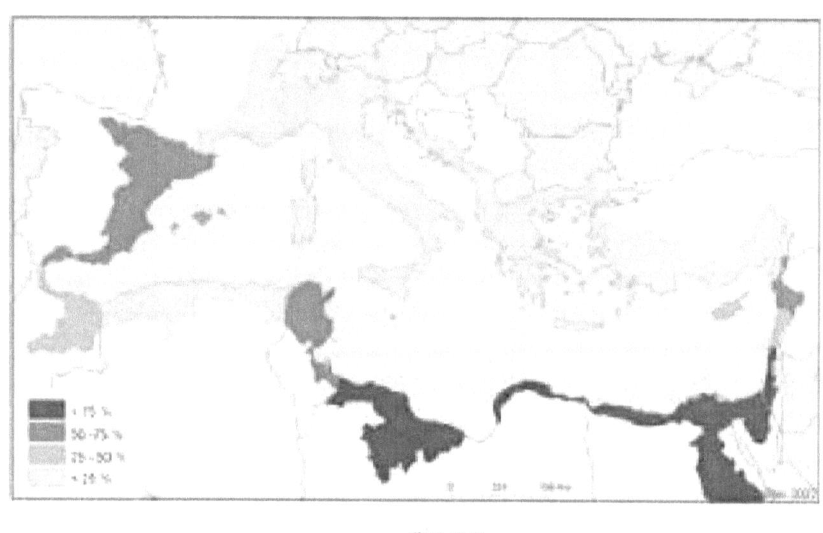

2000

Pressure on water is growing in the South and East

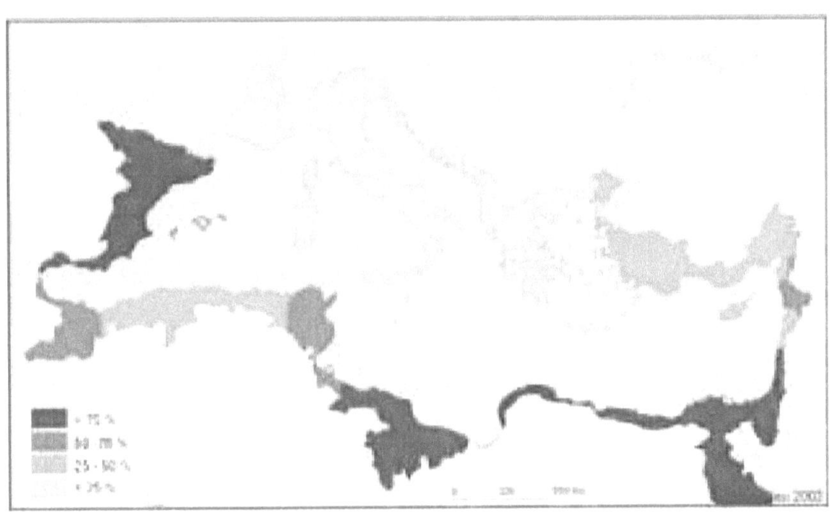

2025

☺ Pressure is decreasing in the north, except in Spain

The confirmation of these markers in the Mediterranean district combines the investigation, attributable to the transcendence of horticulture in water interest. Groundwater overexploitations which clarify ebb and flow abuse files >100% in certain nations are clear deficiencies manifestations. The high abuse lists can be dared to show that water requests can't be totally covered anything else by the regular assets double-dealing and should somewhat utilize non-inexhaustible assets or non-customary stock sources (wastewater re-use, desalination).

Almost all the Mediterranean nations of the South and the Middle East are correct now in pressure circumstance or deficiency as per these public markers. In 2025, the pressure circumstance will have happened in Syria and Egypt will move toward the lack circumstance. A better regionalization uncovers also circumstances of more neighborhood lack present in a few nations of the South (Algeria, Morocco) or North (Mediterranean Spain, South Italy, Greece, Turkey).

It is more hard to regionalise water assets projections per capita

reasoned from the populace projections (2025) - and minored by likely decreases because of environmental change, particularly in the South - and figure advancements of water requests in pattern scenarios.

However these projections predict deficiency expansions and aggravations in a few nations, in the Maghreb and the Middle East.

In 2025, the populaces in water pressure circumstance or water lack, as per the marker "assets per capita", will ascend to 244 million, 44% of the absolute populace of the Mediterranean nations on this date, in normal projection (without including specific nearby circumstances in nations of the North).

Can one survey the future water deficiencies by considering the "shortfalls" assessed: excesses of the extended requests, in benchmark situations, on the exploitable sustainable resources?

Calculations of contrasts among requests and assets generally by nation are huge just in the nations where the arrangement of assets and utilizations is brought together, either naturally (Egypt), or by water projects (Israel, Libya); somewhere else these public correlations can cover nearby shortages (Maghreb, Syria).

n the entire of the South and the Middle East nations, the deficiencies could be around 50 km3/year (remembering 30 for Egypt, 7 in Libya, 1 in Israel) in 2025."

nvironmental change is a worldwide issue, and pretty much every country faces the possibility of significant changes.

China

China is seen by numerous individuals as the country that will be the driving force of worldwide financial development in the 21st century and then some. That development is compromised by changes in environment and pollution.

hina is the world's most crowded nation and a significant producer of ozone depleting substances. Subsequently, much examination has zeroed in on China's effect on environmental change yet fairly less has been expounded on the effect of environmental change on China. China experienced dangerous monetary development in late many years, however with just 7% of the world's arable land accessible to take care of 22% of the total populace, China's economy is incredibly powerless against environmental change itself.

The effect of environmental change in China is now extensive, and its belongings are relied upon to assume a significant part in the existences of the Chinese in the 21st century and then some. A provincial environmental change model (PRECIS), created by the UK's Hadley Center for Climate Prediction and Research, was utilized to recreate China's environment and to foster environmental change situations for the country. Results from this undertaking recommend the normal temperature expansion in China before the finish of the 21st century might be somewhere in the range of three and four degrees Centigrade. Projected occasional changes were additionally fused into the accompanying environment situations utilized for demonstrating the effect on the rice, wheat, maize and cotton.

"For rice, without the CO2 direct impact in the recreation, normal yields are probably going to fall under both the A2 and B2 discharge situations. However, found the middle value of the nation over, yields are for the most part displayed to increment under the A2 outflows situation while decline under the B2 emanation situation when the CO2 direct impact is remembered for the reproduction (for example transformation included).

For maize, without the CO2 manure impact, the normal yield for both rainfed and flooded maize is probably going to succumb to both A2 and B2 discharge situations, If the immediate impact of CO2 is considered, normal yields are displayed to increment for rainfed while decline for inundated maize under both the A2 and B2 emanations scenarios.

For wheat, without CO2 treatment, wheat yields are relied upon to be some 20% and 10% lower by 2080 contrasted and current yields for the A2 and B2 outflows situations independently, If the impact of CO2 preparation, for example variation, is incorporated, normal wheat yields are displayed to increment in many spaces of China by 2080 under the A2 outflows situation for rainfed wheat and flooded wheat. However, for inundated wheat to profit from the impacts of CO2 preparation, adequate water and sustenance should be accessible to the plants.

For cotton, primer outcomes propose that cotton yields could increment marginally in the northern locale of the North China Plain, yet continue as before in the cotton spaces of the Yangtze River catchment and lessening in the north edge and east piece of south Xinjiang region."

From 1970 - 2010, the noticed spillover from the six biggest waterways in China showed a steady diminishing. The Huayuankou station along the Yellow River likewise recorded this pattern with a lessening pace of 5.70 % per decade."

Results from a VLC (variable spillage limit ） model recommend the normal spillover in the Ningxia, Gansu, Shaanxi, and Shanxiof spaces of the Yellow River catchment might fall by 2 - 10% by the 2050s.

Over the following 50 - 100 years, environmental change will cause more genuine water deficiencies for the Yellow River catchment region, the decrease in water volumes may arrive at 20 - 40%. This issue will be exacerbated assuming neighborhood populace increments in accordance with projections, alongside expected industrialisation and going with financial development.

Future environmental change is very likely unavoidable, so variation ought to be the main way to deal with manage environmental change. Specifically, it is prescribed the state finds a way ways to reinforce agribusiness substructure,
for example further developing water system and seepage frameworks, foster water saving innovation and high-effectiveness water use innovation, maintainable manure utilization, foster new high-temperature and vermin safe yield species through super advanced reproducing research, foster new advances including biotechnology to help crops, woods, domesticated animals, fisheries manage dry season, irritations and environment fluctuation, change crop establishing circulation dependent on the

environment designs considering the likelihood of a hotter environment in north-eastern China by the center of the 21st century and setting up a

program to recuperate meadows and stay away from further desertification.

Evidence is mounting that environmental change has as of now impacted human wellbeing straightforwardly and in a roundabout way in China, including mortality from outrageous climate occasions, changes in air and water quality, and changes in the biology of irresistible diseases.

Heat waves and other outrageous climate conditions have been connected to expanded wellbeing hazards in huge Chinese urban communities, like Beijing and Shanghai. Higher death rates during temperature limits have been credited basically to cardiovascular and respiratory illnesses, particularly among the elderly.

The issues brought about by high temperatures are significantly exacerbated by extreme air contamination and this type of contamination is promptly recognized as a significant ecological and general wellbeing challenge in Chinese cities"

Climate change is known to influence environment touchy irresistible sicknesses conveyed by creature hosts or vectors. In China, these incorporate schistosomiasis, Japanese encephalitis, Dengue fever, intestinal sickness, and Angiostrongylus cantonensis.

The effect of environmental change on water assets has been recognized by the Chinese government as a developing concern.

Water assets serve Chen Lei tended to a roundtable gathering on environmental change in China in 2011 and expressed a worldwide temperature alteration has turned into a significant ecological issue for the country - with water being one of the areas most straightforwardly affected.

China faces an irregularity between the market interest of water to help its quick friendly and financial turn of events, while securing the indigenous habitat and biological systems," said the pastor. "Worldwide environmental change could additionally compound existing issues over water security, water supply and cultivating irrigation."

e proceeded to clarify China encounters a water lack of 40 billion cubic meters a year, with 66% of the country's urban communities confronting expanding shortage of water.

According to Chen, China's per capita water assets are just 28% of the worldwide normal. Plainly, the nation can not stand to lose more water

assets. Its whole monetary and social improvement program is at stake.

Khalid Mohtadullah, a senior consultant of Global Water Partnership, an overall association zeroing in on the incorporated administration of water assets for supportability, brought up one of the most noticeably terrible issues confronting China today is water contamination. China quick and apparently inflexible financial development to turn into the world's second biggest economy has not been coordinated by endeavors to appropriately oversee squander water.

"China is defenseless against the effects of wild environmental change as its water framework is powerless or caught off guard for such changes," clarified Mohtadullah. "Policymakers need better data about the local effect of environmental change on water supplies, and on methods of adjusting to it, any other way it will negatively affect China's economy and could prompt a decrease in financial growth."

Chen has brought up the Chinese government is set to contribute 4 trillion yuan ($612 billion) in water conservancy projects by 2021. It has additionally settled severe water asset the executives measures to restrict the size of water abuse, work on the effectiveness of water utilization, and check water contamination. This would be a positive turn of events, given the new guidelines are enforced.

more likely than not, Mohtadullah was being thoughtful. The genuine outcomes of neglecting to carry out squander the executives change and tackle contamination will be far more regrettable. Assuming urban communities become appalling and land and water excessively harmed to develop crops there will be no economy by any means. By and large, the response of a gathering of individuals to the acknowledgment that the spot they occupy is not generally fit for reason has been to forsake their homes and move some place better.
Where could individuals of the world's most crowded country move to? Moving a huge number of individuals inside China's lines and away from those pieces of the country most seriously harmed is a finished non-starter. Moving external China's lines – probably going to Siberia, Japan, Australia and Canada – would more likely than not prompt a destructive conflict. Hence, the remainder of the world might dare to dream that Chen and his

partners truly are having the opportunity to holds with the problem.

ndia

India is viewed as the fundamental adversary to China's financial predominance of the Asian economy, and conceivably even a future world pioneer. It, as well, is extremely

defenseless against the desolates of environment change.

Climate change specialists have cautioned that rising temperatures will prompt more floods, heat waves, storms, rising ocean levels and unusual homestead yields.

Here are the vitally likely impacts of environmental change on a country which is the world's seventh biggest in region and is home to 1.1 billion individuals, a 6th of humanity.

Various examinations show that surface air temperatures in India are increasing at the pace of 0.4 degrees Centigrade consistently, especially during the post-rainstorm and winter seasons. While mean winter temperatures could increment by as much as 3.2 degrees Centigrade by the 2050s, summer temperatures could go up 2.2 degrees Centigrade.

xtreme temperatures and hotness spells could adjust examples of storm downpours, fundamental for India's farming and water needs. Researchers caution India will encounter a serious decrease in summer precipitation by 2050. The rainstorm represents practically 70% of the nation's all out yearly precipitation. Winter downpours are likewise expected to fall 10-20%. Higher temperatures will likewise prompt quicker liquefying of Himalayan ice sheets and as the dissolving season corresponds with the rainstorm season, any strengthening of the storm is probably going to add to flood fiascos in the Himalayan catchment.

Agriculture will be unfavorably impacted not just by an increment or decline in the general measures of precipitation, yet additionally by shifts in the circumstance of the precipitation. Higher temperatures diminish the absolute length of a harvest cycle, prompting lower yields per unit region, particularly for India's wheat and rice crops.

Soil disintegration, expanded quantities of irritations and weeds achieved by environmental change will likewise influence horticulture in India. For example, the measure of dampness in the dirt will be impacted by changes in elements like precipitation, overflow and evaporation.

Local examinations have been built up by research directed by the United Nation's Intergovernmental Panel on Climate Change(IPCC). As indicated by IPCC director R. K. Pachauri, changes in environment all over the planet are relied upon to trigger a lofty fall in the grain creation. In particular, Pachauri assessed an ascent of 0.5 degree Celsius in normal winter temperatures could cause a lessening of 0.45 ton per hectare in India's wheat creation. The normal per hectare yield in India is 2.6 tonnes.

Climate change will make rainstorm capricious. Most wheat development in South Asia relies upon precipitation as the essential wellspring of water system. Ranchers need trustworthy climate cycles to establish crops at the perfect opportunity. The fall in oat creation will cause food frailty on a public and territorial (let us not neglect India's neighbors Pakistan and Bangladesh will endure to some degree as severely) scale and loss of livelihood.

To exacerbate the situation, the complete space of land reasonable for agrarian use will recoil and surprisingly the accessible land may not stay appropriate for the yields at present cultivated for significantly longer. Ranchers need to investigate choices of changing yields reasonable to winning climate conditions.

early 80 million hectares, out of the nation's net arable homesteads of around 143 million hectares, need water system offices and in this manner depend altogether on downpour water for crop growth.

Over 85% of the beats and coarse oats, over 75% of the oilseeds and almost 65% of cotton are delivered from such terrains. The harvest yields hush up low contrasted with more created portions of the world.

ecords demonstrate the prevalently downpour took care of lots experience three to four dry spells each decade all things considered. Of these, a few dry spells are by and large of moderate force and one is severe.

Moreover, the vast majority of the homesteads that depend entirely on precipitation are in parched and semi-bone-dry zones where yearly precipitation is pitiful and drawn out droughts are very regular in any event, during the rainstorm season.

This makes crop development profoundly hazard inclined. On the off chance that the quantum of precipitation around there drops further or its example goes through any unmistakable, yet unforeseeable, changes in the 21st century, which is the thing that numerous specialists are foreseeing, crop usefulness might decrease further, adding to the misfortunes of downpour took care of farmers.

ccording to A K Singh, agent chief general (regular asset the executives) of the Indian Council of Agricultural Research (ICAR), medium-term environmental change expectations have extended the possible decrease in crop yields because of environmental change at somewhere in the range of 4.5 and 9% by 2039.

Long term conjectures are considerably more negative, with crop yields expected to decay basically 25% by 2099. Neighborhood specialists accept this will detrimentally affect ranchers' pay and buying power, with obvious

down-the-line repercussions. Another chance is that diminished homegrown inventory of food will expand ranch earnings, albeit this would be to the hindrance of the economy as a whole.

Although the precipitation records kept up with by the India Meteorological Department (IMD) don't demonstrate any discernible pattern of progress in generally yearly storm precipitation on a public level, recognizable changes have been seen inside certain unmistakable regions.

At least three meteorological sub-divisions - Jharkhand, Chhattisgarh and Kerala - have shown huge lessening in occasional precipitation however some others have recorded an increment in precipitation too. Since downpour took care of harvests, as coarse grains, heartbeats and oilseeds are developed for the most part during the kharif season, these are impacted by both low and unreasonable rainfall.

The groundnut crop in the Rayalaseema space of Andhra Pradesh in 2008 is an exemplary model. It experienced generous harm since weighty precipitation from the get-go in the season unfavorably impacted the advancement of stakes (which bear groundnut units underneath the dirt), while the moderately drier spell at the later stage hit the improvement of pods.

The uplifting news, all things considered, is the arrangement of the National Action Plan on Climate Change, dispatched in 2008, which targets creating innovations to help downpour took care of horticulture adjust to the changing environment patterns.

At least four of the eight 'public missions' begun under this program will have immediate or backhanded bearing on downpour took care of cultivating. These are the missions on practical horticulture, water assets the board, green India and vital knowledge.

The ICAR-drove public rural examination framework is additionally directing exploration on explicit undertakings under the umbrella program on environment change.

"Aside from the utilization of innovative advances to battle environmental change, there must be sound approach system and solid political will to accomplish this target", announced Singh.

he IPCC report likewise predicts gigantic waterfront disintegration brought about via ocean levels rising roughly 40 cm. The ascent is fundamentally because of sped up softening of glacial masses in the Himalayan and Hindu Kush ranges.

A 10-year concentrate in and around the Bay of Bengal focuses to the ocean rising 3.14 mm a year in the mangrove marshes of the Sunderbans delta contrasted with a worldwide normal ascent of just of 2 mm. This pattern undermines the low-lying region which is home to around 4,000,000 people.

ea levels are increasing at a pace of 1 cm each decade along a large part of the Indian coast. The significant delta spaces of the Ganga, Brahmaputra and Indus streams, which have huge populaces dependent on riverine assets, will be impacted by changes in water systems, salt water interruptions and land loss.

The rising levels of the ocean in the beach front regions will harm nursery regions for fisheries, causing seaside disintegration and flooding.

There is one more arrangement of variables that makes grain yield projections considerably more troubling: India's populace is developing at 1.41% each year. As per the 2011 registration, India has a populace of 1.21 billion. Assuming current development rates endure, it is expected to overwhelm China as the world's most crowded country by 2025. India's populace will surpass 1.6 billion by 2050. Put in setting, the country's populace increments by generally what could be compared to the absolute number of individuals living in more noteworthy London and Paris consistently. India's developing in general abundance really worsens the issue of food adequacy in light of the fact that the more extravagant populace requests better quality and assortment in its eating routine. The country frantically needs to raise food yield, so expected misfortunes in grains should be counterbalanced somewhere else. In spite of making colossal advances in farming since acquiring autonomy, the characterizing issue for India in the

21st century will be as old as most occasions past: how might it feed so many people?

As things stand, soon after the distribution of India's 2011 statistics and going with estimates, the nation needs to face the accompanying situation for the 21st century:

India's populace will increment 25% by 2050, and presumably by 60-70% (gauges for the absolute populace for this period range from 1.85 – 2.18 billion, so let us acknowledge a middle figure of 2 billion) before the century's over. Simultaneously, India's grain creation will fall 25%. Following a few decent back to back harvests, India is just with regards to independent in grains starting at 2011 and 2012. All in all, there is sufficient grain delivered in India in a decent year like 2012 to take care of 1.2 billion people.

By 2100, India will create sufficient grain to take care of 900 million individuals, leaving
1.1 billion individuals requiring grain from outside India. As a matter of fact, the circumstance is

truly much more terrible than those figures infer in light of the fact that they depend on the profoundly unrealistically presumption that India's per capita grain utilization stays static all through the 21st century.

According to the US Department of Agriculture, American utilization of grain (wheat, grain, rye and so on) was 1,046 kg each year, contrasted with 946 kg each year in 2003. Utilization inside the European Union is generally a large portion of that level. In India, per capita utilization is only 178 kg each year. Clearly, Americans don't eat almost 3 kg of bread and breakfast cereal each day.
Much of the dissimilarity in utilization is on the grounds that American grain is utilized to take care of creatures that are subsequently butchered for their meat. Additionally, grain is utilized to make brew and some refined alcohol.

If Indian grain utilization multiplied, it would in any case be way underneath per capita levels for most created countries. However at that point there would be just sufficient homegrown grain yield for around 450 million individuals, and surprisingly more oat would need to be imported. Given the patterns for monetary development and thriving, it is amazingly reasonable India's per capita grain utilization will rise forcefully over the 21st century.

here will this food come from and at what cost? In the present circumstance "value" signifies significantly more than the measure of cash charged. Such reliance on food imports can without much of a stretch lead to political and financial insecurity.

s indicated by a 2006 report on an incorporated energy strategy arranged by a specialist advisory group of the Planning Commission, India needs to support a yearly monetary development pace of 8-10% over the course of the following 25 years in the event that it is to kill neediness and meet its human improvement objectives. Therefore, the nation needs, as a base, to expand its essential energy supply three or four - crease over the 2003-04 level in a similar 25-year period.

As the report expresses, India's financial development would "fundamentally include expansion in (ozone harming substance) outflows from the current amazingly low levels." Any limitations on such emanations by India, regardless of whether direct, via discharge targets, or circuitous would decrease development rates, the report expressed. Notwithstanding, the report likewise added, "India ought to contain her (ozone harming substance) discharges as long as she is made up for the extra expense involved."

at the end of the day, India is ready to forfeit its current circumstance and long-term

food security to meet medium term financial and social improvement targets. Except if different nations will pay India to take on more down to earth and far-located policies.

The authority position of Indian agents at environment strategy exchanges is that in spite of the fact that India is among the main 10 producers of carbon dioxide on the planet, its per capita emanation is as yet one-6th of the worldwide average.

Furthermore, it has dealt with a 8% financial yearly development rate while energy utilization has ascended by just a 3.7%.

his utilization pattern is probably going to change for the more regrettable as India enters the following phase of its modern turn of events. An IPCC report regarding the matter recommends India will encounter the best expansion in energy and ozone depleting substance discharges on the planet assuming it supports a high yearly financial development rate. The International Energy Agency predicts India will turn into the third biggest producer of ozone depleting substances by as right on time as 2015.

India imports huge amounts of petroleum products to meet its energy needs, and the consuming of these energizes represents 83% of India's carbon dioxide outflows. Almost 70% of the country's power supply comes from coal-terminated power stations.

For a long time to come, India is probably going to go against any transition to look for its obligation to lessen ozone depleting substance emanations and will rather request that the created world exchange protected innovation freedoms identifying with clean technologies.

Europe

notwithstanding the report alluded to before on the Mediterranean, the European Union appointed a broad report on the normal effect of environmental change in Europe as entirety. The Projection of Economic effects of environmental change in Sectors of the European Union dependent on Bottom up Analysis (PESETA – the manager is Spanish) included information that was gotten and introduced in a somewhat dubious way, particularly that from the Climate Research Unit and the University of East Anglia, yet the general ends are difficult to question: Europe and Europeans are helpless against environment change.

The finish of the report is as per the following:-

"The PESETA incorporated appraisal
focuses on better comprehension the
geographical
and sectoral examples of the physical and financial impacts of environmental change in Europe. PESETA considers the effects of climate change in farming, stream bowls, waterfront frameworks, the travel industry and human wellbeing. Other key effects, like consequences for ranger service, impacts in environments and biodiversity and catastrophic occasions, have not yet been investigated. In
addition, the harms because of environmental
change has been assessed, without considering
the
reality that financial development will mean
higher openness and weakness to environment
change.

Therefore, the PESETA project underestimates

the effects of environmental change in Europe generally. The
review has executed a nitty gritty base
up philosophy utilizing high resolution
environment information (50 km x 50 km, day by day)
and area explicit effect models. Such methodology
permits evaluating likely effects of environment
change
at territorial and sectoral aspects important for leaders in variation policy.

he appraisal has been made for the 2020s and
the 2080s. Four future environment scenarios
are considered for the 2080s to represent the
vulnerability in outflow drivers and environment
displaying. The ocean level ascent (SLR) in the
situations ranges between 49 cm and 88 cm.
The extended increment of worldwide temperature
by the 2080s, contrasted with that of the 1970s, is
in a reach between 2.3°C (B2 SRES situation) and
3.1°C (A2 SRES situation). Note that contrasted with the preindustrial level,
the worldwide temperature increment of the PESETA situations are in a
reach somewhere in the range of 2.6°C and 3.4°C.

According to the local environment models of the task, the
temperature expansion in the EU contrasted with the 1970s would be bigger,
in a reach somewhere in the range of 2.5°C and 5.4°C. In the text the four
2080s scenarios

considered are named after the EU temperature increment: 2.5°C, 3.9°C,
4.1°C and 5.4°C.

Without public variation to environmental change and if the environment of
the 2080s happened today, the yearly harm of environment change
to the EU economy as far as GDP misfortune is
assessed to be between 20 billion € for the 2.5°C
situation and 65 billion € for the 5.4°C situation
(Figure 41). Harms would occur
basically in the Southern Europe and Central Europe North regions.

Yet those figures belittle the losses
as far as government assistance. For example the
fixing of harms to private structures because of
stream floods builds creation while decreasing the

utilization prospects of families and, thusly, their
government assistance. The future environment as
today would prompt an EU yearly government assistance misfortune (Figure
42) of between 0.2% for the 2.5°C situation and 1% for the 5.4°C situation
with high SLR (88 cm). When contrasted with the memorable EU annual
development of government assistance (around
2%), environmental change could lessen the
yearly government assistance improvement
rate to between 1.8% (for the situation with a 0.2% government assistance
misfortune) and 1% (for the situation with a 1% government assistance
loss)."

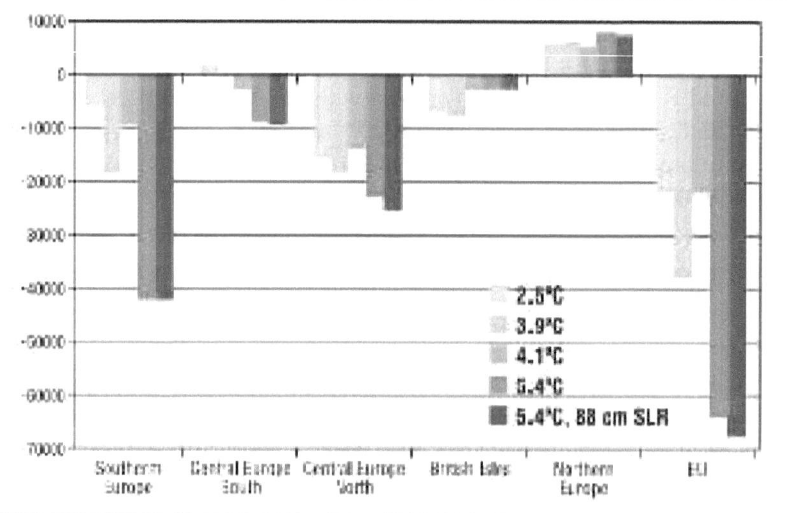

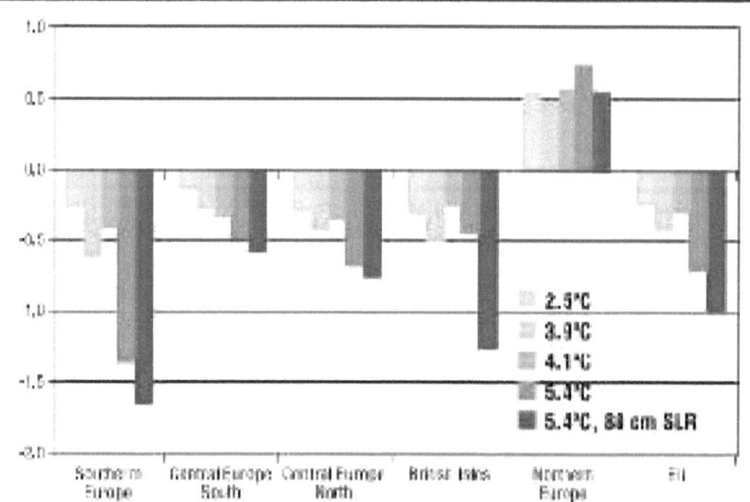

Another finding of the review is that the collected appraisals of impacts mask large sectoral and regional variability (Figure 43). Under the 5.4°C scenario with high SLR (5.4°C in Figure 43), most losses occur because of the damage in the agricultural sector (production losses), river floods (damage to residential and commercial buildings) and, particularly, coastal systems (sea floods and migration costs).

Figure 43: Sectoral decomposition of regional welfare changes

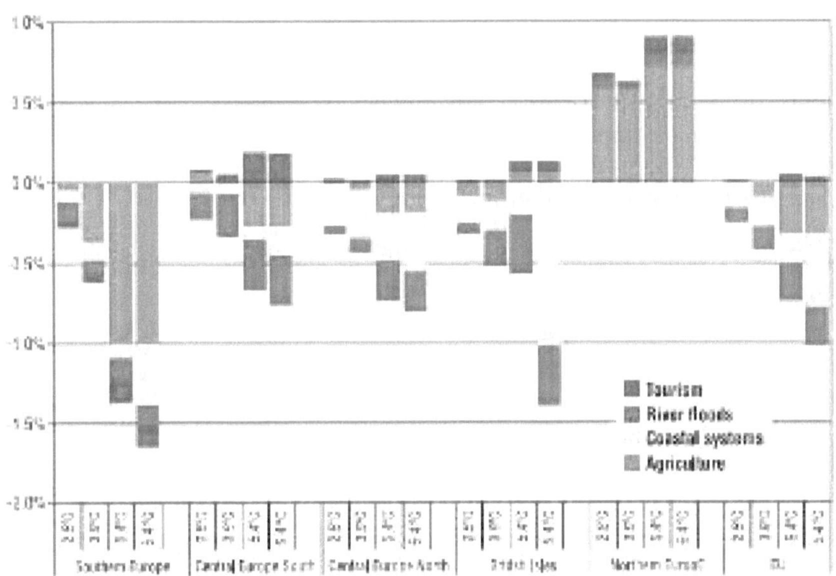

The exploration uncovers Southern European region is the district expected to experience the most noteworthy government assistance misfortunes, running somewhere in the range of 0.3% and 1.6%. Government assistance in this district steeply crumbles in the situation with the most elevated temperature increment. All effect classes are negative, while harm to the rural area is viewed as the most genuine. The travel industry incomes could decrease up to €5 billion for each year.

Central Europe is additionally seriously impacted by environmental change. The government assistance misfortunes in PESETA's Central Europe South locale range from 0.1% to 0.6%. The harm brought about by waterway floods is by all accounts the main effect classification. The hottest situation would likewise incur genuine damage on the agrarian area. The travel industry area would be relied upon to profit from environment change.

The Central Europe North locale would encounter government assistance misfortunes of 0.3% - 0.7%. The significant adverse consequences are harm to waterfront frameworks. Harm from waterway floods could cost of €5 billion yearly. The extended effect on the travel industry area is marginally positive.

The British Isles would confront government assistance misfortunes on a comparable scale to Central Europe, with the special case of the 5.4°C situation with high SLR, where the government assistance misfortune would move to 1.3%. The sway from stream floods is very negative in all situations, just as the effect on waterfront frameworks, especially under a SLR of 88 cm. The travel industry area would profit from a hotter environment, with up to €4.5 billion in extra yearly revenue.

Northern Europe is the main region inside the EU expected to encounter government assistance gains in all situations, running between .5% and 0.7%, essentially on account of the positive effect on the agricultura Lower harms from waterway floods are normal and the travel industry incomes should rise. In any case, harm to beach front frameworks could be significant.
Public transformation measures have just been generally assessed in the seaside regions evaluation, because of deficient information and systemic limits in the remainder of sectors.

PESETA has likewise concentrated on the effect of environmental change on human wellbeing during the 2080s without acclimatization. The assessed scope of expansion in yearly hotness related mortalities is somewhere in the range of 60,000 and 165,000, while the scope of reduction of cold-related mortalities is somewhere in the range of 60,000 and 250,000. Acclimatization to hotter summers would lessen the projected mortality changes by a component of five. Heat waves have not been considered in the estimations. As such, on balance, there would be no general adverse consequence based on the EU in conditions of human wellbeing, and most likely some benefits.

ompared to some prior investigations, the PESETA harm gauges are lower predominantly in light of the fact that the attention on sway with market impacts is smaller in the PESETA, and non-market parts of the harm are not taken into

consideration.

he Fankhauser and Tol report of 1996 assessed the general GDP misfortune for the EU at 1.4%, utilizing a situation multiplying the CO2-identical focus (to 550 ppmv), contrasted with pre-modern levels. The PESETA 5.4°C situation with high SLR, prompting a fixation level of 710 ppmv, has an expected yearly GDP and government assistance deficiency of 0.5% and 1%, respectively.

North America

North America has not endured however much most regions of the planet from the impacts of environmental change, yet that doesn't mean the area is impenetrable to worldwide trends.

Within the North American district (characterized for the motivations behind this book as the piece of mainland North America south of the Arctic Circle and north of the U.S.- Mexico line), weakness to environmental change shifts essentially from one area to another and from sub-locale to sub-region. Recognition of this fluctuation or sub-local "surface" is significant in understanding the likely impacts of environmental change on North America and in concocting suitable reaction strategies.

The attributes of the sub-areas and areas of North America propose neither the impacts of environmental change nor the reaction choices will be uniform. Involving the vast majority of Canada and the mainland United States, this huge region is different as far as its land, environmental, climatic, and financial constructions. Temperature limits range from well below - 40°C in northern scopes throughout the cold weather a long time to more noteworthy than 40°C in southern scopes throughout the mid year. Local climatic dissemination is administered essentially by upper-level westerly breezes and subtropical climate frameworks, with hurricanes at times affecting on the Gulf of Mexico and Atlantic coasts during summer and harvest time. The Great Plains (counting the Canadian Prairies) and south-eastern U.S. experience more extreme climate as tempests, cyclones, and hail-than some other locale of the world.

The IPCC's Third Assessment Report has a segment committed to North America. In its leader rundown, the report proposes the accompanying environmental change scenario:

"For a scope of emanation situations delivered for this Third Assessment Report, model outcomes recommend that North America could warm by 1–3°C throughout the following century for a low-outflows case (B1). Warming could be just about as much as 3.5–7.5°C for the higher discharge A2 case. Distributed local effect studies have utilized environment situations with worldwide temperature changes that are like these new cases, yet local situations may not be straightforwardly comparable."

Not every one of the expected impacts of environmental change in North America are negative. Accepting the progressions are moderate for the main portion of the 21st century, total yields of downpour took care of farming are relied upon to rise 5-20%, however with significant inconstancy among districts and sub-locales. One of the significant difficulties confronting ranchers in this period is a few harvests are now moving toward the constraint of their temperature resilience. Different yields rely upon exceptionally specific water system frameworks that current water assets probably won't have the option to help in future.

Higher temperatures in western mountains will prompt a diminished snowpack and, subsequently, more winter flooding, and decreased summer streams. This will worsening contest for over-extended water assets. Flood avoidance and fixes will require extra financial plans at public and common levels.

Infestations from bugs and related infections will add to the general medical care trouble, and will likewise have a destructive effect on horticulture. It is potential ranchers may depend on expanded utilization of ever-more grounded pesticides to battle this issue. Shockingly, this procedure is probably going to prompt more medical care and natural problems.

As the IPCC report focuses out:

"Changes in precipitation are profoundly questionable. There is little understanding across environment situations in regards to changes in all out yearly spillover across North America."

So what North America faces is a hundred years of – to summarize Donald Rumsfeld – "obscure questions". This isn't extremely useful, however it is sensible to assume a few regions will have more precipitation than previously and others will get less.

Forest flames are a common issue in North America, and higher summer temperatures will just worsen the circumstance. Metropolitan spread brings homes nearer to what in particular used to be wild, and expands the danger of towns and

towns enduring fire damage.

The uplifting news according to the viewpoint of ranger service, is the IPCC's appraisal of the subject:

"Environmental change is relied upon to build the areal degree and efficiency of woodlands over the course of the following 50–100 years (medium certainty). Outrageous or potentially long haul environmental change situations demonstrate the chance of broad decay (low confidence)."

s in Europe, the expansion in passings and genuine ailments brought about by hotter summers in North America will presumably be more than offset by the improvement in medical problems during cold weather months for example less individuals passing on or getting normal winter illnesses.

According to the IPCC report, more than 65% of the number of inhabitants in North America is delegated living in seaside districts. As ocean levels proceed with their normal ascent in the 21st century, north of 200 million individuals face the possibility of waterfront disintegration, salt water interruption into water tables, expanded openness to storm floods and harm to foundation and sea shores. This last thing probably won't appear to be especially significant, however when you consider an ocean side is frequently viewed as a superb vacation destination, it implies nearby resources are endangered.

The Environment Protection Agency summarized the issue on its site (http://epa.gov/climatechange/impacts/beach front/index.html) as follows:-

Ocean level is ascending along the vast majority of the U.S. coast, and all over the planet. Somewhat recently, ocean level rose 5 to 6 inches more than the worldwide normal along the Mid-Atlantic and Gulf Coasts, in light of the fact that beach front grounds there are dying down…

… Higher temperatures are relied upon to additional raise ocean level by extending sea water, liquefying mountain icy masses and little ice covers, and causing bits of Greenland and the Antarctic ice sheets to dissolve. The International Panel on Climate Change (IPCC) gauges that the worldwide normal ocean level will ascend somewhere in the range of 0.6 and 2 feet (0.18 to 0.59 meters) in the following century (IPCC, 2007)…

… Nationwide, around 5000 square miles of dry land are inside two feet of elevated tide. Albeit most of this land is right now lacking, numerous waterfront districts are developing quickly. Land inside a couple of feet over the tides could be immersed by rising ocean level, except if extra embankments and bulkheads

are built. A two foot ascend in ocean level would kill roughly 10,000 square miles of land…

… including momentum wetlands and recently immersed dry land, a region equivalent to the joined size of Massachusetts and Delaware…

… Sea level ascent likewise builds the weakness of waterfront regions to flooding during storms for quite a long time. Initial, a given tempest flood from a storm or northeaster expands on top of a higher base of water. Thinking about just this impact, a Report to Congress by FEMA (1991) assessed that current advancement in the U.S. Waterfront Zone would encounter a 36-58 percent expansion in yearly harms for a 1-foot ascend in ocean level, and a 102-200 percent increment for a 3-foot rise. Shore disintegration likewise expands weakness to storms, by eliminating the sea shores and hills that would somehow or another shield seaside property from storm waves (FEMA 2000). Ocean level ascent likewise increments beach front flooding from rainstorms, since low regions channel all the more leisurely as ocean level rises."

ccording to a report distributed by the US Global Change Research Program:

"Worldwide ocean level has as of now ascended by 4 to 8 inches (10-20 cm) in the previous century and models propose this ascent is probably going to speed up. The best gauge is that ocean level will ascend by an extra 19 inches (48 cm) by 2100, with a vulnerability scope of 5 to 37 inches (13-95 cm). Geographical powers (like subsidence, in which the land falls comparative with ocean level) assume an unmistakable part in provincial ocean level change. Sped up worldwide ocean level ascent is relied upon to have emotional effects in those areas where subsidence and disintegration issues as of now exist."

Another likeness North America imparts to Europe is that it is clear enormous amounts of cash should be spent/contributed over the course of the following not many a very long time to handle issues brought about by environmental change. What isn't clear at everything is the place where that cash will come from. Nor is it clear who will – or ought to – be responsible for the spending. Ought to there be a halfway controlled – government – program to handle the difficulties, or should neighborhood specialists and individuals adjust programs that suit their region best?

South America

South America is more helpless against serious environmental change, and this is at

least mostly because of human exercises, for example, deforestation.

Latin America is home to various quickly emerging countries and tremendous tropical woodland holds, putting it under the careful attention of the worldwide local area. Four nations in this locale make the worldwide top 30 rundown of most elevated yearly CO^2 producers, specifically Brazil, Argentina, Mexico, and Venezuela (utilizing 2008 information). Brazil rapidly ascends to the best five assuming discharges from deforestation are incorporated. The locale additionally faces a scope of environment impacts, including dangers to drinking water assets because of the contracting ice pack in the Andes mountains and expected decreases in crop yields and flooding because of ocean level rise.

Tropical deforestation is a significant reason for environmental change; and, tragically, Latin America is no more unusual to this issue—more timberlands have been obliterated around here than in some other since the United Nations Framework Convention on Climate Change was embraced in 1992.

The quantity of individuals in Latin America and the Caribbean impacted by outrageous climate occasions, including high temperatures, woods fires, dry seasons, tempests and floods developed from 5 million during the 1970s to in excess of 40 million somewhere in the range of 2000 and 2009, as indicated by a United Nations report that graphically subtleties the impacts of environmental change in those regions.

The 2010 report by the United Nations Environment Program (UNEP), named "Fundamental Climate Change Graphics for Latin America and the Caribbean," portrays the significant indications of environmental change in the area, its actual effects and works out ebb and flow levels of ozone depleting substance outflows and opportunities for alleviation.

nfavorable climate conditions have cost the locale more than $40 billion in the decade going before the report, which was disclosed at the UN environmental change gathering in Cancún, Mexico.

roduced as a team with the Sustainable Development and Human Settlements Division of the Economic Commission for Latin America and the Caribbean (ECLAC) and UNEP's Polar Research Center, the report additionally predicts future environment situations for the region.

A vital gauge in the report expresses that by 2050, expansions in sea surface temperature will bring about more regular fading of coral reefs, with an adverse consequence on the travel industry and fishing. Such information would be understood as bad

news in the USA, however for some nations in the Caribbean and Latin America, these are the principle industries.

Rising temperatures likewise cause genuine medical conditions. In 1970, just few nations in the locale were home to mosquitoes that communicate yellow fever, dengue fever and intestinal sickness. By 2002, the report noticed by far most of the area was impacted by these tropical diseases.

By now, most sensibly very much educated individuals know that environmental change has prompted dissolving of the Andean icy masses, the demise of many plants inside the Amazonian rainforests (extraordinarily exacerbated by uncontrolled logging) and rising ocean levels and the immersion of low-lying districts along Colombia's Caribbean coast.

Less consideration has been paid to the harm environmental change could unleash on the locale's agribusiness. As indicated by a World Bank report, the world's absolute agrarian result could fall 3-15% because of worldwide environmental change. One of the spots most noticeably awful impacted would be Latin America's central belt.

While it is valid, expanded degrees of CO_2 should help crop richness, this addition is more than offset by expanded harm from vermin and more serious and unsound climate conditions.

The World Bank report has assessed income misfortunes in Latin America's agrarian area could go from 12 - 50 percent by 2100, even in the wake of representing a specific degree of innovative transformation to environment change.

This sensational decrease will add to a gigantic worldwide food emergency on the off chance that means aren't taken expeditiously to capture it, in light of the fact that the food sending out nations of the district have food exchange adjusts as high as 12% of GDP, like Guyana. This implies they feed the world, despite the fact that a portion of those nations likewise have high food instability - which means their own kin can't manage the cost of fundamental nourishment. The United States Development Agency gauges there are 46 million individuals in Brazil who are food-insecure.

The circumstance looks significantly more critical when one limits the concentration to individual countries.

"Environmental change can have very extreme ramifications for Colombian horticulture," remarked Walter Vergara, an environmental change master. He anticipated that in the most dire outcome imaginable, Colombian ranch creation would nearly stop completely because of temperature ascents of 2.5 - 5 degrees Centigrade

and a 10% variety in yearly rainfalls.

In practically every one of the situations explored, Brazil, Peru, and Ecuador were seriously impacted, fundamentally in view of their nearness to the Equator. Central nations are especially defenseless against environmental change in light of the fact that most yields developed there at or close to the ocean level are now near the restrictions of their capacity to endure outrageous temperatures.

Colombia is a tropical country that has high countries shaping piece of the Andes mountain chain. The nation depends on frigid water system for its yields, similar as Ecuador and Peru. These three have contributed a small part of the world's ozone harming substances contrasted with industrialized countries, yet they remain to experience huge losses.

Venezuela would crushed by most pessimistic scenario environmental change situations. Ruinous communist approaches executed by Hugo Chavez have unleashed sufficient harm even without environment issues. Higher temperatures and less precipitation would essentially convey the final blow. It is assessed land esteems would plunge 75% and agrarian result by 38% by the 2080s. As Venezuela imports the greater part of its food and depends on deals of waning oil stores to pay for its imports, the future looks exceptionally troubling for this country.

exico is relied upon to encounter a decrease in horticultural creation of up to 35%. The results of such a difficulty have suggestions for pretty much every country that has a critical part of its horticultural area dedicated to corn/maize.

The foundation of Mexico's cultivating industry are the corn crops developed on resource plots—milpas. This immense organization of little plots has made a natural vault which ranchers all over the planet can access for required seed-stock. They may require seeds more impervious to environmental change, outrageous climate, like dry seasons, or curses, for example, the one that tormented the American corn crop in 1970, clearing out 15% of complete output.

otanist H. Post Wilkes calls the milpa fix an "transformative nursery," and agronomist James Boyce has brought up "because of environmental change and recently advancing strains of vermin and plant infections" corn can advance progressively and react to outside ecological changes. The process for cultivating that has created among Mexican maize cultivators results in a "significant positive externality to humanity—the in situ protection and development of hereditary variety" in one of the world's most significant cereal

crops.

ustralia

Australia is one of the world's driving exporters of food. It is no occurrence the Cairns Group of countries that are net food exporters is named after an Australian city. Any danger to Australia's food creation would have worldwide outcomes. As the nation is one of only a handful of exceptional excess puts on earth that could oblige an altogether bigger populace, extraordinary consideration should be paid to the effect a lot bigger metropolitan populace in Australia would have on public assets and local climate.

Fortunately, the Australian Government has treated the issue of environmental change extremely in a serious way, and one outcome has been the Technical Report on Climate Change in Australia, distributed in 2007. The material on the accompanying pages of this book are drawn generally from this report.

by and large, the temperature in Australia has expanded by 0.9°C starting around 1950, with critical local varieties. The recurrence of "hot evenings" has expanded and the recurrence of cooler evenings has declined. Precipitation patterns from 1900 to 1949 were for the most part rather powerless and spatially incoherent.
ainfall patterns starting around 1950 are both huge and spatially coherent.

he eastern coast, the province of Victoria, and southwest Australia have all accomplished significant decreases in precipitation beginning around 1950. Across New South Wales and Queensland precipitation patterns have been to some degree mutilated by an exceptionally wet period around the 1950s, and a bizarrely dry period in the principal decade of the 21st century. Conversely, north-western Australia has encountered an increment in precipitation over this period.

Trends in outrageous every day precipitation differ across Australia. From 1950 to 2005, there have been expansions in north-western and focal Australia and over the western tablelands of New South Wales. This has been balanced by diminishes in the south-eastern, south-western and focal east coast. Patterns in most outrageous precipitation occasions are rising quicker than patterns in the mean.

Since 1900, the period with the least precipitation was from the 1930s to the mid 1940s. Notwithstanding, dry seasons in the early long stretches of the 21st century have been more blazing, with both the greatest and least temperatures higher than in the previous dry periods.

Maximum winter snow profundity at Spencers Creek in the Snowy Mountains has fallen marginally starting around 1962, and the snow profundity in spring has declined all the more notably (by around 40%).

Table 1: Average number of days per year above 35°C at selected sites for present (1971-2000) climate and best estimate values for 2030 and 2070, with ranges of uncertainty in brackets. The mid, low and high emissions are A1B, B1 and A1FI.

	Present average (1971-2000)	2030 average (mid emissions)	2070 average (low emissions)	2070 average (high emissions)
Sydney	3.5	4.4 (4.1-5.1)	5.3 (4.5-6.8)	8.2 (6-12)
Melbourne	9.1	11.4 (11-13)	14 (12-17)	20 (15-26)
Adelaide	17	23 (21-26)	26 (24-31)	36 (29-47)
Brisbane	1.0	2.1 (1.5-2.5)	3.0 (2.1-4.5)	7.5 (4-21)
Hobart	1.4	1.7 (1.6-1.8)	1.8 (1.7-2.0)	2.4 (2.0-3.4)
Perth	28	35 (35-39)	41 (36-45)	54 (44-67)
Darwin	11	44 (25-69)	89 (49-153)	230 (143-308)

Substantial warming has happened in the three seas that encompass Australia. Southern Ocean temperatures have ascended since the 1950s to a profundity of 1,000 m in certain areas. The warming is related with a 50 km toward the south relocation of the Antarctic Circumpolar Current. Seawater close to the lower part of the sea off Antarctica has quickly become less pungent and less thick. This proposes generously expanded softening from Antarctic glaciers.

Long term perceptions off Maria Island close to Tasmania uncover a warming pattern far more noteworthy than the worldwide normal, however this might be because of changes in the East Australian Current.

The best gauge of yearly warming over Australia by 2030 comparative with the environment of 1990 is a public normal increment of around 1.0°C. Seaside regions are relied upon to encounter increments of 0.7-0.9°C in coastal

regions though inland regions will endure increments of 1-1.2°C. Mean warming in winter is relied upon to be minimal not exactly for different seasons, and ought to be pretty much as low as 0.5°C in the far south. The scope of vulnerability is around 0.6°C to 1.5°C in each season for the majority of Australia.

hese conjectures depend on the A1B discharge situation, yet considering a more prominent scope of emanation situations extends the reach just marginally - warming would in any case be whatsoever 0.4°C in all locales and could be pretty much as extensive as 1.8°C in some inland regions.

ater in the 21st century, the temperature projections are more subject to the expected outflow situation. By 2050, yearly warming evaluations for Australia range from around 0.8 to 1.8°C (best gauge 1.2°C) for the B1 (low emanations) situation and 1.5 to 2.8°C (best gauge 2.2°C) for the A1FI (high discharges) situation. By 2070, the expected temperature increment goes from around 1.0 to 2.5°C (best gauge 1.8°C) for the B1 situation to

2.2 to 5.0°C (best gauge 3.4°C) for the A1FI situation. Local variety follows the example seen for 2030, with less warming in the south and north-east and all the more inland. In 2070, the danger of a temperature expansion in abundance of 4°C is higher than 30% over inland Australia under the A1FI situation, though under the B1 situation the increment is probably going to be under 2.0°C besides in the north-west.

The Australian Government is very much aware of these gauges, which is the reason it has attempted to pass enactment to forestall or enhance the effect of environmental change. One can squabble over the adequacy of the actions proposed, or regardless of whether it is really conceivable to keep the conjectures from becoming reality, yet government programs and new laws should be assessed in the setting that Australia is accepted to be at genuine danger from environmental change and the state is taking a stab at solutions.

Africa

One of the way of life right now under more clear danger from environmental change is that of the Horn of Africa. Ethiopia, Somalia, Eritrea and portions of Kenya have been tormented by dry season for the majority of the twentieth and 21st hundreds of years. This adjustment of the environment has been exacerbated by monstrous deforestation and battles in the region.

Forest inclusion in Ethiopia, for instance, declined from 40% to beneath 2% in

only 30 years. So the trees and shrubs that tight spot the land, forestall desertification and that hold and channel water, are no more. This additionally implies that evapotranspiration is significantly decreased.

Regular dry seasons have for quite some time been viewed as an element of eastern Africa, however in the course of recent years the recurrence of these dry spells has observably expanded. As indicated by new examination distributed in Climate Dynamics, this is probably going to proceed as worldwide temperatures proceed to rise.

If this expectation is right it implies that an expected 17.5 million individuals in the Greater Horn of Africa are in danger of potential food shortages.

The forecasts are the consequence of a review did by researchers from the US Geological Survey (USGS) and the University of California, Santa Barbara. They inferred that the expansion in temperature of the Indian Ocean that caused diminished precipitation in eastern Africa was connected to worldwide warming.

hey accept that as the world heated up during the last century, the Indian Ocean heated up especially quick. The hotter air rose, however the expanded dampness delivered more incessant precipitation around there. Having lost the vast majority of its dampness the air then, at that point, streamed westwards and plunged over Africa, causing dry season conditions in Kenya and Ethiopia.

This new exploration that shows proceeded with dry spell, goes against past situations made by the Intergovernmental Panel on Climate Change, which kept up with that precipitation in eastern Africa would really increase.

The USGS and the US Agency for International Development are restless to distinguish spaces of possible dry season and starvation to target food help and to give data on agrarian turn of events, natural protection and the preparation of water resources.

USGS researcher Chris Funk says that considering the anticipated expansion in worldwide temperatures it is expected that precipitation sums in Kenya and Ethiopia will keep on diminishing or will stay underneath the verifiable normal. This abatement in precipitation is especially articulated in the March to June season, he reports, when this is when significant precipitation generally happens. Notwithstanding, dry season isn't the main justification for food deficiencies; the advancement of farming has deteriorated and populace has kept on developing, so there are basically more mouths to feed.

Park Williams, a researcher from the University of California, Santa Barbara

brings up that anticipating the fluctuation of precipitation from one year to another is incredibly troublesome. Solid endeavors are being made to further develop unwavering quality by connecting worldwide change and precipitation in explicit districts. By doing this it is trusted that more exact projections of future precipitations can be developed.

ark Williams additionally focuses on that while ocean temperatures in the Indian Ocean are relied upon to keep on rising, consequently causing a normal decline in eastern African precipitation, since there are numerous different variables that impact precipitation, extremely wet seasons will in any case happen from time to time.

In request to show up at their discoveries, researchers saw information to see what was driving environment varieties. A large portion of the Indian Ocean warming was viewed as connected to human exercises, especially ozone depleting substance and spray discharges. The Indian Ocean has warmed especially quick since it is rapidly being infringed upon by the Tropical Warm Pool, which is a region with the hottest sea surface temperature in the world.

It should be focused on that a component that has contributed enormously to the district's dry spell is that beginning around 1974, the populace in the Horn of Africa has multiplied, and the pace of populace development is really expanding. This prompts further annihilation of the delicate environment, which thusly exacerbates the dry season. There is presumably no way around La Nina and that current's effect on environmental change. Populace control and the executives of assets is another matter.

It is impossible there will be numerous perusers of this book in the Horn of Africa, so maybe the possibilities for this area are not a significant reason for concern. All things considered, what about a gander at regions under danger that are nearer to home.

The circumstance in the Horn of Africa is somewhat bleak, yet the remainder of the mainland is incredibly helpless against environmental change. This weakness and the restrictions of helpless nations to adjust to environmental change difficulties were featured in Climate Change 2001, the Third Assessment Report of the Intergovernmental Panel on Climate Change (IPCC).

The report set up how human action (consuming non-renewable energy sources and changes in land-use) is altering the worldwide environment, with temperature rises anticipated for the following 100 years that could influence human government assistance and the environment.

The chronicled environment record for Africa shows a temperature rise of

around 0.7°C over the greater part of the mainland during the 20th century; a diminishing in precipitation over huge bits of the Sahel (the semi-dry district south of the Sahara); and an expansion in precipitation in east-focal Africa. Over the course of the following century, this warming pattern, and changes in precipitation designs, are relied upon to proceed and be joined by an ascent in ocean level and expanded recurrence of outrageous climate events.

Most of Africa depends on downpour took care of agribusiness. Thusly, it is exceptionally helpless against changes in environment fluctuation, occasional movements, and precipitation designs. Any increment in mean yearly temperature will prompt expanded water pressure. Generally 70% of Africans rely upon cultivating professionally, and 40% of all commodities from the mainland are horticultural items (WRI 1996).

Temperature ascends over numerous spaces will be more prominent than the worldwide normal. The overall anticipated ascent is 4°C by the 2080s. To exacerbate the situation, temperatures could ascend to 7°C in southern Africa and 8°C in northern Africa

- practically twofold the worldwide normal. The difficulties defying Africa can be summed up as follows:-

- Significant changes in precipitation are normal all through the landmass, with the space around the Sahara and in southern Africa prone to encounter the most serious declines.
  - Desertification is probably going to increment around the Sahara, driving populaces to migrate.
- Higher temperatures, far reaching water pressure, expanded recurrence and seriousness of dry seasons and floods, and rising ocean levels will seriously hinder progress on advancement objectives in Africa.
- Cereal harvest yields could fall 10 – 30% by the 2050s contrasted with 1990 levels.
  - Heat waves will prompt more wounds, infection and death.
  - Vector-and water-borne sicknesses like intestinal sickness, dengue fever and cholera will presumably increment. An extra 67 million individuals in
  -
  -

    Africa could be in danger of intestinal sickness pandemics by the 2080s.

s environmental change is a worldwide issue, it will undoubtedly significantly affect pretty much every country on the planet. Created nations are probably going to give need to distributing their assets to handle the homegrown effect of environmental change. Whatever the nearly wealthy have passed on to help other people should be shared by an expanding number of individuals in every mainland who face ruin assuming the middle environmental change forecast demonstrate correct.

Europe has various very well off nations that would be relied upon to help neighbors out of luck. North America and the Caribbean have generally relied upon the USA and Canada for help. South Americans would most likely look to Brazil, and perhaps Chile, to lead any recuperation program. Asians can hope to Japan, Taiwan and Korea for help, despite the fact that there are numerous of all shapes and sizes Asian countries that are creating to where they could help themselves generally. Australasians would anticipate that Australia and New Zealand should deal with them.

Who could the Africans go to in their hour of need? South Africa has the landmass' greatest economy, and would most likely be leaned to help everything it could. Be that as it may, it would be unimaginable for any nation to give significant, enduring help to multiple times its own populace.

Considering that South Africa is relied upon to battle with the effect of environmental change inside its lines, it is outlandish to anticipate that the country should give a lot of help to its neighbors, particularly those outside southern Africa.

so, the future looks exceptionally bleak for Africa in case the environmental change projections of the IPCC and others demonstrate accurate.

The Immediate Threat

So far all of the environmental change issues referenced have represented a danger that will not be seen until after 2020 at the soonest. As a rule, the most noticeably terrible impacts will not become evident until 2050, 2070 or even 2080. At the end of the day, not in the expected lifetimes of most perusers of this book brought into the world in the twentieth century.

This is a problem for our children and grandchildren to worry about. Very unfortunate of course, but unlikely to affect us directly. This makes it very unlikely serious effort will be made to address the issue of climate change until enough people in wealthy, developed countries are directly affected. By that time, the crisis will be upon us and probably impossible to avoid.

The bad news for all those hoping to pass on the problem of tackling climate change to the next generation, or possibly the one after that is there is a specific and genuine threat from climate change that could wipe out entire regions in a single day. Any day. Even tomorrow. Many of the world's richest countries and those with the largest economies are at risk, including America, Mexico, Britain, Ireland, France, Spain, Portugal, China, Taiwan, Japan, India, Indonesia and possibly Australia and New Zealand.

This threat is essentially the same one that the events in the Storegga area off the coast of Norway posed to Doggerland. In many ways, the result would be just as catastrophic. Essentially, the Storegga Slide (and this applies to whether there were two, three or four such slides) was a consequence of a sudden release of huge quantities of methane hydrates from just below the seabed and a subsequent movement of the marine floor in reaction. This led to severe earth tremors and massive tsunamis – far, far worse than anything that happened in the Indian Ocean on December 26, 2004 or on March 11, 2011 off the coast of Japan. The accompanying devastation could also be much worse.

Even today, there are substantial methane hydrate deposits off the coast of Norway and centred on the area around the Storegga Slide. The good news is recent surveys have indicated this particular site no longer poses a threat. The bad news is there are plenty of other places on the ocean floor that have large methane hydrates deposits, and theoretically, any one of them could cause a similar disaster.

To get an idea of the global scale of the problem, the map below, provided by US Navy Research Lab, suggests methane hydrate can be found along virtually every continental shelf in the world.

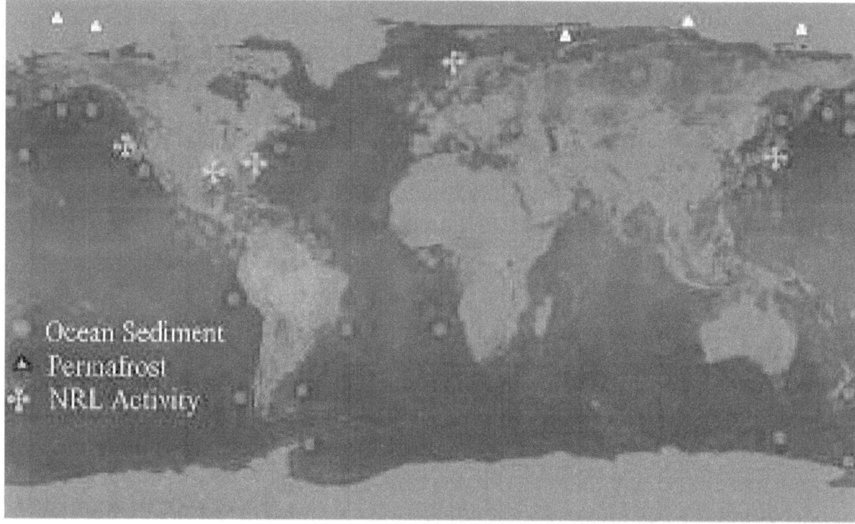

Some methane hydrate deposits are in permafrost. It is unlikely they will cause serious earthquakes or tsunamis, but the release of methane into the atmosphere will have a far more serious impact on climate change than carbon dioxide. This alone is cause for concern.

But let us focus on the ocean floor methane hydrate deposits and the consequences of a chain of events similar to the Storegga Slide in one of the wealthiest parts of the world.

There are methane hydrates deposits all along the eastern coast of America. The best known is at Blake Ridge.

Blake Ridge is a bathymetric high located on the Atlantic continental rise approximately 400 km east from Charleston, South Carolina. The sedimentary feature is situated in water depths between 2,000 to 4,800 metres and is approximately 500 km in length. Over the past 30 years, the

Blake Ridge has become perhaps the best-studied occurrence of methane hydrate in the United States.

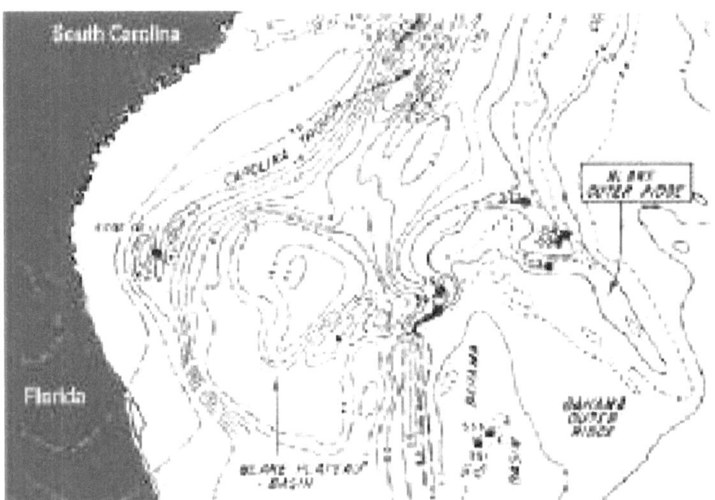

Location of Blake Ridge with respect to Atlantic coastline.
Source: B. E. Tucholke, R. E. Houtz, and W. J. Ludwig, 1982, Sediment thickness and depth to basement in the western North Atlantic Ocean basin, AAPG Bulletin 66:1393.

In 1970, the Deep Sea Drilling Project (DSDP) began drilling in the Blake Ridge as part of their effort to understand the evolution of the world's oceans and oceanic processes. Sediment cores recovered during drilling contained high concentrations of methane. The correspondence between the presence of methane and the observation of anomalously high seismic velocities led to the hypothesis that methane hydrates exist at Blake Ridge. Confirmation of hydrate presence occurred in 1980 when a hydrate sample was retrieved from beneath the ocean floor.

The Blake Ridge formed through the deposition of sediments carried parallel with the shoreline by ocean bottom currents. During the Palaeocene, the initiation of the Gulf Stream brought warm waters northward along the Atlantic coast. The opening of the Greenland Sea in the Oligocene allowed cool, dense water from the Arctic Ocean to flow south (Western Boundary Current) along the western Atlantic margin. Blake Ridge marks the spot where these two major currents interact, lose speed, and drop a portion of their sediment load. If one of these currents were to diminish, it would lead to a significant change in water temperatures around Blake Ridge almost instantly. Such a change – higher or lower – would be far above any average rise or fall in regional temperatures. The affect of this sudden change could change the world as we know it. More on this a little later.

o date, no sediments older than Miocene have been recovered from Blake Ridge. Miocene sediments cored at Blake Ridge are siliceous gray-green muds. Middle Miocene through present sediments are commonly carbonaceous gray-green muds with varying amounts of silts and sands.

The occurrence of hydrate at Blake Ridge is connected to the high rates of sedimentation in the area. Estimates of sedimentation rates range from 160-350 metres per million years for the Miocene to 40 metres per million years for the Pleistocene. Such high rates of sedimentation allow for relatively quick and deep burial of organic matter that is transported to the site. At depth, bacteria convert the organic matter to methane and release it into the sediments. In addition, deeper marine shales and carbonates may provide methane for hydrate formation.

A large amount of methane is believed to be trapped within the hydrate layer and beneath the hydrate as free gas. Repeated episodes of deep hydrate burial, hydrate dissociation, methane release and recapture is recognised as a method to explain the relative concentration of free gas and hydrate at Blake Ridge.

Scientists from the United States Geological Survey have mapped the distribution and thickness of methane hydrate deposits at Blake Ridge using seismic lines and side-scanning sonar. Maps of depth to the BSR (Bottom Simulating Reflector) reveal thinning of the hydrate layer linked to disruptions of the sea floor. Because hydrates are sensitive to changes in temperature and pressure, external forces that affect these parameters, such as a drop in mean sea level or a mass movement of sediment, can initiate hydrate dissociation which may lead to pressure build-up and subsequent methane release and seafloor disruptions.

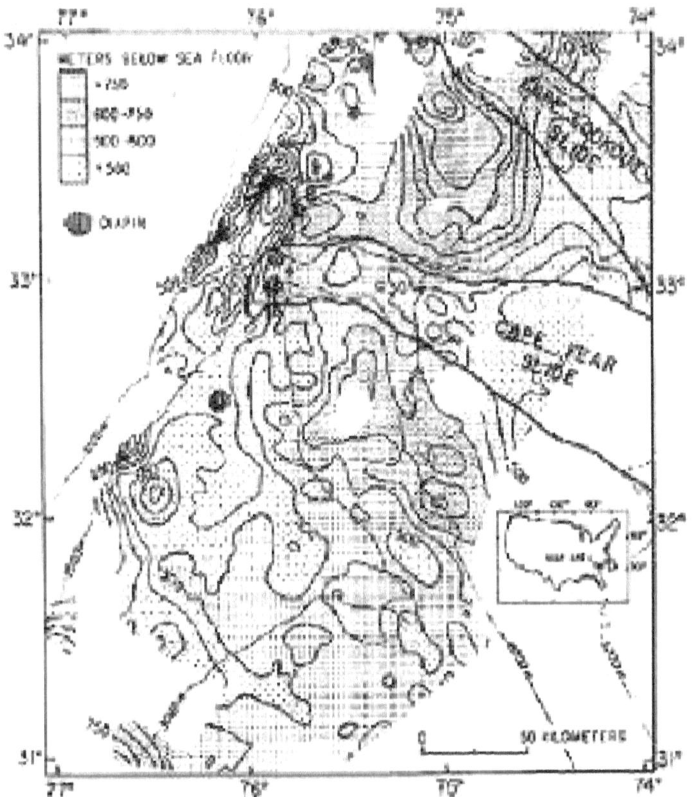

Topographic map showing the locations of landslides and diapirs on top of the BSR in the Blake Ridge area.
ource: W. P. Dillon and M. D. Max, 2000, The U.S. Atlantic Continental Margin; the Best-Known Gas Hydrate Locality, in M. D. Max (ed.), Natural Gas Hydrate in Oceanic and Permafrost Environments.

The picture below shows Blake Ridge from a side perspective and was supplied by the United States Geological Survey:

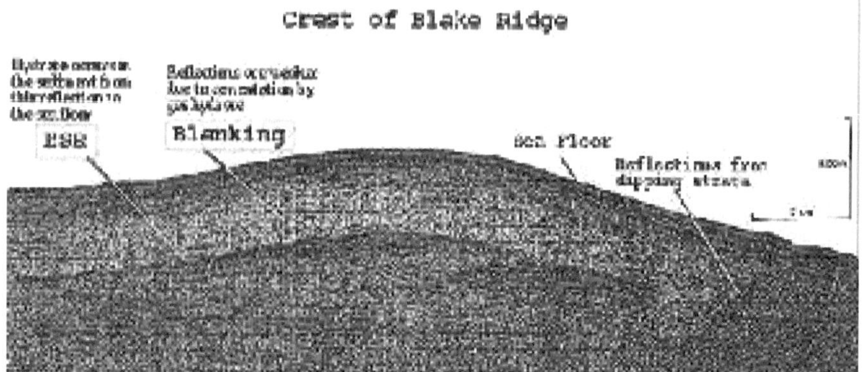

The picture makes it very clear there is a "bulge" in the rock structure at Blake Ridge and that it has been caused by pressure from methane hydrate. The image resembles a cross section of a volcano and lava. The methane hydrate might seep out of the rocks above over a long period of time, or burst through the seabed, rather like Krakatoa.

Cape Fear Slide and Cape Lookout Slide are two mass movement features near Blake Ridge (see Seismic Line figure above). Seismic lines show weaker and shallower BSRs beneath the slides compared to undisturbed adjacent areas. It is likely decreased overburden pressure upon the sediments beneath the slides resulted in dissociation of hydrate. Although hydrate dissociation may not have triggered the slides, dissociation may have involved more sediment in the mass movement.

ne of the most intriguing aspects of the Blake Ridge is the presence of a major depression on the crest that may be linked to methane dissociation and release. Although its development history is not fully understood, two theories currently exist to explain the structure. One stresses catastrophic expulsion of gas and sediment. During an unspecified glacial episode, the fall in sea level led to reduced pressure and consequent hydrate dissociation. owever, the gas was unable to effectively dissipate due to the low permeability of the Blake Ridge sediments. Pressure built up, the structure inflated, and eventually blew out. A second theory suggests the feature is composed of rapidly deposited sediment waves that allowed for more gradual methane expulsion through high-permeability pathways linking the zone of hydrate dissociation to the sea-bottom.

Essentially, the first theory suggests two events rather like the Storegga Slides have taken place at Blake Ridge. The second theory is based on the assumption the release of methane was less abrupt and presumably less damaging in its aftermath.

If we base our assumptions on the first theory, the Blake Ridge features two known slides plus a feature that might well represent another site of a previous sudden release of major quantities of methane hydrates. What would be the impact of another major release from this site?

For starters, take a look at a map of the Google Earth map that shows the location of Blake Ridge:

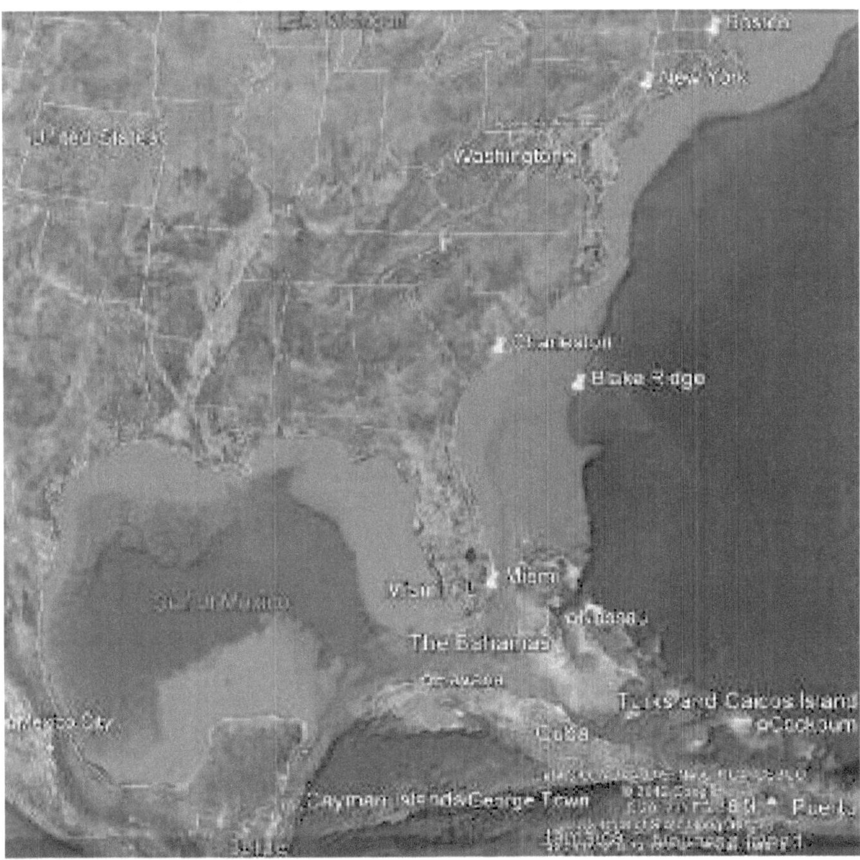

Look at all the major cities along that coast: Boston, New York, Washington, Charleston, and Miami are just the biggest cities. How would they cope with a tsunami the height of a five-storey building rushing towards them. If we shift our focus further south, just about every major town and city in Florida is at or near sea level. Events from the 2004 tsunami have proven such waves can go around corners, so New Orleans and the entire Louisiana coastline would also be extremely vulnerable. Houston and much of Texas would not be much better off.

o put it into perspective, imagine the devastation Hurricane Katrina had inflicted in 2005 had been applied almost simultaneously to the entire eastern coastline of America, with Nova Scotia and parts of Mexico also badly hit. That is how widespread a worst-case scenario would be.

Let us consider the possible consequences of a mega-tsunami being unleashed from Blake Ridge. Perhaps, we should start by reminding ourselves what the word tsunami actually means. It is a Japanese word. "Tsu" means "harbour" and "name" means "wave". This is because the wave in question is especially damaging when it enters a harbour because the shallowness of the water causes the wave to slow down and grow taller. The sides of a harbour act like a funnel to amplify this growth so when the wave reaches land, it is often many times higher than it was in open water.

n extreme cases, such as the March 11, 2011 tsunami in Japan, the waves can reach in excess of 100 feet or 30m. when they reach the shore. The force of such a huge wave can be awe-inspiringly destructive, as many images from the 2011 event attest. To make matters worse, many harbours have rivers flowing into them, and these waterways can carry a tsunami miles inland.

There is clear evidence the tsunami caused by the Storegga Slide penetrated as much as 50 miles/80km inland in parts of Scotland. The March 11, 2011 tsunami in Japan also penetrated six miles/10km inland in flat coastal areas.

Each tsunami is unique, so there must be an element of guesswork when trying to calculate the effects of one of these waves on a particular place. Nevertheless, this book will attempt to give an idea of what could happen if there was a methane hydrate eruption at Blake Ridge.

irst, let us look at Boston. The map provided by cityofboston.gov shows how many of that city's districts are exposed.

Many of the residential areas closest to the shoreline will be the most expensive homes in Boston, so the richest citizens would be the hardest hit. With such an extensive shore and riverside, greater Boston is horribly exposed to the kind of mayhem a tsunami can cause.

Firstly, the port itself would be badly hit. Ships, containers, imported and exported goods would all suffer extensive damage. Oil and gas tankers are often located close to the sea, and those would all be extremely vulnerable to a tsunami.

Power stations would also be obvious casualties. There are three nuclear power stations near Boston and the Atlantic coast: Pilgrim Power Plant in

Plymouth, Massachusetts, Seabrook Station in Seabrook, New Hampshire and Millstone Power Station in Waterford, Connecticut. With the memory of the disaster that befell the nuclear power stations in Japan still fresh in our collective minds, it is easy to envisage a tsunami on the Atlantic coast causing a similar level of radioactive mayhem.

Mass transit systems would be very badly hit: roads and railways, bridges, and - worst of all – the underground railway would all suffer extensive damage. The possible impact on the city at the height of rush hour does not bear thinking about.

Logan International Airport is beside Boston Harbour, so it is unlikely to remain intact if a tsunami passes by.

In summary, a worst case scenario would lead to much of greater Boston being completely destroyed, hundreds of thousands of people dead or injured, possibly no electricity, raw sewage contaminating the drinking water supply, no mass transit systems in operation, many hospitals badly damaged and the rest overwhelmed by people demanding urgent treatment, the port and airport in ruins, along with roads, railways and bridges, making evacuation of people and supply of urgent provisions very difficult, to say the least. If the incident took place in winter, there would also be the cold to contend with.

Another unpleasant factor to consider is that in March 2011 Japan's population displayed stoicism and a sense of civic duty and cooperation that would not be very likely in America or almost any other country. Such a disaster in America would very quickly lead to a breakdown in law and order and a sharp increase in tensions between communities. One only has to consider the aftermath of the relatively localised Hurricane Katrina to know the situation in America would be far worse than anything witnessed in Japan.

There is a counter argument that might suggest this forecast is wildly over-pessimistic. A key point being the March 11,1 2011 tsunami caused terrible damage to only a portion of Japan's eastern coast and major cities like Tokyo were spare much of the wave's impact. It is true the precise epicentre of a tsunami and the nature of its cause has a profound influence on the chain of events. This is why the December 26, 2004 tsunami in Indonesia inflicted such terrible carnage from Burma to Tanzania.

Predicting the outcome of a methane hydrates eruption and a (possible)

resulting slide of the surrounding seabed is almost impossible. All we can do is make forecasts based on evidence from previous examples, and the Storegga Slide(s) provides ample data for what a worst case scenario might look like. The tsunamis of 2004 and 2011 provide further – recent – evidence of what tsunamis can do to coastal areas.

urthermore, Blake Ridge is just one of many sites along America's Atlantic coast that have substantial methane hydrates deposits. There are similar, known sites from Maine to the Gulf of Mexico. Anyone of them could be considered a possible cause of a tsunami, and there might even be a chain reaction of multiple methane hydrates eruptions.

What could happen to Boston is made even worse by the possibility that at almost exactly the same time, a tsunami might also be approaching New York.

New York is rather similar to Boston in the sense that the city is built around an extensive harbour, with many small bays and islands and a large river, the Hudson, flowing into it.

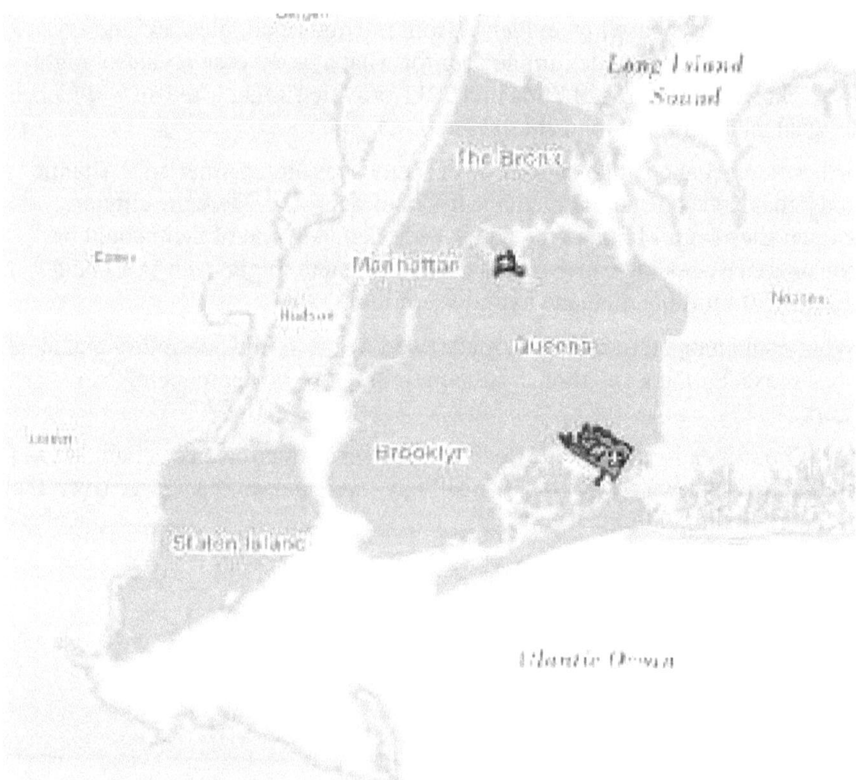

As the map from nyc.gov clearly shows, the city's main airport, JFK International, is horribly exposed to the Atlantic coast. So too, is much of Brooklyn. Any tsunami that reached Manhattan would have to do so via the Hudson estuary. It would take a stroke of terrible bad luck for the trajectory of a tsunami to carry the wave to Manhattan, but a worst case scenario would be every bit as devastating to America's commercial capital as the probable impact on Boston.

t is more likely, residential areas on Long Island would be worst affected, along with New York's port and airport facilities.

The 2011 tsunami in Japan showed the world what can happen when a tsunami strikes an area with nuclear reactors. The following map has been adapted from Google Maps and shows commercial nuclear power stations near Boston and New York:

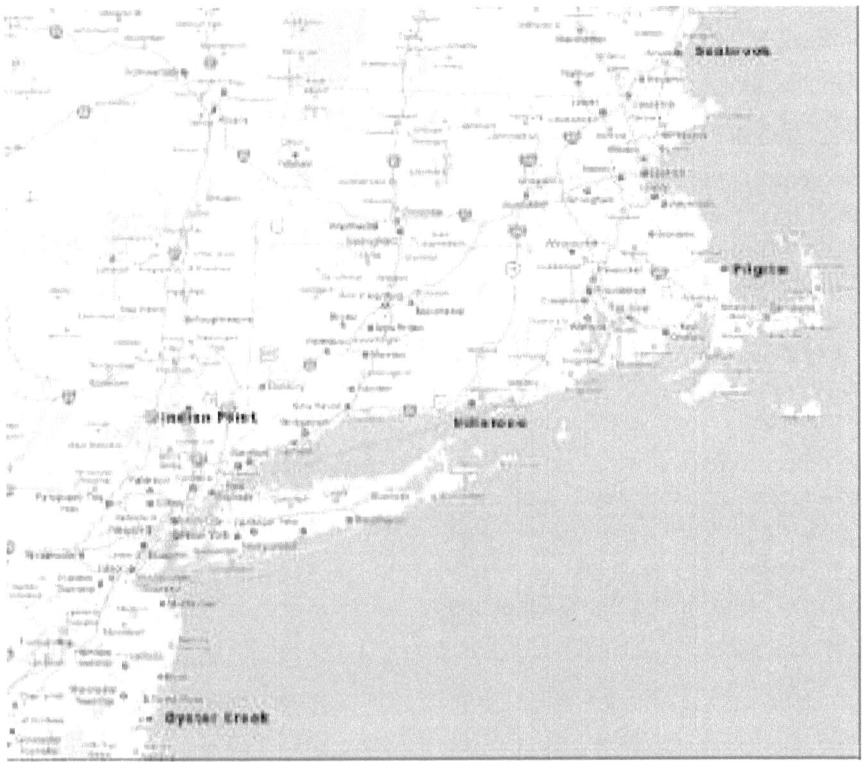

There are a number of nuclear reactors on the coast near New York. To the North, lies Millstone. To the South, there is Oyster Creek and Hope Creek/Salem (these power plants occupy the same site). The latter is slap bang in the middle of a harbour shaped like a funnel pointing directly out to sea. In terms of possible physical impact, if ever there was a nuclear power plant in the worst possible place for a tsunami to strike, Salem is it. Hope Creek, almost within walking distance of Salem, is equally exposed. The three nuclear reactors at Indian Point Energy Center are 38 miles/55km north and upriver of New York.

Further down the coast is America's capital, Washington. The city itself would almost certainly be spared a direct hit by a tsunami because of the land ridges protecting most of Chesapeake Bay, plus the fact that the Potomac twists more than once from the city to the sea. Even Ronald Reagan International Airport should be spared if a tsunami were to strike the Atlantic coast.

The bad news is Washington is just as vulnerable to the aftermath of a nuclear power station being destroyed by a tsunami as any other place on America's East coast. To the North, lie the Salem and Hope Creek plants. Just outside the capital, on the shore of Chesapeake Bay lie the twin nuclear reactors at Calvert Cliff. While the bay is largely protected by a strip of land at its entrance, if a tsunami were to penetrate the bay, its most obvious path would lead it directly to the Calvert Cliff.

he Dominion Surry nuclear power station is even closer to the mouth of Chesapeake Bay, but in a smaller inlet. It is probably just as vulnerable to a tsunami, and just as likely to cause radioactive havoc with Washington and its suburbs.

In other words, a tsunami could lead to the sudden, permanent abandonment of America's capital city and related infrastructure even if not so much as a single drop of water made it to the city.

he following map has been adapted from Google Maps and shows nuclear power stations in the Washington area:

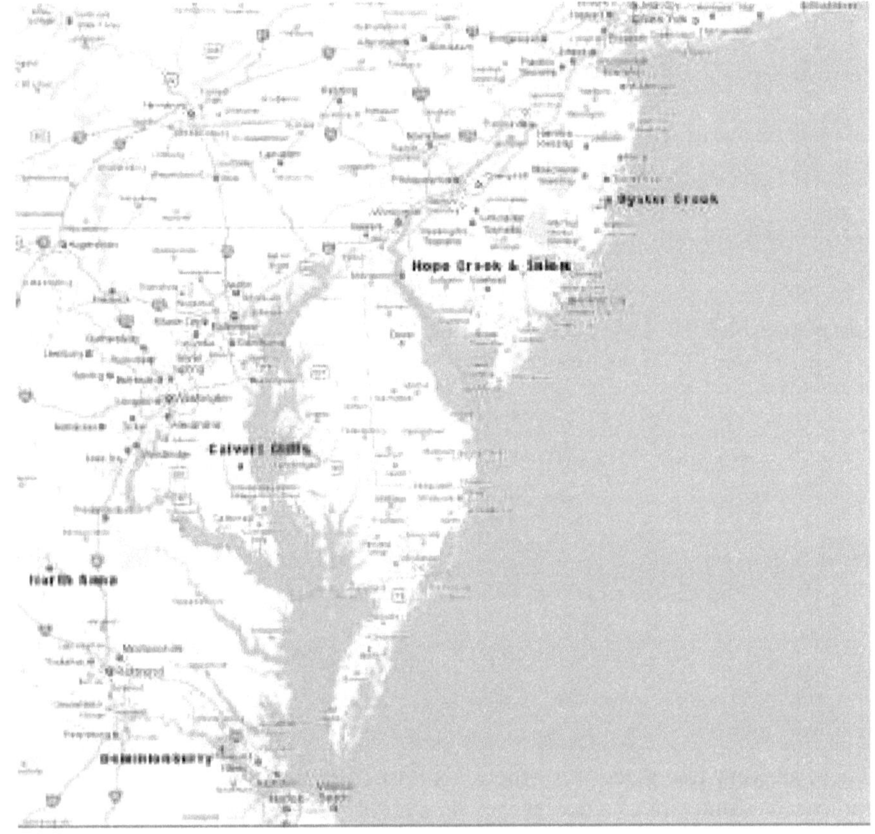

The following map has been adapted from Google Maps and shows nuclear power stations in the south-eastern part of the United States:

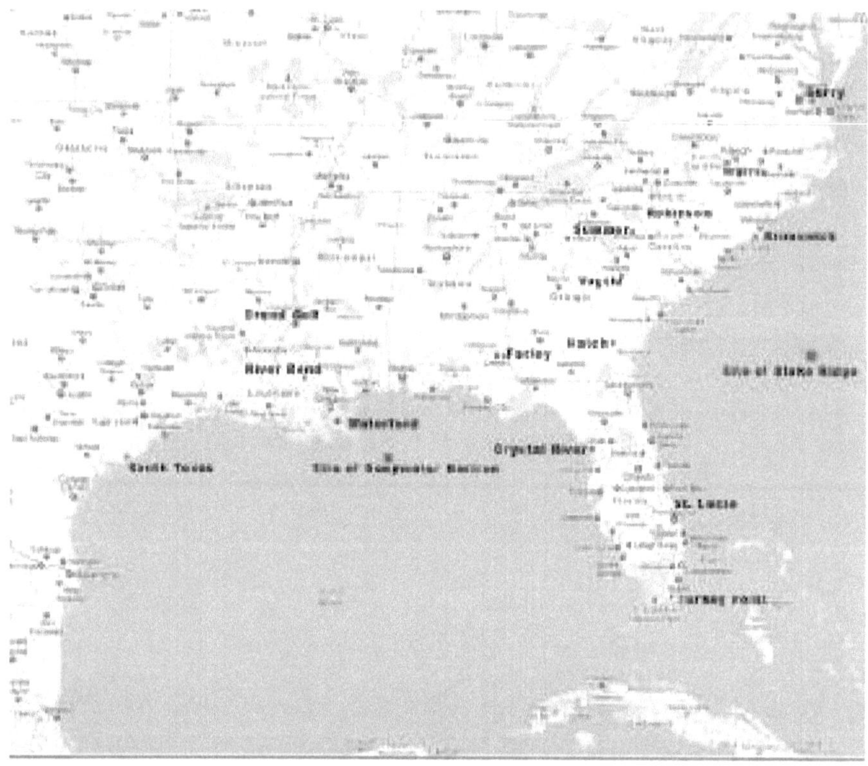

There are very few places on America's East coast that are not within the radioactive footprint of a nuclear power station. The following section describes each site active in 2011, with most of the details provided by Greenpeace.

Starting with the most northerly nuclear plant on the coast, we have Seabrook in New Hampshire. This plant is at beside a small bay that opens directly on to the Atlantic. This bay offers no protection from a tsunami as the plant is directly opposite its entrance. This bay would simply amplify the effects of the wave, so it is likely to be worst hit part of the regional shoreline.

South of Boston lies the Pilgrim plant in Massachusetts. The plant is beside the sea in Cape Cod Bay. A narrow strip of land offers some protection from waves coming from the South, but as the plant is almost level with the end of that protective barrier and tsunamis often travel around obstacles, it must be said this plant is highly vulnerable.

hen, we have two reactors at the Millstone plant in Long Island Sound. As the plant is exceptionally near the finish of Long Island, this hindrance would offer insignificant assurance from a tsunami.

In New Jersey, there is the Oyster Creek plant, close to somewhere between New York City and Atlantic City. An extremely restricted segment of land extends for a significant distance on the beach front toward the North and South of the plant, however it is dubious this would offer more than token security against a tsunami.

A little toward the South, lies the Delaware Bay. A characteristic harbor, formed rather like a channel. At its tightest point lie the Salem and Hope Creek reactors. On the off chance that a torrent were to enter the straight, the wave would be at its generally ruinous in the space involved by these reactors.

he Calvert Cliffs power station lies on the western shore of Chesapeake Bay, and is in a more shielded situation than a significant number of the plants on this rundown. All things considered, assuming a tidal wave were to enter the inlet, the wave would have a genuinely clear way to the two atomic reactors at this site.

Surry Power Station is on a headland on the James River which streams into the Chesapeake Bay close to its entry. In principle, a wave could enter that far upstream, yet it would be very improbable to show up with adequate power to cause major damage.

On the North Carolina coast, there is the Brunswick thermal energy station. In spite of the fact that there is some low lying land between the plant and the sea, this would not offer a lot of assurance in case of a tidal wave striking the coast.

The following thermal energy plant on the coast is in Florida. The twin reactor St. Lucie Nuclear Power Plant is right on the sea and depends on the ocean for water to be utilized as a coolant for its optional framework. There is no insurance from a torrent heading for the space. One would trust the way that this piece of America is presented to various typhoons and storms has prompted proficient security gauges set up on the off chance that a crisis closure is required.

Almost on the southern tip of Florida lies the Turkey Point Nuclear Generating Station. There are five power producing units at this site: two atomic reactors, two oil/flammable gas terminated units and a joined cycle gas-terminated unit. The uplifting news is this station endure flawless an immediate hit from Hurricane Andrew and is worked to withstand wind paces of up to 235 mph/380 kmh. The awful news is the atomic reactors have a somewhat awful record of "occurrences". The more terrible news is an immediate hit by a torrent would be undeniably really wrecking that a hurricane.

Traveling North along Florida's western coast, we show up at the Crystal River Nuclear Power Plant. It has been shut starting around 2009 while fixes are being completed on its substantial radiation control divider. The plant is exceptionally near the ocean, and keeping in mind that intended to withstand storms, it is presented to the full effect of a tsunami.

The following thermal energy plant on America's eastern shore is in Louisiana. The Waterford Nuclear Generating Station is in suburbia of New Orleans. At the point when Hurricane Katrina was moving toward the space in 2005, the plant was shut in before the tempest showed up and no harm was reported.
Unfortunately, waves don't give a few days early notification before they strike. The huge measure of harm brought about by that storm makes it clear New Orleans would endure awfully assuming a tidal wave were to strike.

Blake Ridge is the opposite side of Florida from Louisiana, yet there are known stores of methane hydrates in the Gulf of Mexico. As a rule, where you observe oil and gas stores, methane hydrates isn't far away.

The River Bend thermal energy plant is a couple of miles inland from Baton Rouge, which thusly is somewhat further away from the coast than New Orleans. Almost elsewhere on the planet, that should put it out of danger from a wave, yet the idea of the territory and the levees that keep the ocean under control mean even this site could be considered under threat.

The keep going plant on the coast is the South Texas Project, around 90 miles/145km South-west of Houston. It is around 10 miles/16km from the ocean, setting it at the external edge of a risk zone. The twin reactor station has a 7,000 section of land/28 km² supply utilized for as an option in contrast to cooling towers. Indeed, even a reasonably amazing wave that arrived at that repository could prompt enormous amounts of radioactive water contaminating the area.

Including the Crystal River plant, there are 15 business thermal energy plants (21 reactors) along America's Atlantic shoreline that could be thought of as defenseless against the effect from a torrent. The odds of every one of them being hit by similar series of tidal waves is for all intents and purposes zero, however the chance of a tidal wave hitting a stretch of coast that included more than one reactor ought not be excused. Moreover, the thermal energy stations inland

at Indian Point, North Anna, Harris, Robinson, Summer, Vogtle, Hatch, Farley and River Bend are likewise helpless for reasons that will be clarified later in this book.

We have convincing proof of what can happen when a tidal wave hits a thermal energy plant on the coast in light of the March 11, 2011 wave in Japan. The most noticeably terrible impacted regions will be dreadful until at minimum some point during the 2030s. Luckily for Japan in general, the torrent struck a region that was moderately inadequately populated. Likewise, there are no atomic reactors inside 100 miles/160km of Tokyo or Yokohama, which implies the nation's political and monetary heartland is generally protected from atomic defilement brought about by a harmed reactor. Osaka is more helpless as a result of a series of reactors on Honshu's north-western coast that are inside 50 miles/80km of Japan's second city at their nearest point.

Some of America's greatest urban communities are undeniably more defenseless. Boston, Philadelphia, New York and Washington all have atomic reactors close by on the coast. They are sufficiently close to one another that one torrent could hit them all.

lately, various spots on America's Atlantic coast have been forced to bear cataclysmic events. Storm Katrina is maybe the most high profile illustration of what can turn out badly. Katrina is additionally a profoundly important model since a significant part of the harm was caused by a tempest flood up to 30 feet/nine meters high, which intently looks like the impacts of a tsunami.

The tempest flood infiltrated as much as 12 miles/20km inland as the levee framework developed to keep the region dry fizzled. Over a month after the fact, huge spaces of more noteworthy New Orleans were as yet submerged. There was no power in many areas. Individuals who needed to leave their homes took shelter in the city's (American) football arena and were regularly helpless before packs of plunderers and general criminals.

ost of the shore of Texas, Louisiana, Mississippi and portions of Florida experienced broad and delayed harm. Around 3,000,000 individuals lost admittance to power. Countless individuals lost their homes because of the effect of Hurricane Katrina. It is assessed that around 1,000,000 individuals were dislodged from the focal Gulf Coast because of that tempest – the biggest diaspora in America's history.

In the interceding years, a considerable lot of those individuals have gotten back to the space, but

even today, urban communities like New Orleans have a lot more modest populace that before.

The public authority reaction to Hurricane Katrina has come in for far reaching analysis, and get what happened in light of the fact that this has direct bearing on the expected consequence of a torrent hitting America's east coast.

Acting In understanding with government law, President George W. Shrubbery educated the Secretary of the Department of Homeland Security, Michael Chertoff, to organize and direct the Federal reaction. Chertoff relegated Michael D. Brown, top of the Federal Emergency Management Agency (FEMA), as the Principal Federal Official to lead the organization and coordination of all government reaction assets and powers in the Gulf Coast region.

Many of the well known people engaged with the crisis reaction came in for serious analysis. President Bush, Chertoff and Brown were faulted for what some apparent as an absence of arranging and coordination. Brown guaranteed Louisiana Governor Kathleen Blanco opposed their endeavors and was pointless. Lead representative Blanco and her staff questioned this.

Governor Blanco and New Orleans Mayor Ray Nagin likewise came in for their portion of analysis from people in general. A grievance that summarized the inadequacy of Blanco concerned endeavors by private causes and guardians to empty New Orleans. A significant number of them depended on transport organizations and rescue vehicle administrations for clearing and couldn't empty individuals in their consideration since they needed to stand by excessively ache for transportation. Louisiana's Emergency Operations Plan Supplement 1C(Part II, segment II section D) calls for utilization of school and other public transports in departures. In spite of the fact that transports that later overwhelmed were accessible to ship those ward upon public transportation, insufficient transport drivers were accessible to drive them as Governor Blanco didn't sign a crisis waiver to permit any authorized driver to ship evacuees on school buses.

agin and Blanco were scrutinized for neglecting to execute New Orleans' departure plan and for requesting occupants to a safe house after all other options have run out with practically no arrangements for food, water, security, or sterile conditions. Maybe the main analysis of Nagin was that he deferred his crisis clearing request until 19 hours before landfall of the typhoon, which prompted many passings of individuals who at that point couldn't track down any exit plan of

the city.

resident Bush looked for $105 billion to take care of fixes and reproduction costs in the consequence of Katrina. The generally monetary expense of the typhoon is assessed at about $150 billion for Louisiana and Mississippi alone. Streets, spans, rail routes, levees, electrical cables, houses, schools, medical clinics, manufacturing plants were completely obliterated on an exceptional scale. Nine petroleum processing plants were seriously damaged.

The natural effect ought not be neglected. The tempest flood caused generous ocean side disintegration, at times totally annihilating waterfront regions. In Dauphin Island, roughly 90 miles (150 km) east of where Katrina made landfall, the sand that contained the hindrance island was moved across the island into the Mississippi Sound, pushing the whole island towards land. The tempest flood and waves from Katrina likewise wrecked the Chandeleur Islands, which had additionally been impacted by Hurricane Ivan in 2004. The US Geological Survey assessed 217 square miles (560 km2) of land was changed to water by the tropical storms Katrina and Rita (the accompanying year).

The terrains that were lost were favorable places for marine warm blooded animals, earthy colored pelicans, turtles, and fish, just as transient birds, for example, redhead ducks. Around 20% of neighborhood swamps were forever overwhelmed by water because of the storm.

Damage brought about by Katrina constrained the conclusion of 16 National Wildlife Refuges. Breton National Wildlife Refuge lost a large portion of its space in the tempest. Therefore, the typhoon impacted the living spaces of ocean turtles, Mississippi sandhill cranes, Red-cockaded woodpeckers and Alabama Beach mice.

The tempest caused oil slicks from 44 offices all through south-eastern Louisiana, which came about in more than 7 million U.S. gallons (26 million liters) of oil being spilled. While a few spills were only a couple hundred gallons; the biggest was at Cox Bay where 14,300,000 liters were spilled. The vast majority of the spills were contained nearby, yet some oil entered the biological system. The town of Meraux was especially severely hit as it was overwhelmed with a mix of water and oil.

Thus far, the harm caused for the space by the tropical storm can be credited to a catastrophic event, compounded by human mistake. The breakdown in lawfulness was completely owing to the inhabitants of the space who settled on cognizant choices to perpetrate wrongdoing. There can be no denying the way that some parts

of the world contain individuals more inclined to guiltiness than others, and this should be considered in to harm computations while surveying the weakness of a space to significant harm by a catastrophic event, including a torrent. Assuming one is searching for proof to help or question this statement, each of the one needs to do is contrast the outcome of Hurricane Katrina and that of the March 2011 wave in Japan.

When military and police work force must be redirected from search and salvage missions to halting plundering and even sharpshooter assaults, the general harm cause by the torrent will be greater.

In the result of Hurricane Katrina, plundering, brutality and other crime were intense issues. While the vast majority of the consideration of the specialists zeroed in on salvage endeavors, public security in New Orleans debased quickly. By August 30, 2005, plundering had spread all through the city, regularly without trying to hide and in the full perspective on police officers.

New Orleans City Councilwoman Jackie Clarkson was cited as saying:

"The plundering is wild. The French Quarter has been assaulted. We're utilizing depleted, scant police to control plundering when they ought to be utilized for search and salvage while we actually have individuals on rooftops."

ncapacitated by the breakdown of transportation and correspondence, just as mathematically overpowered, cops could do essentially nothing to stop wrongdoing, and businesspeople and entrepreneurs who stayed behind were left to fight for themselves in the guard of their property. Plunderers were not simply relaxed residents who chose to perpetrate violations spontaneously – they included packs of furnished shooters, and gunfire was heard in different pieces of the city. Alongside vicious, furnished burglary of trivial significant products, there were numerous episodes were of inhabitants basically taking food, water, and different wares from unstaffed supermarkets. There were additionally reports of some cops looting.

There were reports of marksman fire all through New Orleans, some of it focused on salvage helicopters, help laborers, and cops. Sometimes, it is accepted the marksman fire was expected as protection from migration or departure. One improvement that didn't help the rule of peace and law circumstance was the choice by 33% of New Orleans cops to abandon the city long before the tempest, a large number of them getting away in their specialty possessed watch vehicles. This additional to the disarray by extending law implementation even more

daintily. Moreover, a few NOPD officials were captured in the weeks after Katrina on doubt of vehicle theft.

The City of Gretna on the West Bank of the Mississippi got impressive exposure when, in the result of Hurricane Katrina, dislodged and got dried out survivors who endeavored to escape from New Orleans by strolling over the Crescent City Connection span over the Mississippi River were turned around at gunpoint by City of Gretna Police, alongside Crescent City Connection Police and Jefferson Parish Sheriff's representatives, who set up a road obstruction on the extension soon after the tropical storm. It ought to be brought up that a large portion of the individuals who were endeavoring to cross the waterway were African Americans and those dismissing them were white.

On August 31, New Orleans' 1,500-part police power was requested to leave search and salvage missions and concentrate toward controlling the inescapable plundering. The city likewise forced an obligatory check in time. Chairman Nagin called for expanded government help with a meandering aimlessly broadcast request in which he requested that administrative organizations "accomplish something", following the city's powerlessness to control plundering. Simultaneously, Governor Kathleen Blanco declared the appearance of a tactical presence, expressing that "they have M-16s and are locked and stacked. These soldiers realize how to shoot and kill and I expect they will."

Despite the expanded law requirement presence, wrongdoing kept on being an issue. Aid ventures were continually disturbed by brutality, and there were reports of gatherings of furnished men spinning out of control through the roads, plundering and looting unattended structures and stores. Good cause Hospital, one of a few offices endeavoring to empty patients, had to stop the work subsequent to going under weapon discharge. By September 1, 6,500 National Guard troops had shown up in New Orleans, and on September 2, Blanco mentioned a sum of 40,000 staff for help with clearing and security endeavors in Louisiana.

Two ongoing occasions – one in southern California, and the other on the New England coast – exhibit how even a slight "issue" with power supply in one little region in America can rapidly prompt power outages influencing a large number of individuals, regardless of whether they are extremely distant from the underlying reason for supply disruption.

In the August 2011. The last part of Hurricane Irene unloaded rather a great deal of

downpour on the territory of New York. Twists blasted up to 60 mph (almost 100 kmh). What ought to have been a somewhat wet and unsavory end of the week ended up being 5-10 days with no power or in any event, running water for a huge number of individuals in perhaps the most affluent put on the planet. A large number of those spots were not immense metropolitan regions with high-thickness lodging and different elements that would make a power outage justifiable, yet rural private networks in Long Island and Vermont. The explanation? A flimsy condition of framework and no cash to further develop it. Extreme layers of organization at public, state, area and even town levels don't help at all.

Just a couple of days after the fact, on the contrary shoreline of America, 6,000,000 individuals in southern California and Arizona were passed on without power because of an intentional power outage. The prompt reason was broken hardware at a sub-station in the town of Yuma in Arizona. The abrupt power lack at Yuma caused the current on the Southwest Power Link from Arizona to California to unexpectedly switch bearing. The subsequent serious vacillation in line voltage stumbled wellbeing switches at various sub-stations in the San Diego (California) area.

n absolute, 15 power stations in the district shut down naturally to shield themselves from voltage swings, including the 2,200MW San Onofre thermal energy station up the coast close to San Clemente. With the San Onofre plant disengaged and the association with Arizona cut off, the gently adjusted matrix serving San Diego and its adjoining districts immediately became unsound. Such issues ought to be settled by tightening up the result of encompassing power stations. Be that as it may, with lacking base-load limit nearby, backup plants for fulfilling top need couldn't be turned up quick enough to settle the voltage. The over-burden network then, at that point, slammed, making power outages spread across the locale and even into Mexico. Power was not reestablished until the accompanying morning.

During the power outage, sea shores in San Diego must be shut in light of the fact that crude sewage had saturated the ocean. Travelers on trains stuck among stations and caught in lifts must be saved by the police. Departures from San Diego International Airport were dropped because of an absence of runway lighting. With traffic signals messed up and gas stations unfit to siphon, drivers deserted their vehicles and added to the gridlock that burned-through the streets. Schools, clinics, workplaces, industrial facilities, shops and cafés were completely shut as lighting, cooling and other fundamental gear stopped to work.

The underlying cause of the problem is that the private companies that supply electricity to Americans have kept generating capacity to an absolute minimum. Investment in supply and maintenance are restricted to what the suppliers are absolutely obliged to spend and no more. The average age of transformers at substations is approximately 40 years. These are the most critical components of the grid and they are past their sell-by date.

Long-haul power lines are frequently made to handle more power than they were designed to, as wholesalers sell their electricity over longer and longer distances. Consequently, the grid suffers far greater fluctuations in electricity flow than before privatisation. The continual cycling of power plants up and down to meet demand from elsewhere in the country causes generating and transmission parts to heat up and cool down repeatedly. Therefore, they then wear out faster than expected.

t is clear America will suffer increasingly severe blackouts regardless of whether a tsunami strikes the coast, but it is equally obvious such a natural disaster could affect people hundreds - or even thousands – of miles from the point of impact.

Try to imagine a United States of America with population centres along its western shore without electricity, its air contaminated with radioactive fallout from stricken nuclear power stations, the waterways contaminated with raw sewage, oil and radioactive waste, its seat of government abandoned, its main stock and commodity markets closed indefinitely, the commercial powerhouses New York, Boston and Philadelphia in chaos and even its tourist attractions in Florida off limits.

In all probability, those states not directly affected by the immediate impact of a tsunami would organize replacement power supplies for their citizens and do their best to ensure life carried on as close to normal as possible. But would they all pull together or would it be every state for itself? What about the inevitable flood of refugees. Where would a central government be based? Would we witness the break up of America into a number of smaller countries based along ethnic majorities, regional ties and similarities. In other words, could a climate change-induced tsunami lead to the end of a civilisation?

In essence this is two questions: "could a tsunami cause that much damage?" and "is such a tsunami at all likely in the first place?"

We have no way of knowing the answer to the first question until after the event. All we can do is compare recent disasters around the world and in America itself, and make guess. The simplest answer is the worse the event, the more likely the answer to the3 first part of the question is "Yes". Perhaps it is more pertinent to answer the second question.

First, let us take another look at Blake Ridge. The map below is adapted from a Google Earth image. We can see the site is on the very edge of the continental shelf. It is clear that if a tsunami did start from this point, the coastline from North Carolina to Florida would be the worst hit in America. Blake Ridge is far enough offshore – approximately 250 miles/400 km – that a tsunami could generate sufficient momentum to be absolutely devastating by the time it reached the shore. Even more crucial to any evaluation, it would be likely to travel around the "bulge" formed by North Carolina and continue along the eastern shore. By contrast, the epicentre of the March 2011 earthquake and tsunami was just 45 miles/70 km offshore and Tokyo was protected by a similar ridge of land.

One consolation is the western coast of Florida, Louisiana and Texas would probably be spared much damage, even though tsunamis can go "around corners". As there are known methane hydrates deposits in the Gulf of Mexico, these areas are still vulnerable.

lake Ridge is one of the most studied locations with methane hydrates deposits in the world. Therefore, there are a number of important things we can say with a great deal of confidence in their accuracy. This sedimentary feature is approximately 310 miles/500 km long and lies in water 2,000 –

4,800 metres in depth. The site is the meeting point for cool dense water flowing from the Arctic Ocean and the warmer Gulf Stream. Even a slight adjustment to one of the currents could mean a substantial shift in water temperature.

Methane hydrates deposits are sensitive to changes in temperature and pressure. Blake Ridge is no exception. Its similarities to the Storegga area in terms of overall size, quantity of methane hydrate deposits, the type of ocean currents flowing over and around it plus climate trends over the past 50 or more years mean we should take the possibility of another major slide/eruption at Blake Ridge very seriously.

This does not mean a natural disaster will take place. Nor can we give a

timeframe for a series of events that could trigger such an event. But we do know what has happened in the past, and it appears increasingly likely another such event may take place.

n June 2011, a landslide 200 miles/320 km of the coast of Cornwall is believed to have led to a tsunami that struck a 200 mile section of the southern English coast. This tsunami was only two feet/60 cm high, and caused no damage. However, the event demonstrated such landslide-induced tsunamis could happen at any time, and in more than one part of the world. It should be noted that the landslide theory has not been proven beyond reasonable doubt as the sole cause of the tsunami. On the other hand, the suggested area of the landslide was at the end of the continental shelf and a place believed to have significant methane hydrates deposits. Could this be a sign that bigger eruptions of methane hydrates and submarine landslides are imminent?

o, how often do such events occur? Approximately 10% off all tsunamis are caused by submarine landslides. This figure is based on research conducted by Dr. Viacheslav K.Gusiakov, head of the Tsunami Laboratory at the Institute of Computational Mathematics and Mathematical Geophysics, Siberian Division, Russian Academy of Sciences. There have been numerous tsunamis in the 20th and 21st centuries that are attributable to landslides and which have led to many deaths and destruction of property. In some cases, like the 1968 tsunami that struck Papua New Guinea, thousands of people have died.

Perhaps a more relevant question would be: how often are submarine landslides caused – directly or indirectly – by climate change? On a slightly different tack, how often has methane hydrate been linked to a major disaster?

Perhaps the biggest and best known submarine slide in North America – to date – was the Cape Fear Slide which was actually a series of at least five submarine slides from 12,000 – 30,000 years ago. The slide area is about 120 miles/200 km South-east of Cape Fear, North Carolina and is quite close to Blake Ridge. The eruption of methane hydrates is believed to have been the cause of at least some of the slides at the site.

A report published in 2007 by Matthew J. Hornbach (Institute for Geophysics, University of Texas), Luc L. Lavier (Institute for Geophysics,

University of Texas) and Carolyn D. Ruppel (U.S. Geological Survey) came to the following conclusion:

"Analysis of new multibeam bathymetry data and seismic Chirp data acquired over the Cape Fear Slide complex on the U.S. Atlantic margin suggests that at least 5 major submarine slides have likely occurred there within the past 30,000 years, indicating that repetitive, large-scale mass wasting and associated tsunamis may be more common in this area than previously believed. Gas hydrate deposits and associated free gas as well as salt tectonics have been implicated in previous studies as triggers for the major Cape Fear slide events. Analysis of the interaction of the gas hydrate phase boundary and the various generations of slides indicates that only the most landward slide likely intersected the phase boundary and inferred high gas pressures below it… Using new constraints on slide morphology, we develop the first tsunami model for the Cape Fear Slide complex. Our results indicate that if the most seaward Cape Fear slide event occurred today, it could produce waves in excess of 2 m at the present-day 100 m bathymetric contour."

Off America's western coast, the Humboldt slide took place just a few miles offshore in northern California in the same period the Cape Fear slides occurred. Again, there were multiple slides – perhaps as many as nine. More pertinent, studies have indicated the slides took place in an area with methane hydrates deposits. A research article by U. Tinivella, M. Giustiniani, and D. Accettella of the Istituto Nazionale di Oceanografia e di Geofisica Sperimentale published in the Journal of Geological Research in 2011 claim the Cape Fear, Humboldt, Storegga and several other major slides all have the same root causes, of which the eruption of substantial methane hydrates deposits is one. The report also indicates submarine slides have taken place off the western coast of Africa, in the fjords of British Columbia and on the Alaskan Beaufort Sea continental margin.

Off the Gulf of Cadiz between Spain and Morocco lies an area of seabed littered with huge pockmarks. There are proven methane hydrates deposits there, although the cause of many of the pockmarks is disputed. One of the biggest such marks, the Caleton BV, is believed to have been described in a 2009 report "Pockmarks, collapses and blind valleys in the Gulf of Cadiz" by . Javier González Sanz:

"This structure could be related to a massive dissociation of hydrates. Indeed the Caleton BV is on the track of an important fault and is affected by a warm undercurrent."

America's National Aeronautics and Space Administration (NASA) has published a report on a much earlier massive eruption of methane hydrate:

"A tremendous release of methane gas frozen beneath the sea floor heated the Earth by up to 13°F (7°C) 55 million years ago...

Generally, cold temperatures and high pressure keep methane stable beneath the ocean floor, however, that might not always have been the case. A period of global warming, called the Late Paleocene Thermal Maximum (LPTM), occurred around 55 million years ago and lasted about 100,000 years. Current theory has linked this to a vast release of frozen methane from beneath the sea floor, which led to the earth warming as a result of increased greenhouse gases in the atmosphere.

movement of continental plates, like the Indian subcontinent, may have initiated a release that led to the LPTM, Schmidt said. We know today that when the Indian subcontinent moved into the Eurasian continent, the Himalayas began forming. This uplift of tectonic plates would have decreased pressure in the sea floor, and may have caused the large methane release. Once the atmosphere and oceans began to warm, Schmidt added, it is possible that more methane thawed and bubbled out. Some scientists speculate current global heating could eventually lead to a similar scenario in the future if the oceans warm substantially. "

This report was followed up by NASA scientists Gavin A. Schmidt and Drew . Shindell who authored a report entitled "Atmospheric composition, radiative forcing, and climate change as a consequence of a massive methane release from gas hydrates". Key extracts as follows:

The Paleocene/Eocene Thermal Maximum (PETM) event was characterized

by extreme global warmth and a rapid, pronounced decrease (of up to -3‰ d^{13} C) in the mean carbon isotopic ratio of the global carbon cycle [Kennett and Stott, 1991; Koch et al., 1992; Katz et al., 1999; Bains et al., 1999]. Deep ocean warming of about 4–6 °C has been inferred in many cores. Estimates of surface warming from foraminiferal oxygen isotopes are from 5 °C to 8 °C in the high latitudes (ODP 690, Maud Rise, South Atlantic, ~ 65 °S), 1–4 °C in the subtropics (DSDP 527, Walvis Ridge, South Atlantic, ~35 °S), and 1–2
°C in lower latitudes...

... A compelling explanation for the carbon isotope excursion is a massive release of methane gas (CH4) from hydrates along continental margins..."

Up to this point, our description of the effects of a methane hydrates eruption on the seabed has focused exclusively on the possibility of submarine landslides and the possibility a slide triggering a tsunami – a tsunamigenic landslide. This is not the only way a methane hydrate eruption could cause a tsunami. At standard air pressure and normal room temperature methane hydrate is a gas. When solid methane hydrates escape from the seabed and experience a rapid increase in temperature combined with a drop in pressure, it expands by about 164 times its size when frozen in a very short time. In other words, it explodes.

Given that the amount of methane hydrates that is known to have erupted on occasions towards the end of the most recent ice age has left craters that measured thousands of square miles on very rare occasions and numerous smaller craters that covered hundreds of square yards/metres, some of these explosions must have been on a par with nuclear explosions. This force would surely be sufficient to trigger a tsunami.

Atlantis Conclusion

Before considering the implications for the future, let us revisit the legend of Atlantis one last time. This book's title has taken advantage of the curiosity the name Atlantis has inspired over thousands of years, and now this book can include its own theory as to the reality behind the myth.

According to Plato, Atlantis was "beyond the Pillars of Hercules", which is usually interpreted to mean "west of the Strait of Gibraltar". If you are travelling from the Mediterranean and passing through the Strait of Gibraltar, the Gulf of Cadiz is the immediately to your North and West. There is even a submerged island – Spartel – in the gulf that was submerged by an earthquake-tsunami double strike around 10,000 BC i.e. when Plato claimed

Atlantis was supposed to have been destroyed. The area is believed to have suffered eight major earthquakes since then.

Earthquakes are a probable cause of the demise of Spartel, but as the seabed of the gulf is littered with mud volcanoes and bears the signs of major methane hydrates eruptions, could a localized eruption have caused the downfall of Atlantis?

few things are certain: if Spartel was Atlantis, it was a much smaller place than the fantastic kingdom described by Plato. Also, if the island was inhabited, the population would almost certainly have consisted of fishermen eking out a rather primitive and precarious living on the fringes of prehistoric society. Several archaeological studies of the area have failed to discover anything significant in the area.

On the opposite side of the Strait, archaeologists have had better luck. Expeditions by Georgeos Diaz-Montexano and Jonas Berghman in the first decade of the 21st century have uncovered evidence suggesting a bronze age civilisation had existed off the Atlantic coast of Morocco several thousand years BC, possibly – just possibly – old enough, large enough and advanced enough to qualify as Atlantis. They claim to have found copper and bronze artefacts, stone building blocks and other remnants of bronze age life on the seabed in an area they believe was dry land around the time Atlantis supposedly existed.

acques Collina-Girard of the University Aix-Marseille I in France has come up with a similar theory that Atlantis was on a group of islands off Cape Spartel in Morocco.

If Atlantis was there, it would have been close enough to the Gulf of Cadiz to be very badly affected by earthquakes, mud volcanoes, methane hydrates eruptions and tsunamis that originated in that region.

n conclusion, there is not enough evidence to date for a definitive statement on whether Atlantis ever existed, let alone its precise location. But there were some type of settlements out there beyond the Pillars of Hercules in ancient times and those places are no longer on the map. Conditions in the Gulf of Cadiz are unusually conducive towards creating the kind of catastrophe that would destroy a civilisation in a single day. Another uncertainty is whether the destruction was related to climate change. We know the areas explored by Georgeos Diaz-Montexano and Jonas Berghman are under water today because of rising sea levels which are related to climate change, but as the

Gulf of Cadiz is in a tectonic fault area, this is one destruction that could have causes completely unrelated to climate change based on our present understanding of the nature of tectonic faults and mud volcanoes. On the other hand, the calamity that brought the settlements off the Moroccan coast to such an abrupt end might have had the same climate-related factors as the Storegga Slide.

There is evidence the area was devastated by a tsunami around 9500 BC, which ties in nicely with Plato's writings. More research is needed before the argument can be settled, however, this book might as well provide its own theory to add to the countless other attempts to explain the legend. So, prolonging the conclusion, here it is:

The Moroccan media has occasionally made claims about finding ancient ruins, such as Arghilas, that are supposedly around 15,000 years old. While these reports seem a little far fetched, there are enough cave paintings, pottery shards and beads etc. to prove humans have been in the area for about 80,000 years. The area was sufficiently far away from the glaciation that covered most of Europe during the Ice Age that people living in what is now north- western Morocco might have had a head start on other groups of people when it came to starting a permanent settlement.

There are many gaps in the evidence, such as an absence of agriculture, but might the forests covering the Atlas mountains, the game grazing on the savannah-like plains of the Sahara, plus the bountiful Atlantic Ocean have provided enough food to support a society similar in sophistication to Göbekli Tepe? If that group of people chose to make their base on Spartel and a couple of coastal settlements, they would have been in the right time and the right place to match some of Plato's account of Atlantis. The choice of a coastal base or capital for the territory of Atlantis makes sense for a couple of reasons. If the people depended on fish and other seafood for part of their diet, this would only be practical if the settlement was very close to the sea. There was no refrigeration in those days, so fresh fish would have to be consumed almost immediately. Fruit, vegetables and even most other types of meat would last longer and thus could be transported further.

The other reason is that if Atlantis did make seaworthy boats, they had to have a port. The notion of Atlanteans exploring the Mediterranean and even further afield is not impossible. Polynesians were able to explore the Pacific Ocean using very basic wooden craft (thanks to an understanding of astronomy, ocean currents and bird flight patterns that Atlanteans might have had). Plenty of cultures have demonstrated the kind of qualities needed to explore places thousands of miles from their original home. The key difference in most cases is that the movements were migratory. If Atlantis was home to the first people to travel hundreds and occasionally thousands of miles in order to trade, these pioneers would have helped the exchange of

something other than products – thoughts, strict convictions, language and innovation could likewise have been spread over extremely wide regions in a generally brief time frame. Individuals who could achieve this would have been held in wonder by those they visited, regardless of whether the main things they were exchanging comprised of stone tomahawks and arrow points, earthenware and fired globules, creature stows away and possibly a few sorts of saved food. A solitary boat with a group of twelve going along the Mediterranean might have come into contact with a bigger number of networks than a multitude of adventurers bridging north Africa.

The size of the domain for this rendition of Atlantis is a lot more modest than the size ascribed by Plato, however assuming they considered the grounds north of the Atlas Mountains as their own, that would in any case add up to a huge realm by Ancient Greek norms. Consider the idea that a portion of their hunting and exchanging undertakings ashore may have gone far south of the Atlas mountains, and the region they overwhelmed might have been extensive by any norms. The section of centuries and oneself serving accounts began by any overcomers of the annihilation of Atlantis could undoubtedly clarify how the achievements of this somewhat humble culture became extinguished of all proportion.

catastrophic event starting from the Gulf of Cadiz might have overpowered Atlantis in a solitary day. Rising ocean levels could then have lowered the proof that Atlantis at any point existed in any case. All that remained was an impressive legend that interested Plato adequately for him to compose a couple of pages regarding the matter. That, thus, begun another legend that proceeds to this day.

So why has Atlantis never been found? The most probable answer is archeologists and travelers have been searching for some unacceptable thing. Disregard marble castles and brilliant sculptures. Without a doubt, Atlantis had no stone structures and no metal carries out. The depiction of Spartel as assortment of low lying islands simply off the coast proposes a region that is somewhat marshy.

In different areas of the planet that are comparable, it has been conventional to assemble homes out of woven reeds, with marginally sturdier wood used to make house outlines. Reeds enjoy the benefit of being adequately light to ship a couple of miles to an appropriate spot for a town and simple to transform into dividers and material. It would likewise take far couple of individuals to construct a town or unassuming community this way than the large numbers required for the stone designs at Göbekli Tepe, Tell Qaramel or Nevalı Çori, which proposes the number of inhabitants in Atlantis might

have been more modest. Lamentably, the odds of houses and public structures made of reeds making due after almost 12,000 years lowered in the Atlantic Ocean are not good.

The layout of waste waterways and moors may endure such a significant stretch, however as it were "might". It relies upon nearby conditions, in addition to the idea of the occasion that finished residence at the site. Graves may make due, accepting individuals of Atlantis covered their dead. A catastrophe that killed many individuals simultaneously may leave bodies tossed over the site, or they may have been cleaned out to the ocean. As I would like to think, Atlantis won't ever be found. that will not stop wayfarers searching for it, though.

The following map from Google Earth shows the location of Spartel:

The land that (may have) involved Atlantis would have comprised of the region north of the A2 and west of N99, in addition to what is currently the Strait of Gibraltar and some more land toward the west of Cape Spartel. This is roughly a similar size an advanced Greece – not even close to the size portrayed in legend, however greater than any known realm/domain for the period, and a lot greater than the statelets that made up Ancient Greece millennia after the fact. In the event that hunting parties and migrant herders consistently voyaged south of the Atlas Mountains (and the Sahara Desert would not have

been the obstruction it has been since a few thousand years after this period), individuals of Atlantis might have guaranteed the vast majority of northern Africa for themselves.

Other Places at Risk

America isn't the main huge, prosperous country in danger from the consequence of a methane hydrates emission. Allow us to consider the effect on India and China.

The greatest city on India's western coast is Bombay ("Mumbai" in Hindi). Like such countless significant business and modern focuses on the planet, it is based on a huge regular harbor. Likewise, it is just shy of 100 km from the main dynamic atomic reactors on the western coast, Tarapur. This office comprises of two bubbling water reactors, like the Fukushima reactors obliterated by a tremor and wave in March 2011, and two current compressed substantial water reactors. Starting at 2011, the bubbling water reactors had as of now been working 16 years past their design.

The Google Earth guide of Tarapur above shows how uncovered the atomic reactors would be to a tidal wave. One just needs to think about what befell indistinguishable reactor types at Fukushima in March 2011 to understand the expected harm. Likewise, one would need to address whether security and support norms at Tarapur are pretty much as solid as Fukushima.

As with such countless huge urban communities on the coast, Bombay/Mumbai spreads around a huge regular harbor. The business focus of the city and its air terminal are amazingly defenseless against the effect of a wave. The Google Earth picture above shows the city and encompassing areas.

t is India's eastern coast that is more in danger dependent on research on methane hydrates stores. The Krishna Godavari bowl, off the south-eastern India state has some amazingly huge methane hydrate stores, alongside raw petroleum that has drawn in interest from significant worldwide oil firms.

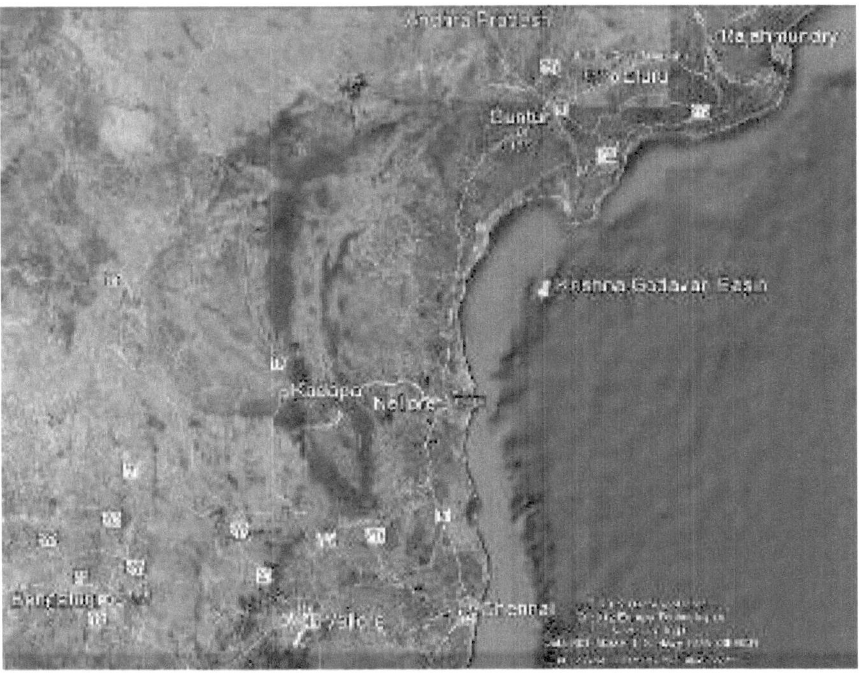

As the guide from Google Earth shows, the region containing the stores is near the shore, which restricts the conceivable effect of a torrent on the Indian coast. Madras/Chennai may in any case be vulnerable.

nother significant store has been found at the Mahanadi bowl a little toward the north of Krishna Godavari, and representing a comparative danger. Luckily, both of these stores lie near somewhat meagerly populated coastline.

Possibly the most unfathomable and thickest methane hydrate store yet found is off the Andaman Islands. Look at the guides underneath of the Andaman store from Google Earth and the guide of the 2004 Boxing Day tsunami.

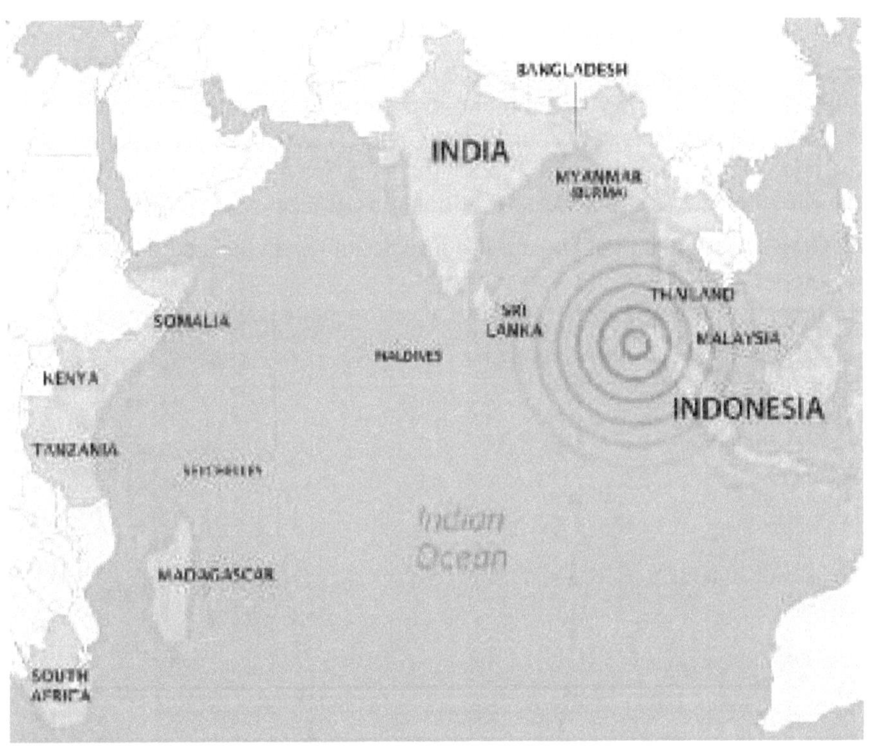

Map from Cantus of Wikipedia showing 2004 wave epicentre.

hifting the focal point of a tidal wave two or three hundred miles north would bring about a very much like degree of demolition for practically the very region that was annihilated in 2004. A few spots, similar to Thailand, Malaysia, Burma and Bangladesh would likely experience more, while India's western coast and the greater part of East Africa may keep away from any negative consequences.

To all goals and purposes, a significant methane hydrates ejection at the Andaman store would presumably prompt a rehash of the 2004 Boxing Day wave. Maybe there would be a diminished death toll on account of wave early notice frameworks introduced in certain spaces since that disaster.

Despite its colossal size, China has generally scant oil and gas saves. In case you factor in methane hydrates, the circumstance looks undeniably more encouraging for the country's energy industry. Beside huge coastal stores in Tibet, there are considerable seaward stores in the South China Sea. Starting around 1999, various stores have been found in northern piece of the ocean for example the part nearest to central area China. A 2007 Chinese report closes the methane hydrates found in the South China Sea up to that point may be the exploitable energy likeness 10 billion tons of oil.

he Google Earth map underneath is of the South China Sea and the land that encompasses it.

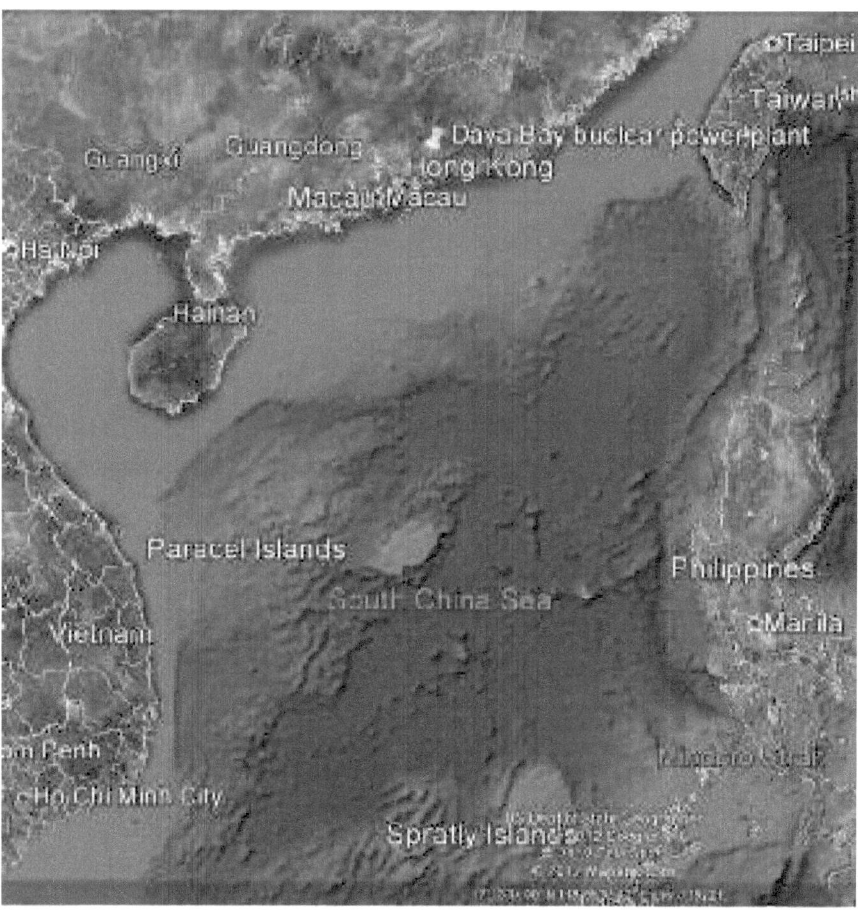

The guide shows unmistakably the edge of the mainland rack and as that is the place where most seaward methane hydrates stores are found, it is sensible to assume the northern edge of the rack is the place where the methane lies. The shore is home to large numbers of China's driving ventures and the port of Hong Kong. Just a single thermal energy station is functional at the hour of composing – the Daya Bay Nuclear Power Plant in Shenzen, Guangdong. The plant has two 944 MWe PWR atomic reactors dependent on the Framatone ANP French 900 MWe three cooling circle plan. It is incredibly near Hong Kong and Macau, and numerous inhabitants of these urban communities are not mollified by the reality the plant has one of the most amazing security records in the world.

The Google map underneath shows the coast around Hong Kong, with Daya Bay thermal energy station. Remember a torrent may come closer from due South or from the South-east or South-west.

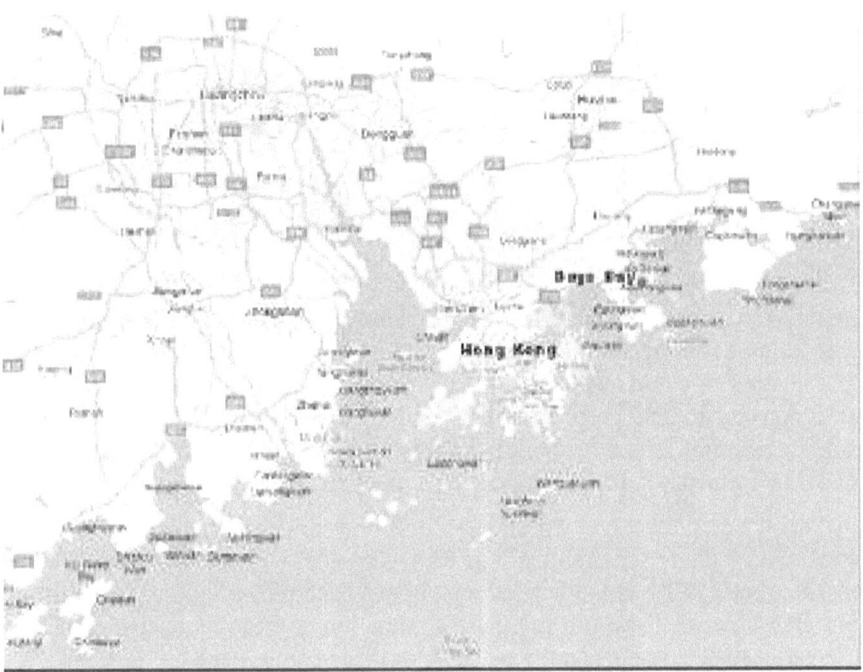

The Danger from Above

Up till now, our admonitions on the risks of methane hydrates have zeroed in on a fierce emission of the material and resulting tidal waves that might follow. There are two additional issues straightforwardly identified with methane hydrates that could make destruction the world. Initially, on the off chance that a huge square of methane hydrates escapes from the sea depths without causing a torrent, the methane will quickly ascend to the sea surface and dissipate. The methane will bond with water fume and structure clouds.

These mists are combustible, yet hazardous. To place the harm potential in setting, during the 1960s the Soviet Union concocted a thermobaric bomb (typically alluded to as a "fuel air bomb") as a modest and non-radioactive option in contrast to atomic weapons. This weapon relies upon the dispersal over the ground of a fume haze of exceptionally combustible gas or moment drops of combustible fluid that are lighted by a traditional unstable charge once an adequately huge "cloud" has been created.

Most of the harm to life and property is brought about by the resultant huge shockwave, with discharge an optional reason for harm.

In 2007, the Russian military reported it had made the world's greatest and most remarkable non-atomic bomb. This weapon has a fabulous time range of 300m. As such, the fume cloud made by the weapon is around 600m wide. Expecting the cloud was 600m wide, long and profound, it would be 216 million cubic meters in volume.

Under "awesome" conditions, it would take 1,317,073.17 cubic meters of methane hydrates to firm a haze of that size. As a square of methane hydrates estimating 110m by 110m by 110m would extend to somewhat more than that number of cubic meters and the world has encountered methane hydrates emissions estimating great many cubic kilometers previously (albeit not as a solitary piece of frozen methane), it appears to be almost certain such a cloud could be framed, yet on a significantly greater scale.

ow terrible could that be? Around 250 million years prior, the world encountered its most extreme elimination occasion, with 96% of every marine specie, 70% of land-based vertebrates becoming wiped out. It is the possibly time when there was a mass elimination of creepy crawlies. There are various speculations on the reasons for this calamity, and there is a developing agreement that an unexpected arrival of huge amounts of methane hydrates assumed a significant part, and that would definitely mean there were immense firestorms of methane seething all over the planet sufficiently long to kill most animals on earth (for those wishing to concentrate on the occasion in more detail, if it's not too much trouble, gaze upward the "Permian-

Triassic Extinction").

Anything near a rehash of the occasions 250 million years prior would have outcomes far more terrible even than the breakdown of civilisation. At the end of the day, the most dire outcome imaginable for a methane hydrate emission from a site, for example, Blake Ridge is the apocalypse and the elimination of mankind.

Calculating the likelihood of such a result is incredibly troublesome. Everything we can say with full confidence is such an occasion has occurred in some measure once in our planet's set of experiences and the material that caused it is still with us. Definitely, it is on the planet's aggregate interest for this issue to be approached in a serious way and for a thorough, co-ordinated set of studies implemented.

bviously, even a monstrous methane hydrate ejection need not undermine humankind as an animal groups. Aggregately, we have endure the Storegga Slide(s). However, what are the ramifications for those near such an eruption?

ake a glance at the sky. On the off chance that you can see any mists, envision they are impregnated with methane because of a methane hydrates emission. Presently investigate your environmental elements and attempt to envision the results of that cloud detonating. The impact on individuals, creatures, structures, spans, transportation, yields and domesticated animals, power and water supplies.

Such a cloud could travel inland, delivering urban areas a long way from the coast or central area methane hydrate stores profoundly defenseless against the impacts of an eruption.

Combine a torrent with billows of methane, and the situation cuts to the chase where there is no perceived construction – common or physical – left to empower the occupants to pull together and recuperate without assistance from somewhere else on a scale never endeavored in history.

Take one more gander at America's East Coast. What might be the impact on Boston, Philadelphia, New York, Washington and other significant populace habitats in case they were struck by waves in addition to what could be compared to various fuel air bombs exploding at random?

Before considering the final outcome of an enormous ejection of methane hydrates, let us think about what different regions of the planet are vulnerable.

The most straightforward answer is that, except for a couple of somewhat shallow and

restricted inlets, pretty much every stretch of coastline on the planet is uncovered. There will never be a way out. Each city, port, thermal energy plant (or traditional power station), ranch, industrial facility, school, street, rail line, scaffold or passage close to the coast is presented to a torrent or potentially combustible methane cloud brought about by a methane hydrates emission. Key position might secure against a wave, yet not against fire and blasts pouring down from the clouds.

The other adverse consequence of a methane hydrates ejection is that it would prompt an increment in the measure of environmental methane and methane is an incredibly intense "nursery gas".

As referenced before, the Storegga Slide prompted an unexpected and significant expansion on the planet's in general barometrical methane, which thusly ended a time of cooler environment. As the world's ice cover was undeniably more broad around then, that ice would have directed the impacts of the methane. Put another way: assuming a comparable occasion happens under conditions common in the mid 21st century, that methane will cause a more elevated level of warming.

Such an occasion would influence everybody all over, albeit the effect would not be consistently negative. Indeed regions like the Siberian and North American tundra may be changed into areas equipped for creating huge amounts of arable yields and even leafy foods, with a lovely, calm environment. This accepts precipitation and other contributing elements are reasonable for such a scenario.

There is no denying the way that for the greater part of the world an unexpected, sharp expansion in temperature would have terrible outcomes. Gigantic wraps of land would become appalling in light of either to an extreme or too little downpour. We have a lot of authentic instances of what befalls civilisations that meet that destiny. Likewise the discussion on "regular" environmental change has given a sizable amount of contentions about the outcomes of an extreme change in climate.

We realize methane hydrates ejections have caused very genuine catastrophic events on various events before, with at minimum a portion of these emissions connected to the worldwide environment getting hotter. We likewise know there are various destinations all over the planet that have enormous methane hydrates stores and that large numbers of those locales have encountered the sort of avalanches that were no doubt brought about by emissions thousands, or now and again millions, of years prior. Have there been any significant episodes including methane hydrates in

late times?

here is a developing doubt that the April 2010 Deepwater Horizon oil rig fiasco was brought about by an abrupt emission of methane from the well as architects were currently fixing it. The Deepwater Horizon was boring in a piece of the Gulf of Mexico that is known – not accepted, yet known – to contain considerable methane hydrates stores. Besides, this data is notable in the oil and gas industry.

In September 2009, Dan Zimmerman, a natural dissident/analyst, sent an exhaustive report to the US Minerals Management Service (the government organization answerable for guaranteeing wellbeing and security of the climate at seaward boring locales) that zeroed in on the risks of oil drills interacting with methane hydrates. The report warned:

"The essential driver of victories, spills and uncontrolled arrivals of gases from seaward tasks is boring into methane hydrates, or through them into free gas caught below."

The report proceeded to say that from 1992 – 2006, right around 2,500 deepwater wells were bored and, agreeing MMS mishap reports, there were 39 victories. Everything except one of those victories occurred in the Gulf of Mexico. All in all, there would one say one was victory for each roughly 60 wells.

iven the idea of the material that caused the issue, definitely an out and out catastrophe will undoubtedly happen sometime? Could it be the locale had a nearly fortunate break with the Deepwater Horizon victory? We know a ton of oil and methane got away, however there was no tidal wave or hazardous billows of methane and the well gives off an impression of being forever sealed.

Zimmerman isn't persuaded the Deepwater Horizon victory issue is over.

"My anxiety is that cratering has now happened and a stream way has been set up external the very much bore. In case this has happened we are in some hot water, more than we as of now think."

"Assuming there are crest of gas and oil ascending from the ocean bottom around the pipeline," Zimmerman said, "that would be a sign. They have submarines. They ought to analyze the region around the blowout."

To exacerbate the situation, investigations of the seabed around the Deepwater site and the spillages of both oil and methane propose the region is profoundly temperamental and a submarine avalanche could happen at practically any time. Regardless of whether such a slide

would have an impact like the one of Cornwall in 2011 or the Storegga Slide of ancient occasions is extremely difficult to determine.

What we do know is the state of the Gulf of Mexico implies the Western bank of Florida, Alabama, Mississippi, Louisiana and Texas would be in every way crushed by a regular tidal wave. Mexico's eastern coast and Cuba's northern coast, including Havana, would presumably experience similarly to such an extent. Best case scenario, individuals living on the American shore would have recently under an hour's notice to empty. In case the tidal wave is joined by enormous billows of dangerous methane, clearing may not be possible.

uch a debacle probably won't be very as damaging to America in general as a similar episode occurring at Blake Ridge, yet it would be far more terrible than any catastrophe the nation has encountered previously. More terrible – in a literal sense – than Hurricane Katrina. Indeed, even the 2004 Boxing Day Tsunami didn't incur the sort of gore we are guessing about with at Deepwater Horizon or Blake Ridge.

The following map was modified from a Google Earth image:

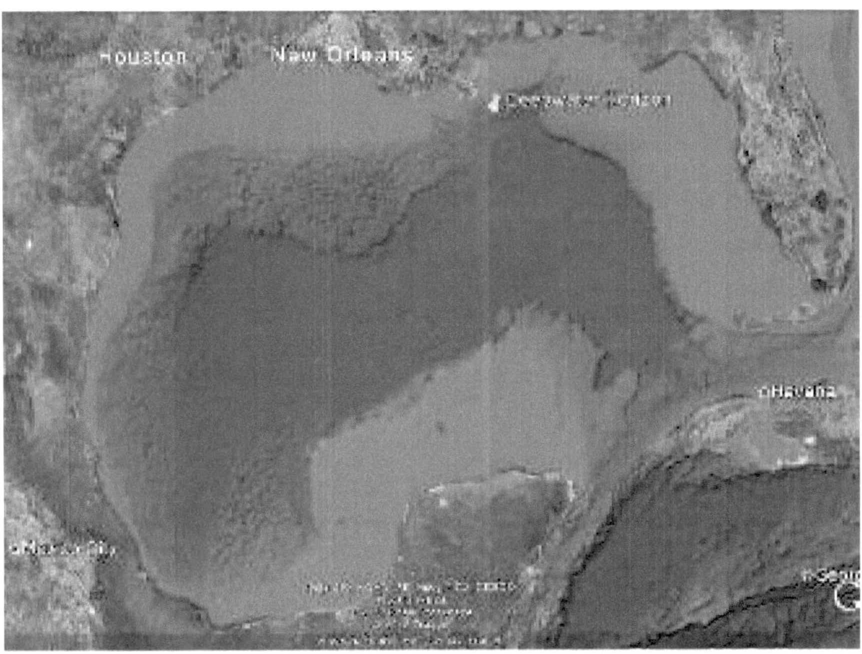

as far as actual harm incurred and monetary effect, it is assessed Hurricane Katrina caused $250 billion in harm to America. That figure depends on issues as various as the expense of fixing harmed houses, tidying up contamination and loss of pay that would have occurred under "ordinary" circumstances.

Let us accept a methane hydrates ejection happens nearby Deepwater Horizon and causes a practically indistinguishable measure of harm. Leave theory about an Armageddon-type occurrence to the side and spotlight on what we definitely know.

here are three issues that mean such a calamity would indeed cause undeniably more mischief Hurricane Katrina. Right off the bat, individuals living in the way of the storm had a lot of caution to empty. Nearby government made various basic blunders in giving transportation and different offices, yet the vast majority had the chance either to move to security or secure everything and brave the tempest. Accordingly there were just shy of 2,000 recorded fatalities for the impacted region.

he distance between Deepwater Horizon and the American coast is roughly as old as the focal point of the gigantic quake that struck Japan in March 2011 and the Japanese coast. As all that individuals could expect would be an hour long admonition (and that accepts there is torrent recognition hardware set up and experienced staff to give the alerts over an appropriate correspondence organization), it is sensible to expect undeniably more individuals would kick the bucket just on the grounds that they would not have adequate admonition to clear the area.

Approximately 16,000 individuals were affirmed suffocated or missing in the consequence of Japan's quake and wave, with maybe 1,000 extra passings credited to the tremor. As the torrent was bound to a genuinely limited, and delicately populated region, it is sensible to expect the cost along the Gulf of Mexico coast would be far higher. Maybe a superior marker would be the 2004 Boxing Day Tsunami that caused more than 100,000 fatalities on the Indonesian island of Sumatra alone.

In many areas of the planet, the groups of the people who have died in catastrophic events anticipate some sort of monetary help or remuneration from the public authority. America is the same in this regard. Accepting 100,000 Americans kicked the bucket (a doable number assuming you consider there were a few natural

debacles all over the planet in the main decade of the 21st century that caused in abundance of that number of passings), it would mean a few billion dollars would be required just to pay survivors for the deficiency of family members.

Since Hurricane Katrina, it has become very troublesome and costly for individuals residing in America's storm belt to get homes and different structures protected. That implies assuming property was harmed by a torrent, the nearby and central government would need to pick between trusting individuals would fix and supplant harms themselves or stepping in with state assets to do the work. Assessments of the expense of harm to property directly following Hurricane Katrina range from 80-125 billion dollars, of which around half was insured.

ortunately a torrent unaccompanied by methane mists would not infiltrate as far inland as a tropical storm, thus harm would be bound to the waterfront regions, in addition to places like New Orleans that rely upon dykes and levees to remain dry. The not-great news is a more extensive space of the coast would presumably get around a similar degree of damage.

The third issue is a particularly episode would immediately discount America's seaward oil and gas industry for an unforeseeable period. The oil apparatuses would likely not experience a lot of damage, however dread of rehashed catastrophes, conceivably far more detestable than the one we are mulling over, would drive the public authority to boycott seaward exercises with quick effect.

urricane Katrina contrarily affected America's oil and gas industry and made worldwide oil costs rise a few dollars. It was clear the impacts would be transitory, and as investigation and creation continued, costs got back to normal.

A total restriction on seaward investigation and creation would have undeniably more genuine repercussions. The monetary effect on America is genuinely self-evident – homegrown supplies radically diminished would prompt expanding costs for oil and a tremendous scope of downstream results like petrochemicals, plastics, paints and fuel. As worldwide result of oil is generally exceptionally near worldwide interest, an abrupt reduction in supply – that could be exacerbated by comparative seaward boycotts all over the planet – would cause a flood in worldwide oil costs that could dive the world into serious financial contraction.

Bear at the top of the priority list Hurricane Katrina struck in a time of sensibly solid monetary development. The public authority at the time was not choked by its tremendous obligation and serious enormous aggregates to fixing the harm and relocating

impacted individuals. Given the realities that the recovery expenses would nearly be considerably higher than Hurricane Katrina even with a comparative degree of harm, could the public authority at state and government level stand to make great the harm that had been finished? Likewise, in light of the financial real factors of 2011, where might the cash come from? Might America's banks conclude this was an obligation too far?

As referenced before, generally a large portion of the property that was harmed or annihilated by Hurricane Katrina was guaranteed for such an occasion. Sometime in the not so distant future, the level of safeguarded properties will be far lower. Would a destitute government be capable or able to go to their rescue?

Since the mid 1970s the populaces of urban areas like Detroit, Michigan and

Gary, Indiana have plunged as individuals deserted their homes. Environmental change was not to fault in these cases. Difficult monetary reality, combined with increasing wrongdoing was the reason. The central issue is that countless individuals settled on an aggregate choice to forsake various American towns and urban communities, and have started a trend. Might an administration arrive at the resolution the least difficult, least expensive and most functional answer for a fiasco brought about by a methane hydrates ejection is forsake gigantic wraps of the shore and let nature follows through to its logical end? Would that administration have an attainable alternative?

here are ethnic issues that must be tended to. In the repercussions of Hurricane Katrina, there was significant strain between some solely white networks and gatherings of African Americans escaping the demolition of their areas and the groups of hoodlums that had dominated. A large part of the piece of the country that would be impacted by a methane hydrates emission at Deepwater Horizon is an interwoven of networks that are white, Hispanic or African American.

For the most part, the white networks would be on somewhat higher and better secured ground. Properties are bound to be protected. The occupants are more affluent, and probably better associated. In the fallout of a cataclysmic event, these networks would go up against one another for salvage and restoration assets. Such a situation could trigger out and out race riots and conflict.

Put another way, assuming that America was adequately debilitated as a solitary government element, may a portion of its residents, maybe helped and abetted by neighbouring

nations, try to split away. Also would the national government be capable or potentially ready to stop them? Honestly, this situation sounds extremely fantastical in 2011, however more abnormal and more unlikely things have happened.

f a choice was taken to leave portions of America's shoreline, the dislodged individuals would need to be ingested, and at first in any event, this would include exile camps and the sort of help Americans are accustomed to giving to the Third World. States, districts and individual towns may decline to take enormous quantities of individuals in, or be exceptionally specific with regards to the ethnic character, abundance and training of those they acknowledge. In case nearby crime percentages are seen to go up, even those that were permitted to resettle may observe their hosts becoming threatening very quickly.

The intricacy and delicacy of present day North American and European social orders makes them profoundly defenseless to the sort of inward and outside anxieties that evidently less created social orders could deal with far more prominent ease.

China is a reasonably monocultural country with an exceptionally concentrated type of government. India is a multi-ethnic, fairly turbulent popular government. The two nations are presented to comparative dangers of methane hydrates emissions, and the two nations have a large portion of their business and modern focuses along their coast.

Without having the option to offer much in the method of proof, I accept the two nations would recuperate from the pulverization of a methane hydrates ejection faster and more totally than America. The deficiency of Bombay or Shanghai would be similarly just about as ruinous as New York being cleared off the guide, however India and China would most likely adapt much better. It is in their public minds to ingest misfortunes that crash many thousands – and at times many thousands – of individuals and continue on. It's anything but an issue of being crude of cutting edge as a culture, more an instance of individual and public person. The response of the mind-boggling larger part of individuals to the quake, torrent and atomic reactor emergencies in Japan in 2011 is an exemplary illustration of individuals of an Asian country arranging and doing what must be done to recover.

Could America take a conceivably knockout blow and skip back? Could American culture of the mid 21st century handle such adversity?

These are questions that are presumably difficult to reply with any certainty

except if or until an out and out emergency emits. The nation has had the favorable luck to keep away from large numbers of the perils going up against the greater part of the world. Its states and specialists have generally worked effectively in limiting realized dangers to individuals and property, for example, known tremor zones.

most dire outcome imaginable in the result of a remarkable catastrophic event could be that the interior burdens and clashes inside American culture quickly ascend to the surface and overpower it. Another chance is Americans may settle on an aggregate choice that specific pieces of their nation are too costly to even think about keeping up with and the most ideal choice is to forsake that domain. These circumstances are a long way from certain, not on the grounds that we can not be certain beyond a shadow of a doubt a methane hydrates ejection will happen. The world still can't seem to perceive how America responds in the wake of getting a conceivably knockout blow.

There are a few surenesses that should be considered. The world's environment is evolving. It has consistently changed and it generally will. Given the way that during a large portion of this current planet's set of experiences there have been no polar ice covers, any reasonable person would agree the environment has been hotter than during the mid 21st century as a rule. According to the intermittent mass terminations that have happened all through the world, it is clear a few animal types have adjusted better compared to others.

One of the most ideal ways of guaranteeing humanity has the most ideal shot at enduring an increment in worldwide temperatures is for that increment to be just about as continuous as could really be expected. The greatest danger to a reasonable expansion in temperatures is an abrupt expansion in "nursery" gases, most particularly methane. Regardless of whether there is no methane hydrates ejection, and no tidal waves or inflammable mists, it's undeniably true that methane hydrates from the tundra districts and submarine stores is vanishing into the atmosphere.

he danger presented by a methane hydrates emission is an unexpected, pulverizing power being released on vulnerable networks. The risk from barometrical methane levels expanding strongly in the 21st century are not even close as savage, in any case more deadly. Nobody gets away from an adjustment of the environment. The world has encountered mass terminations previously, and methane is accepted to have assumed a significant part in no less than one of them. One may even question whether endurance of such a situation would be alluring, considering that it would require no less than a few million years for nature to recapture its equilibrium.

Solutions

It is all very well calling attention to how the world may experience the ill effects of an uncommon type of catastrophic event. Showing individuals their approaching destruction isn't exceptionally useful on the off chance that you can't give any arrangement. Luckily, there might be an extremely certain method of managing the issue of methane hydrates. Beyond a shadow of a doubt, methane hydrates should be "managed". Leaving alone and remaining optimistic will not do on the grounds that these methane hydrates stores are releasing ozone depleting substances at an inexorably hazardous rate.

The uplifting news is methane hydrates are a bountiful wellspring of methane, which has numerous business utilizes as a burnable gas. The awful news is significant oil organizations have been attempting to work out a protected, cost effective technique for removing this item absent a lot of progress. Starting at 2011, there is only one site where coastal methane hydrates is extricated for modern use and none offshore.

Deep in the Arctic Circle, in the Messoyakha gas field of western Siberia, lies a pioneer in methane hydrate extraction. Beginning in 1967, Russian (Soviet, back then) engineers started siphoning gaseous petrol from underneath the permafrost and channeling it east across the tundra to the Norilsk metal smelter, the greatest modern venture in the Arctic. In 1978 they chose to unwind the activity. As per their studies, they had drained virtually all the methane from the store. In any case, those appraisals refuted and the gas just continued to come. The gas field was re-opened and keeps on controlling Norilsk today.

Alaska and northern Canada share much for all intents and purpose with Siberia, including the predominance of methane hydrates. In 2007, a US project observed methane hydrates holds in Alaska with 80 % of the ice's pore space loaded with methane. Tim Collett, a methane hydrate expert at the US Geological Survey who was essential for the group, says there might be holds up and down the Alaska North Slope, including underneath existing oil establishments at Prudhoe Bay and the Arctic National Wildlife Refuge. Collett gauges there is somewhere in the range of 0.7 and 4.4 tcm (trillion cubic meters) of methane hydrate in Alaska alone. Indeed, even the low finish of that reach could warm 100 million homes for 10 years for example the greater part of northern America. As expressed before, leaving the stuff in the ground isn't a lot of a choice since hotter temperatures is prompting the stores vanishing and tainting our atmosphere.

In 2004, a German and Chinese group observed methane venting from the seabed off the bank of Taiwan in the South China Sea, and in 2006 Indian analysts observed a layer of methane hydrates 130m thick off its east coast in a space known as the Krishna-Godavari bowl. Collett calls these "one of the world's most extravagant marine gas hydrate accumulations".

In September 2009, an immense store of methane hydrates was found in the Chinese region of Qinghai, Tibet. Qinghai is home to roughly 70% of China's 2.15 million sq km of permafrost. The region is helpless against seismic action, so removing methane would be significantly more troublesome than expected. The Chinese Government may conclude the potential prize legitimizes the risks.
The methane hydrates stores in the Tibetan level are assessed to approach something like 35 billion tons of raw petroleum - enough to control China for the around 90 years.

Zhang Hongtao, boss specialist at China's Ministry of Land and Resources, was cited in March 2010 as saying he expected business abuse of methane hydrates in Qinghai could start inside 10-15 years. This declaration was followed up by CNPC - China's biggest oil and gas maker - consenting to an arrangement with Qinghai common government to put 23 billion yuan in the region over the accompanying five years. A portion of this venture would be utilized to support CNPC's Qinghai oilfield creation, however the organization has likewise consented to furnish Qinghai with 15 billion cubic meters of petroleum gas from 2010 to 2015.

Estimates change, yet moderate figures place worldwide stores at approximately 3 trillion tons of already undiscovered carbon - - more than is caught in the wide range of various realized non-renewable energy source holds set up, says Klaus Wallmann of the Leibniz Institute of Marine Science in Kiel, Germany.

hat would go on around 1,000 years assuming we keep on utilizing flammable gas at the current rate. Regardless of whether the methane from hydrates supplanted every single petroleum derivative, and not simply gas, it would in any case keep going for no less than 100 years. However, with this methane held in delicate ice gems and covered profound inside the Earth, would it be able to be taken advantage of securely and economically?

ntil as of late, there were two strategies for extricating methane from hydrates from seaward areas that were thought of as practical. One is to penetrate an opening into the hydrate store to deliver the tension, permitting the methane to isolate out from the clathrate and stream up the wellhead. The second is to warm the hydrate by siphoning in steam or boiling water, again letting the methane out of its frigid abode.

In 2002, Canadian, American, Japanese, Indian and German specialists tried the two methods in the field, at a drill site called Mallik on the external limit of the Mackenzie waterway delta in the Canadian Arctic. Both were effective, yet the energy expenses of the warming strategy almost offset the energy acquired from the methane delivered, making depressurisation the more alluring option.

The capability of depressurisation was affirmed in March 2008, when Canadian designers drove by Scott Dallimore of the Geological Survey of Canada utilized the method to tap 20,000 cm of methane gas more than six days from a store found 1 km underneath Mallik.

Similarly, in 2007, South Korea took advantage of depressurisation to separate methane hydrate from the Ulleung bowl in the Sea of Japan. Authorities accept holds there could meet the nation's gas needs for as long as 30 years, and they intend to start creation by 2015. In the interim Japan, one more country with restricted petroleum product saves, has found up to 50 tcm of hydrate south-east of Honshu Island in the Nankai box - - enough to supply the country with flammable gas for a really long time. In March 2008, the Japanese bureau vowed to start creation by 2016.

There may indeed be a more secure method of tapping hydrates which, if effective, could relieve the apprehensions of most geologists. Since different gases can likewise frame clathrates, it ought to be feasible to siphon one of these gases into the gems to dislodge the methane. Carbon dioxide would be an optimal applicant - the subsequent gem is much more steady than methane clathrate/hydrate, which means one more ozone depleting substance would be put away out of mischief's way.

This procedure has effectively been shown in the lab. In joint examination with the energy organization ConocoPhillips situated in Houston, Texas, Geir Ersland supplanted methane with CO_2 in counterfeit clathrate gems. The trade was fast and didn't harm the clathrate construction, making it the most secure method for extricating the methane yet found (Chemical Engineering Journal, DOI: 10.1016/j.cej.2008.12.028). Subbing methane with CO_2 "will expand the steadiness of the repository dregs just as keeping up with the clathrates in their strong state", Ersland says.

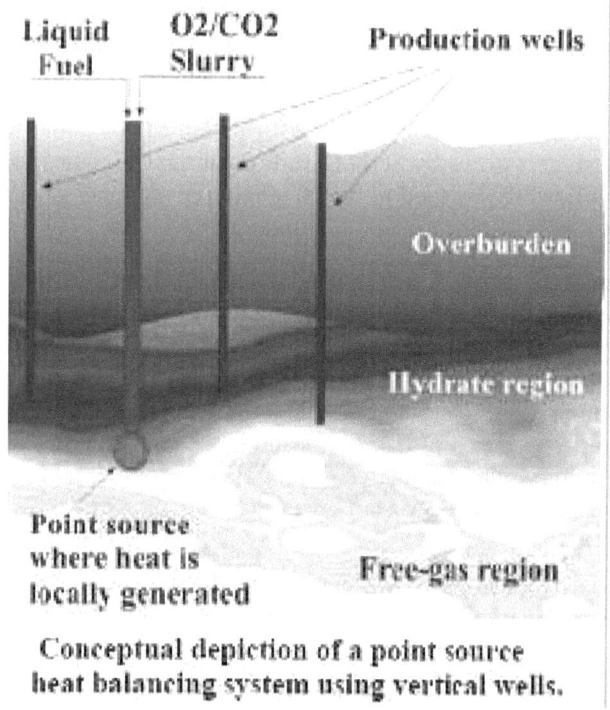

Conceptual depiction of a point source
heat balancing system using vertical wells.

A report named "Land Sequestration and Microbiological Recycling of CO^2 in Aquifers" by Hitoshi Koide of the Geological Survey of Japan proposed three strategies for extricating methane hydrates with the main role of diminishing Japan's carbon dioxide discharges. The diagrammes of these extraction strategies are as per the following:-

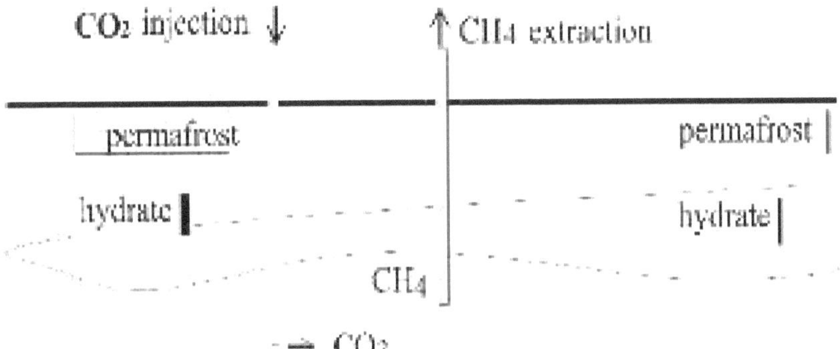

Fig.1 Injection of CO₂ under permafrost layer and extraction of methane.

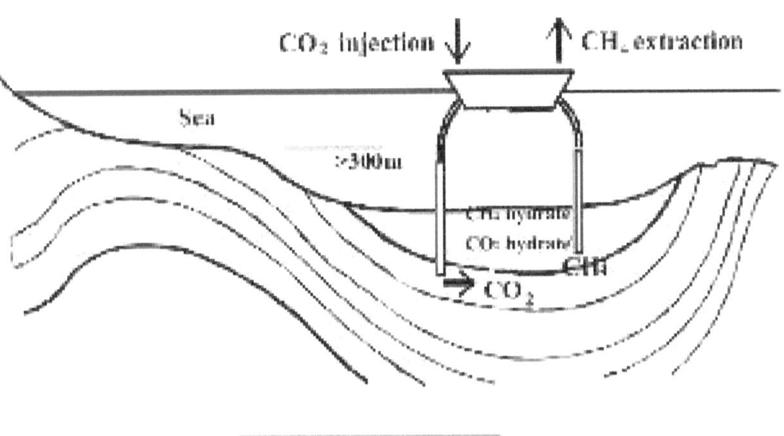

Fig.2 Injection of CO₂ under methane hydrate layer and extraction of methane.

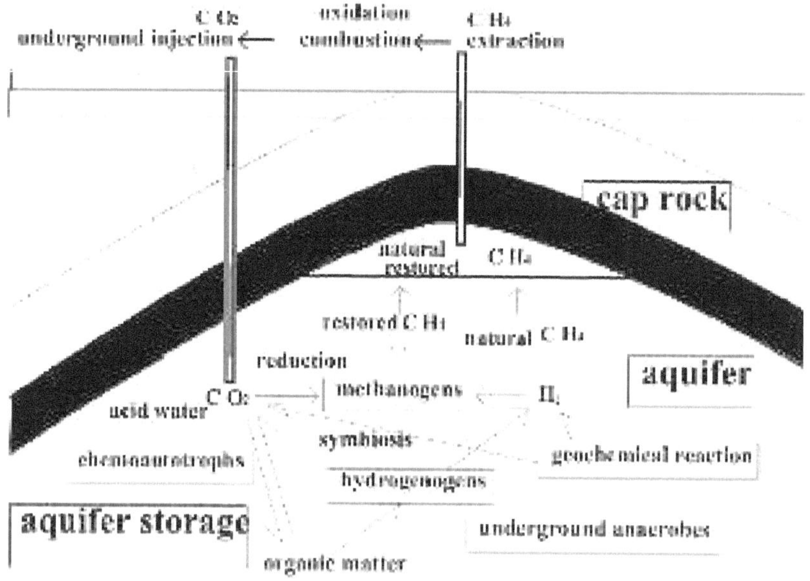

Fig.3 Geological sequestration of CO₂ and microbial restoration of methane deposit.

Regardless of whether the essential intention is decrease of fossil fuel byproducts or extraction of fuel, the final product is something similar. Almost certainly, inside the principal quarter of the 21st century, consuming petroleum products like coal and flammable gas might be adequate assuming that the CO^2 outflows are caught and put away. This moment, there is a hurry to foster a reasonable framework for catching and covering billions of huge loads of CO^2 underground each year. The greatest snag to date is that the immense foundation needed to discard the CO^2 may rapidly make copying petroleum products uneconomic, even contrasted with the genuine expense of choices like sunlight based, wind or atomic power. Discarding CO^2 down a similar line used to raise more fuel could be the appropriate response. Probably, the more carbon dioxide securely arranged, the more methane separated and utilized as fuel.

An incredible number of plans have been proposed with pronounced point of diminishing fossil fuel byproducts. Many are ruinously costly and would make such a disturbance day to day existence as to be totally inadmissible to by far most of individuals who might need to experience the changes. More than a few such projects are actually just a reason to force extra expenses on individuals and businesses.

hese ideas on methane hydrates extraction are unique. They offer positive arrangements for what it's worth: a dangerous climatic impurity is securely extricated from unsteady stores ashore and seaward ; the expense of separating that substance is eagerly paid for by the extractors who then, at that point, own an ample and important fuel; the removed material gives enough (moderately) clean gaseous petrol to drive ventures and networks all over the planet for the remainder of the 21st century and then some; stores of the separated material are appropriated all over the planet, empowering numerous nations that need oil and regular gas stores to become energy free; to sweeten the deal even further, assuming somebody can sort out some way to gather carbon dioxide securely and economically, this ozone depleting substance can be discarded simultaneously and place as the methane is separated. An answer that takes care of such countless issues and pays for itself.

Ultimately, it is the occupation of business undertakings, in meeting with climate security specialists and the enactment given by states that should choose how to handle this issue. The stakes couldn't really be higher, however the prizes assuredly legitimize this work, particularly as those prizes can be shared by pretty much every country on the planet.